A CRITIQUE OF LINGUISTIC PHILOSOPHY

A CRITIQUE OF LINGUISTIC PHILOSOPHY

BY

C. W. K. MUNDLE

CLARENDON PRESS · OXFORD

1970

Oxford University Press, Ely House, London W. 1
GLASGOW NEW YORK TORONTO MELBOURNE WELLINGTON
CAPE TOWN SALISBURY IBADAN NAIROBI DAR ES SALAAM LUSAKA ADDIS ABABA
BOMBAY CALCUTTA MADRAS KARACHI LAHORE DACCA
KUALA LUMPUR SINGAPORE HONG KONG TOKYO

MADE AND PRINTED IN GREAT BRITAIN
BY WILLIAM CLOWES AND SONS, LIMITED
LONDON AND BECCLES

'The knowledge of things is not to be investigated from their names. No; they must be studied and investigated in themselves.'

(Plato, *Cratylus*, 439b)

'Nothing is more common than for philosophers to encroach upon the province of grammarians, and to engage in dispute of words, while they imagine that they are handling controversies of deepest importance and concern.'

(David Hume, *An Enquiry Concerning the Principles of Morals*, Appendix 4)

'Grammar tells what kind of object anything is.'

(Ludwig Wittgenstein, *Philosophical Investigations*, § 373)

'It [Wittgenstein's *Philosophical Investigations*] will consolidate the philosophical revolution for which, more than anyone else, its author was responsible.'

(P. F. Strawson, *Mind*, 1954, p. 99)

PREFACE

I HAVE many debts: to Dr. Reginald Jackson whose lectures I attended at St. Andrews long ago, and who dinned into his students the importance of distinguishing between using and mentioning words; to Professor A. D. Woozley, Mr. J. L. Daniel, and Mrs. K. Scheur for reading earlier drafts and drawing my attention to many passages where I recognized the need for changes and to some more which they would have wished me to change; to several of my students who gave me helpful criticisms of an essay from which this book has evolved; and to the Philosophy Department at the University of Maryland for letting me ruminate there for a semester free from committees. I am also indebted to Miss L. M. Oyler, for her patience in deciphering and typing most of my manuscript; and to my colleague, Professor C. L. Mowat, for his kindness in taking over the Deanship three months before his time.

University College of North Wales, Bangor
July, 1969.

CONTENTS

Abbreviations sometimes used in the Text xi

Section I: Introduction 1

PART ONE: LINGUISTIC PHILOSOPHY IN ITS DIVERSE FORMS

Section II: The target-area reconnoitred and defined 11

Section III: Professor Ayer's former practice of *a priori* linguistics, and how to rid Empiricism of "the" Verification Principle 24

Section IV: Important ambiguities in Professor Ryle's *The Concept of Mind* 41

Section V: Ryle's practice of *a priori* and/or legislative linguistics 54

Section VI: Ryle's misuse of "category-mistake" 68

Section VII: Professor Austin's contributions to Linguistics 78

Section VIII: The use of "concept" in linguistic philosophy 91

Section IX: The misuses of "logic" in linguistic philsophy and a warning about "criterion" 110

Section X: How much linguistic philosophy is *Anglo*-linguistics? 120

Section XI: Mr. Warnock's way of defending linguistic philosophy and Professor Strawson's way of doing it 134

PART TWO: LUDWIG WITTGENSTEIN, THE INSTIGATOR OF THE REVOLUTION IN PHILOSOPHY

Section XII: The rôles of G. E. Moore and Wittgenstein compared 153

Section XIII: Wittgenstein's *Tractatus*, the purest kind of *a priori* linguistics 166

Section XIV: Wittgenstein's later accounts of language and of philosophy 185

Section XV: Wittgenstein's peculiar ways of practising his new kind of philosophy 200

Section XVI: Some answers to important questions raised by Wittgenstein 220

Section XVII: Wittgenstein's legacy 241

CONCLUSION

Section XVIII: A plea for speculative metaphysics 261

INDEX 275

Abbreviations sometimes used in the Text

BBB	for Wittgenstein's *The Blue and Brown Books.*
BJPS	for *The British Journal for the Philosophy of Science.*
C of M	for Ryle's *The Concept of Mind.*
D of L	for W. and M. Kneale's *The Development of Logic.*
DPA	for 'the doctrine of privileged access'.
FEK	for Ayer's *The Foundations of Empirical Knowledge.*
LTL	for Ayer's *Language, Truth and Logic.*
OED	for *The Shorter Oxford English Dictionary.*
PAS	for *Proceedings of the Aristotelian Society.*
PI	for Wittgenstein's *Philosophical Investigations.*
P of GEM	for Schilpp (ed.), *The Philosophy of G. E. Moore.*
P of P	for Russell's *The Problems of Philosophy.*
PP	for Austin's *Philosophical Papers.*
VP	for Verification Principle.

SECTION I

Introduction

THIS book is deliberately provocative. More gentle criticisms made by others have not cut enough ice. It is not only linguistic philosophers who will find its contents in some degree provoking, for complaints will be made about jargon which is now being used by most English-speaking philosophers. If any of my statements are considered tactless, my plea is that tact should not always take priority over saying what one thinks needs to be said. The thought which led me to embark on this project was that Professor J. L. Austin's methods can and should be applied to jargon now being used by philosophers who regard Austin's writings as a model. When this thought struck me, I was surprised that critics of linguistic philosophy had not done this before; had not, for example, compared the everyday uses of "concept" with its uses by linguistic philosophers, who had usually omitted to give any, or any adequate, explanation thereof. I made the first moves in my head, which is, perhaps, how linguistic philosophers normally make their discoveries: I asked myself how people usually use "concept" (how *I* would use it) in everyday talk. I did some field-work by putting a questionnaire to the final meeting of my first-year class in order to find how these students would paraphrase "the concept of . . .". The results showed that confusion reigned as to what their teachers had been talking about when they used the concept-idiom. Since then a similar questionnaire has been used in several Universities, and the results confirm that other philosophy students are far from clear how "concept" is being used by philosophers.

Whatever else the study of philosophy achieves it should promote clarity of thought. Yet most English-speaking philosophers are now expressing their philosophical thoughts in jargon which obscures from their audiences the difference between *using* and *mentioning* a word: between using a word for whatever it is used for, e.g. to talk about the thing(s) it denotes or the properties it connotes; and mentioning a word to talk *about it*, its definition(s), meaning(s) or use(s) *in the language in which it is used.*[1] A philosophical student of language who is not clear about this difference scarcely deserves to become a Bachelor of Arts. One of the subsidiary aims of this book is that philosophers who wish to continue to pursue linguistic studies should do this more openly, and more efficiently, and should more frequently extend their interest from Anglo-Linguistics to Comparative Linguistics.

Ludwig Wittgenstein is almost universally acknowledged as the chief instigator of the linguistic revolution in philosophy. It would, however, have complicated the structure and obscured the purposes of Part One of this book if I had tried therein to do justice to his writings, for these pose formidable problems of interpretation. Sometimes in Part One I allude to remarks of his which have inspired views which I am criticizing. In Part Two I have tried to apply to the two works which Wittgenstein wrote for publication the standards of criticism which professional philosophers normally employ in criticizing each others' work. I argue there that the inconsistencies between Wittgenstein's account of philosophy and his own practice are as flagrant in his *Philosophical Investigations* as in his *Tractatus*; and that he has re-introduced old fallacies, notably that of confusing questions about how we *do* use words with questions about how we *learnt* to use them. This involves what used to be called 'the Genetic Fallacy', and it really is a fallacy. It is, however, a disadvantage of the structure of this book that Part One neglects one common species of more or less linguistic

[1] Since I shall frequently be stressing the need to distinguish between *using* and *mentioning* linguistic expressions, I have tried to impose upon myself the following rules:

(1) To use italics for emphasis and in giving titles of books and journals.
(2) To use double inverted commas only for mentioning a word, phrase or sentence.
(3) To use single inverted commas for all the other purposes for which inverted commas are conventionally used.

I have, however, inconsistently put double inverted commas around the definite article when I speak of '"the" Verification Principle'. This is a way of emphasizing its inappropriateness. For some purposes it would be useful to differentiate further the functions of inverted commas and italics; but it seems to be a step in the right direction to use for different purposes the three devices provided by everyday written English.

philosophy, which involves seeking wisdom by searching for the meanings of Wittgenstein's remarks. I say 'more or less linguistic philosophy' because, although its practitioners usually endorse Wittgenstein's programme of assembling reminders about everyday language, they are often no more faithful to this programme than he was. Some of Wittgenstein's insights are very important indeed, but the philosophers in question proceed as if the solutions to all philosophical problems were hidden in his remarks. (If so they are well hidden.) Such philosophers commonly present their own theses or arguments, sometimes original, as elucidations of texts selected from Wittgenstein. This method of doing philosophy will be considered after we have dealt systematically with Wittgenstein's work. The last section of Part Two contains examples of this new kind of scholasticism, and it is argued there that in this and certain other respects Wittgenstein's legacy has been lamentable.

A critic of an earlier draft of Part One complained that most of the works criticized therein were 'out of date' or 'no longer in the middle of the stage'; and he urged me to devote myself to 'major works which represent linguistic philosophy as it is', his only example being Professor P. F. Strawson's *Individuals*. I had failed to convey to this reader my purpose. This could not be achieved by examining only the now most fashionable form of linguistic philosophy, which is usually presented as a discussion of concepts and categories and their logic. My purpose requires getting behind this and explaining its origin. The works to which I pay most attention have been selected not only because of their great influence, but because I consider them important and believe that they will still be read long after linguistic philosophy is acknowledged as an aberration. This book does not, however, purport to be an adequate history of linguistic philosophy. It does not assess the contributions of all the main practitioners. It ignores the (to me very) elusive thoughts of Professor John Wisdom. It does, however, contain criticism of writings by over twenty practitioners, including, I think, all the most influential, except Wisdom. Many more examples could have been added, but, for therapeutic purposes, enough is enough; and some may consider that more stones could have been left unturned.

While writing this book, I have deliberately avoided research into what other critics of linguistic philosophy have said. When I first recognized that much recent philosophy involves doing what may fairly be called '*a priori* linguistics', and that Austin's methods could be turned upon philosophers whom he had inspired, I decided to take a new look at the facts without, so far as possible, using spectacles provided by others. If I sometimes use arguments which have been used by others, without acknowledgements to their authors, I beg their pardon in advance. I have acknowledged debts of which I am conscious, but others must lurk in my unconscious. There is, however, one important respect in which further inspection of what others had written led me to revise my first draft. In Part Two, I had participated in the 'what Wittgenstein really meant' game, and had adopted what seemed to me the most obvious interpretation of his account of 'names of sensations'. Recent additions to the range of incompatible interpretations of this passage convinced me, however, that it would be pointless to pin on Wittgenstein my own interpretation and criticise only this; that what was needed was to show that, on all permissible interpretations, Wittgenstein was irretrievably inconsistent, and why other interpretations, however ingenious, are not permissible. Mr. George Pitcher's anthology *Wittgenstein, The Philosophical Investigations: A Collection of Critical Essays* (1966), contains a representative sample of rival interpretations. Surely it will lead some students to smell a rat. If, in some future age, a philosopher should come across Pitcher's anthology but not Wittgenstein's book, he would, I think, infer that *if* the authors of these essays are discussing a single book called 'The Philosophical Investigations', they must be referring to different editions involving radical revisions.

Not many references will be found in this book to criticisms of linguistic philosophy made by others. Lest any reader should form the impression that I am, or think that I am, a voice crying in the wilderness, or that I overestimate the originality of this critique, I have collected here a few earlier criticisms of linguistic philosophy which I should have been happy to have written myself; criticisms which have, however, achieved less than they deserved. For a short time, I thought that I owned the copyright of the 'concept' of *a priori* linguistics. I soon recognized however, that, though my phrase is (so far as I know) new, the thought is not. Indeed William and Martha Kneale had used almost the same phrase:

Sometimes, however, philosophers . . . talk of the logic of ordinary language and even of the 'logical behaviour' of particular English words, as though they were engaged in some sort of *a priori* philology. It has been stated for example as a *point of logic* that attention is a polymorphous concept because the English word 'attend' has many different uses . . . but if logic is an *a priori* science it cannot claim this discovery, since the existence of the various uses is a historical accident. In German, as it happens, there is no single word with the same range of application as 'attend', though German is not a notably poorer language than English (*The Development of Logic*, p. 639).

Professor N. Findlay, referring to the later Wittgenstein, has written of:

a radical use-theory [of meaning] carried to extremes, which constructs fables as to how we might have been taught the meanings of words in order to buttress *a priori* doctrines as to what we *must* or *cannot* mean (*PAS*, Supp. Vol., 1961, pp. 241–2).

Professor S. Hampshire, in his review of Ryle's *The Concept of Mind*, wrote:

it is Professor Ryle, and not only Descartes, who displays an *a priori* theory of language involving a conflict with established usage (*Mind*, 1950, p. 241).

And Professor Ayer, in his Inaugural Lecture at Oxford in 1960, when referring to 'reductive analysis', i.e. the kind which he had practised in his *Language, Truth and Logic*, said:

It has a linguistic aspect insofar as it seeks to show that one sort of expression can perform the office of another, but this is the outcome not of any dispassionate study of language, but of an *a priori* conception of reality (*The Concept of a Person*, 1963, p. 14).

This lecture contains the best critique of linguistic philosophy that I have found. Ayer distinguishes several species of linguistic philosophy, and criticizes each for its particular faults. He points out that philosophers who appeal to ordinary language often use a pattern of argument which

rests on a theory of meaning which its advocates commonly fail to make explicit . . . the verification principle on which the logical positivists relied in their elimination of metaphysics (p. 20).

This will be one of my main themes. Ayer has continued to tease linguistic philosophers. Consider how he ends his paper 'Metaphysics and Common Sense':

It is indeed better to tabulate the milestones along the highway of ordinary usage than to rhapsodise about nothingness or the essence of man; but it would be a mistake to forego the more imaginative kinds of conceptual exploration, merely because of the greater risk of getting lost. In philosophy, nothing should be absolutely sacrosanct; not even the ideology of common sense (in *Metaphysics, Reality and Re-Appraisal*, ed. Kennick and Lazerowitz, 1966).

Another critique of linguistic philosophy which deserves mention here is one of the earliest, Professor P. L. Heath's 'The Appeal to Ordinary Language' (*Phil. Quarterly*, 1952). If it had been made compulsory reading for philosophy students, the situation which has provoked this book would surely have been averted. Heath wrote, for example:

Though little or nothing has been done to verify this empirically, writers who appeal to Standard English display a surprising confidence and authority in pronouncing upon the proper, normal, literal, primary, true, correct and dominant meanings of words and phrases. It is surprising, because if you look up what linguists have to say on the subject, you find that this strictly normative conception of vocabulary and grammar is completely out of date, and has been for centuries. To the vast majority of modern linguists, 'Standard English' is no more than a trade-label annexed to a particular dialect, and has no special status or authority, apart from the irrelevant social approval accorded to those who happen to speak it . . . Save *per accidens* there is no logic in the matter, no privilege, no permanence . . . the task of the grammarian is to describe and classify these activities, not to judge them (p. 2).

Mr. L. J. Cohen has made some important criticisms of linguistic philosophy, particularly of Austin's kind, in Chapter III of *The Diversity of Meaning* (1963). Cohen asks what ought *not* to be the business of philosophers with language; and he continues:

The question to be asked is not what they must do or what they actually do, but rather what they may legitimately do without risk of exposure to the charge of amateurism . . . what can philosophers find to study in meanings that philologists, historians, sociologists and other specialists in semantics omit to study? (p. 75).

Cohen reaches the following conclusions:

What is left to constitute the distinctive province of philosophical semantics is the question of value (p. 92).

The question at issue is not so much 'what jobs are at present being done by words' but rather 'how can words do their present jobs better (more clearly, more consistently, more profitably) than they sometimes seem to do?' Philosophical semantics does not [should not?] spring from the disinterested pursuit of truth about word-use, but from the interested pursuit of consistency in it. With regard to the customary usages of ordinary language the job of a philosopher is rather to seek for their own justification, if any, than to seek in them for a justification or refutation of philosophical theses (p. 103).

My main purposes in this book are to exhibit linguistic philosophy as an aberration, to show that its practitioners have often done very badly what they claim to be doing, and to advocate the return to the non-linguistic tasks which philosophers had been tackling for 2500 years. I have also tried to make some contributions to important problems in what is now called 'the philosophy of mind', problems which arise frequently in the samples of linguistic philosophy which are cited and criticized. These problems are now commonly presented as being about our uses of words; but even the most linguistic philosophers, however they describe their occupation, have not in practice lost interest in the traditional problem: how can we justify what we claim to know or believe about minds, mental states, etc., other people's and one's own?

I set out to write a book readable by non-philosophers, sometimes affectionately described by philosophers as 'the vulgar'. I may have failed in this. At any rate, I shall cater only for those of the vulgar who would wish to inspect in detail some of the fruits of linguistic philosophy. I have quoted the words of my targets to an extent which some readers may find tedious. The main reason for this is to avoid a criticism which may be made of an earlier book which attacked linguistic philosophy, *Words and Things* (1959) by Professor Ernest Gellner. Too often Gellner gave his own free rendering of the views he was attacking, and thus exposed himself to the charge that what he criticized was caricature or misinterpretation. Readers will sometimes be invited to laugh. Since Plato introduced the genre, philosophical writings usually give the impression that the kinds of edification or illumination which they offer leave little or no scope for entertainment. (Austin was an exception in this respect). Perhaps philosophers should laugh more often whilst on duty. It might do good if one of our learned journals introduced a column corresponding to the *New Statesman's* 'This England'. Here is a dictum which might qualify for this column. A now very distinguished linguistic philosopher once gave a lecture to the Bangor Philosophical Society. The sweeping claims which he made for the linguistic revolution prompted one member of the audience to ask: have not earlier philosophers been claiming for thousands of years to have discovered *the* method of solving their predecessors' problems? The answer was simply 'Yes; but they were mistaken'. Critics of this book may well find in it statements which deserve to be laughed at where I have failed to see the joke. They have been given every incentive.

PART ONE

LINGUISTIC PHILOSOPHY IN ITS DIVERSE FORMS

SECTION II

The Target-Area Reconnoitred and Defined

CRITICS of linguistic philosophy, including Bertrand Russell, who have argued from premises no longer accepted by those whom they criticize have usually had their criticisms ignored. The premises from which I shall argue would, presumably, be accepted by linguistic philosophers. They are:

(1) Empiricism (to be defined later),
(2) that philosophy still includes the theory of knowledge,
(3) that contradictions are not allowed,
(4) a methodological principle distilled from Austin's work: that technical terms be not multiplied beyond necessity, but that when we need them we should define them and explain their function. (We might call this 'Austin's Razor'.)

If linguistic philosophers would reject any of these premises, I hope they will make this public. Using only these premises, and methods of argument which are employed by its practitioners, I hope to show that linguistic philosophy, in its diverse forms, has been a deviation from traditional philosophy, and that some of its fruits are absurd and educationally harmful.

Critics of this book may want to say that they do not understand how I am using "linguistic philosophy". This has been a stock response to anyone who uses this term—he is told that there is nothing common to the views and methods of the philosophers to whom uninformed outsiders apply it. *Whatever others may have meant by "linguistic philosophy", I am using it, appropriately I think, to refer to philosophers' writings which assert or assume that the subject-matter of philosophy is language, or the uses of words (or of language), or grammar, or concepts* if *talk about 'concepts' turns out, as it commonly does, to be talk about the uses of words.* Linguistic philosophy, in this sense, is now widespread in

English-speaking countries. The common feature described in my definition is surely much more important than the differences in methods and opinions found in the works to which this definition applies. The assumption that language is the subject-matter of philosophy involves a drastic restriction in the scope of philosophy, and, surely, in its importance. Before Wittgenstein wrote during World War One that 'All philosophy is "Critique of Language"' (*Tractatus Logico-Philosophicus*, 4.0031), no important philosopher would have accepted this narrow conception of his subject.

"Linguistic philosophy", as I am using it, is applicable not only to the works of those who, after World War Two, proclaimed a 'linguistic revolution' in philosophy but of those who prepared the way; for example, the early Ayer who wrote, in *Language, Truth and Logic* (1936), that although 'we may speak loosely of him [the philosopher] as analysing facts, or notions, or even things ... we must make it clear that these are simply ways of saying that he is concerned with the definitions of the corresponding words' (p. 59). It is perilous to do what Professor Gellner attempted in *Words and Things*, that is, to describe a single set of doctrines shared, and gambits used, by all linguistic philosophers. I shall not claim that there are any doctrines shared by all the works I shall criticize except the assertion or assumption that the subject-matter of philosophy is language. I shall therefore try to avoid making sweeping generalizations about linguistic philosophy. Linguistic philosophers will be considered one at a time, and each will be criticized for specific things that he has written; and in cases where it might be disputed whether the works in question constitute linguistic philosophy, reasons will be given for so classifying them.

Here are a few samples of the sorts of things against which I wish to protest:

(1) During the last twenty years, linguistic philosophers have often chided other philosophers for using technical terms, and especially for using thus words belonging to ordinary language. But this is precisely what many of them have been doing, without noticing that they were doing this and that their audiences have been left confused. The philosophers whom they criticize usually *have* defined their technical terms, or at least, explained

why they were being introduced. To dispense with technical terms and employ only everyday language would be a self-defeating project for any thinker. It is a prerequisite of critical thinking about any subject, that the thinker should reveal and remove the ambiguities with which ordinary language abounds, should draw and define whatever new distinctions are needed for his own descriptive or explanatory purposes. Some philosophers, however, have claimed that ordinary language provides a test of philosophical truth. Professor Norman Malcolm, for example, has written:

> A philosophical statement cannot be paradoxical and not be false . . . if a philosophical statement is paradoxical, that is because it asserts the impropriety of an ordinary form of speech . . . But it is not possible for an ordinary form of speech to be improper. That is to say, ordinary language is correct language (*The Philosophy of G. E. Moore*, 1942, pp. 361–2).

How odd that a philosopher should think that our problems can be disposed of by reminding us about the ordinary uses of the blunt, multi-purpose tools provided by everyday English, which has slowly evolved to meet the practical purposes of our ancestors. Ironically, many such philosophers, including Malcolm, present their arguments in technical jargon which they have not recognized as such.

(2) Could anything be more incongruous than for a philosopher to tell us to think of language as a tool-kit, and then lay it down that the only use which philosophers may make of verbal tools is to describe, and *not* to theorize about or try to explain, the uses which *other* people make of verbal tools? My target here is the dicta of Ludwig Wittgenstein, in *Philosophical Investigations*, paragraphs 11 and 23; 109, 124, 126 and 128.[1] These statements clearly imply that only non-philosophers may use the verbal tool-kit for intellectually exciting tasks, like trying to solve problems about the world and our place in it; that for philosophers, the study of language is a prison, since they may use the tools it provides only for recording the uses of such tools by free men; and that the philosopher may not even repair or sharpen a free man's tools, but must 'leave everything as it

[1] I shall not quote these passages now, as I do so and discuss them in Part Two.

is'. Wittgenstein seems to have wished philosophers to say only things with which everyone would agree. 'In philosophy we do not draw conclusions . . . Philosophy only states what everyone admits' (*PI*, § 599. Cf. § 128).

(3) In Oxford and most other British Universities, Moral Philosophy has become the study of 'Moral *Language*' (or 'Moral *Concepts*' or 'the *Logic* of Moral Concepts'). For this development two Oxford Professors, A. J. Ayer and R. M. Hare, bear the main responsibility. Both of them are moralists in the good sense in that they have played their part in trying to make the moral attitudes of our society more discriminating and enlightened. But they have also persuaded most of their colleagues that it is not legitimate, for a philosopher *as such*, to make and try to justify moral judgements; that when one is doing moral philosophy, one should remain neutral on all moral issues; that moral philosophy is simply a study of the functions of moral words and the logical implications of moral utterances—a study now usually pursued, at least in intention, by empirical enquiry rather than by *a priori* decree. Sometimes, however, teachers of ethics find it hard to sustain indefinitely the interest of their students in the function(s) of moral words—in asking whether they are primarily expressions of feelings, or exhortations, or commands, etc. Another method of teaching ethics has become popular in parts of Wales and England. This is to read long extracts from Russian novels or Existentialist plays, describing moral dilemmas. When done well, this is an excellent way of starting arguments about *what* you would have done in the problem situations. And, sometimes, about *why*; but this method is generally used to support the conclusion that moral philosophers may draw no general conclusions, since each moral problem is unique. (This conclusion is reached by ignoring the fact that the dilemmas narrated are *moral* dilemmas only because or if, for hearer or hero, they involve a conflict of moral rules, rules as to how *people in general* ought to act.) We have here a point of contact between the thought of Sartre and that of some linguistic philosophers. This mode of doing ethics has doubtless been reinforced by Sartre's ethical theories, but it was inspired by Wittgenstein's views: that the philosopher's function is simply to assemble reminders of how non-philosophers talk, and that philosophers should shun theses or theories

or explanations. (See *Philosophical Investigations*, §§ 109, 116, 127 and 128).

(4) The confinement of philosophy to linguistic studies, *a priori* or empirical, has produced other strange progeny. One result is that it became possible to get a First in Philosophy ('Moral Science') at Cambridge without having opened a book written before 1900. I know a man who did this and is proud of it. There was a compulsory paper on the History of Philosophy, but in the year in question G. E. Moore's writings constituted the history.[2] It looks as if the School of Moral Science had accepted a corollary of Wittgenstein's view that philosophers should confine themselves to describing everyday uses of language (and imaginary language-games). Fortunately Wittgenstein's Oxford admirers have not accepted this corollary. Its Classical Greats School could scarcely dispense with a study of the language-games played by Plato and Aristotle.

A stock response by anyone who is called 'a linguistic philosopher' has been to attribute to the user of this term ignorance of the differences in style, methods and conclusions among the philosophers to whom it is applied. I shall emphasize such differences, shall contrast the diverse forms of linguistic philosophy. These range from what I call '*a priori* linguistics' at one extreme to Professor J. L. Austin's kind of descriptive linguistics at the other, with what I call 'legislative linguistics' a further species sometimes distinguishable from the others. Phrases for teasing linguistic philosophers have been coined by others, for example "language police" (F. Waismann, *Analysis*, 1952, p. 11) and "philosophical Fowlers" (I forget who). The latter phrase fits Austin and his followers, the former those who practise *a priori* or legislative linguistics. I use these last phrases as technical terms, defined in the following ways:

"A priori *linguistics" is to mean the practice of inventing or embracing or presupposing rules about language, proceeding as if these rules are* a priori *and deducing from them that we cannot or may not (properly or significantly) say things that we do say, or that we do not mean by them what we do mean by things we do say.*

[2] The present regulations for Moral Science at Cambridge involve that in Part I (a two-year course), one of the seven papers may be, but none need be, on the History of Philosophy; and that in Part II, two of the eight papers must, and only two can, be on the History of Philosophy.

"Legislative linguistics" is to mean the practice of making false assertions about what we do say, or do not or cannot or may not say, in the interests of some philosophical theory or thesis, but without formulating or being willing to endorse any general rule(s) or principle(s) about language from which these assertions would follow.

Notice that these definitions imply that we may not be able to decide from what a philosopher has *written* whether he is guilty of *a priori* or of legislative linguistics; that sometimes one could settle such a question only by cross-examination, by challenging the writer to justify his false assertions about English usage. This indeterminacy in the application of my technical terms could be avoided, by dropping from the former definition the word "presuppose", and from the latter the clause "or willing to endorse". I have included them because, later on, I shall submit that some philosophers, including Ryle and Wittgenstein, have *covertly* practised *a priori* linguistics; that their counter-factual conclusions about everyday language are derived from, or depend upon, some version of "the" Verification Principle which they have not explicitly formulated—an omission which may be a result of Wittgenstein's prescription that philosophers 'may not advance any kind of theory' (*Philosophical Investigations*, § 109).

"*A priori* linguistics" is an accurate description of much that has been written by English-speaking philosophers in recent years. In Linguistics proper, a rule about usage is a generalization from observations, or a hypothesis to be tested by observations—observations of what people *do* say. Philosophers doing armchair linguistics sometimes produce, out of the blue, rules which they treat as self-evident, and then deduce from these home-made rules what people *cannot* say. Do they mean 'may not'; withholding their permission? Do they mean 'Never do (period)'; categorical imperatives? They often fail to make this clear. When they do explain, their claim is sometimes that so and so is improper or incorrect English, sometimes (what is very different) that it is absurd or meaningless. Whatever they mean, as often as not the things they deduce that we cannot say are things we commonly do say. Ironically, the practitioners of *a priori* linguistics usually subscribe to the slogan that the meaning of a word is its *use*, and the view that language is essentially a *public* institution. The term "*a priori* linguistics" obviously applies to the practices of philosophers who put themselves in this incongruous position.

I shall not be using "*a priori* linguistics" to include an enquiry which might be so described, but which is legitimate and important. I refer to the sort of thing that Professor Strawson has sometimes done—formulating necessary conditions for any language to be usable for a given purpose; for example, showing that a necessary condition for any language to be used to transmit information (true or false beliefs) is that it should have devices for referring to things and devices for describing them, and that a symbol S cannot be used to describe anything if it is applicable to everything, so that non-S must be applicable to something (*Introduction to Logical Theory*, 1952, Ch. 1). This is an *a priori* proof of what is sometimes called 'the polar principle'.[3] Strawson's kind of Kantian approach to language is obviously important for philosophy and for practical purposes like computer-technology. But this kind of investigation must be distinguished from that of Strawson's *Individuals* (1959): from what he there calls 'descriptive metaphysics', an investigation of 'our conceptual scheme'. When Strawson discusses our concept of a person, he does not make it clear to whom he refers by "our", who *we* are. English-speakers? People whose languages are like English in certain relevant respects? I shall argue later that Strawson's account of 'our' concept of a person is different from that which most of us would give, whichever languages we speak.

I hope that Professor A. R. White will forgive me if I use some of his statements to illustrate the most extreme kind of *a priori* linguistics. He writes:

> in *no* circumstances would it make sense to say . . . that someone . . . *found* a half-crown . . . inadvertently or intentionally. The concepts of . . . intention, etc., can *never* go with the concepts of . . . discovering. (*Analysis*, March 1967, p. 116. Strong words. His italics.)

I tried out a few sentences of the pattern here proscribed on a dozen people, including some graduates in English Literature and Professor Ryle, e.g. "I found the coin inadvertently while

[3] This principle was recognized by Aristotle in *Topics*, Book V, § 2, 130b. It provides a useful weapon for criticizing, or clarifying, some philosophical theses, e.g. that all actions are selfish.

arranging the cushions", "I found the thimble intentionally", "I discovered your secret unintentionally". I reported to White that none of them reported qualms about the grammar or style or significance of these sentences. White's answer was that his above-quoted statement was based on what he thought was generally agreed among philosophers, that "to find" is an achievement-verb and that "inadvertently" and "(un)intentionally" only qualify 'verbs of action'. It transpired that White was treating it as 'a rule for categorizing "achievement-verbs"' that they can neither be qualified by the said adverbs nor be preceded by "I did (not) intend to ...".

Consider the implications. White had already adopted rules for defining "achievement-verb" which much reduce the contents assigned by Ryle to this category. Ryle had included in it verbs which 'signify more or less protracted proceedings' like "keeping a secret", "retaining the lead", "keeping a hawk in view" (*C of M*, p. 149). White had earlier expelled all such verbs by adopting the rule that an achievement-verb cannot be used in the continuous present tense (*Attention*, 1964, pp. 23 and 25). He has now adopted a further rule which expels the remainder of the verbs which Ryle gave as exemplars. Take "to score a goal". If the English captain had scored for Germany in the Final match for the 1966 World Cup, surely no one would jib at saying that he did so unintentionally? (We wouldn't suspect *him* of taking bribes.) Notice that White's new rule implies *either* that we cannot (may not?) ask White whether he expelled "to score" *intentionally* or *inadvertently*; *or*, if we can (may) ask him this, that "to expel" is not an achievement-verb. Then what is? As Ryle pointed out (*C of M*, p. 150), some achievements are fulfilments of corresponding task activities, e.g. finding what you were looking for, and others are due to luck or chance. A natural way of drawing this distinction is to describe the former achievements as intentional and the latter as unintentional. One may be said to beget a child, hit a target, lose a game, find a thimble, intentionally or unintentionally. What is left in White's category of achievement-verbs? Apparently only a few cognitive verbs like "know", "understand" and "recognize".

There is nothing sacrosanct about Ryle's use of "achievement-verbs". White is free to define his own use of this term as he pleases. What I find so odd is that White should deduce from his own definition that 'in no circumstances would it make sense' to say anything which transgresses *his* defining rules. A philosopher who argues thus is arguing *as if* he believed that his own classifications of uses of English words constitute *a priori* knowledge about real essences located *in nominibus*, revelations of an objective logical structure inherent in language. But we must ask: which language is it, or which languages are they, whose 'logic' is under discussion? All languages including that of digital computers? Obviously not. All natural languages? No one is qualified to make assertions about this class. Presumably the language under discussion is English. At any rate, linguistic philosophers do not often show signs of having considered the other languages with which they are familiar. Have those like White who 'categorize concepts' recognized that their subject-matter is the same as that of Fowler's *A Dictionary of Modern English Usage*? And are their own uses of "categorizing" and "concept" and "logic" not to count as English usage, and therefore not part of the subject-matter to which their critical acumen should be directed? If they had thought of doing this, they could scarcely have continued to use such jargon obscurely in the course of doing what is supposedly an empirical study of the non-technical uses of words!

The incongruity of White's sample of *a priori* linguistics can be exhibited in another way. If anyone asked White how the category-term "achievement-verb" is *correctly* used, he can scarcely settle this by the method he uses to decide how an everyday word is correctly used, i.e. by finding out how it is most frequently used in the market-place, or by looking up Fowler or the *OED*. The only empirical tests would be: how it was used by the man who invented it, Ryle, *or* how it is usually used now by philosophers. Then it is absurd to define "achievement-verb" in a way which expels from this category almost all the verbs that these others include in it. As we shall see later, the example which White was here following was set by Professor Ryle. Ryle had used his category of achievement-verbs to outlaw various perfectly legitimate sentences. He claimed, for example, that we cannot significantly say that someone 'hit the target successfully' or 'saw the nest rapidly' (*C of M*, p. 151).

Philosophers sometimes make dogmatic and false statements that something is said, or cannot or may not be said, without apparently being willing to endorse any general rules about language from which these statements would follow. This is what I call 'legislative linguistics'. It is not a new phenomenon. Thomas Hobbes, for example, made a habit of it. Thus, in the interests of Egoism, he incorporated in his definition of "gift" his own thesis that gifts are always made for the sake of some *quid pro quo*, and he presented this as *the* meaning of "gift" (*Leviathan*, Ch. XIV). Let us consider two recent examples of legislative linguistics. Both occur in papers written to defend linguistic philosophy and both concern the use of "use". Wittgenstein's influential equation between the *meaning* of a word and its *use*, has made "use" a key term in linguistic philosophy. Wittgenstein's equation was closely connected with his simile between using words and using tools, a simile which he used primarily to stress the variety of the *functions* of, the *purposes* for which we use, our verbal tools. My first example is of interest because its author's motive was to try to defend linguistic philosophy from the charge that it is really *Anglo*-linguistics. Professor A. G. N. Flew has written that:

> if we enquire about the *use* of 'table' then we are simultaneously and equally concerned with the *use* of 'tavola' and other equivalents in other languages . . . if we enquire about the *usage* of 'table' then we are concerned with how that particular *English* word is (or ought to be) employed by those who employ the word, and not 'tavola' (*Phil. Quarterly*, 1955, p. 27. Reprinted in *Essays on Conceptual Analysis*, 1956, Ed. Flew).

There could be no complaint if Flew had presented these statements in the form of a *proposal*; for we need a way of distinguishing when we are talking about (i) the use of a word in the language in which it is used, and when about (ii) the use or meaning of a word *and* of any words which have the same use or meaning in the same or other languages. Flew, however, writes as if he is reporting a fact about English usage, a fact which, he says, Ryle 'curiously neglects' when distinguishing "use" and "usage" in his paper 'Ordinary Language' (*Phil. Review*, 1953). Surely it is not at all surprising that Ryle did not say what Flew asserts. The distinction which Flew wished to make, by contrasting "the use of..." with "the usage of...", was not, and is not, made in this way by others. If we interpret Flew's statements as a disguised proposal, it is one which did not catch on among philosophers. It is, of course, an implication of my definition of "legislative linguistics" that it does not apply to a *stipulative* definition, whereby someone announces how he will, or intends to, use some expression; nor to what is presented as a *recommendation* as to how some expression should be used for a certain purpose. We are each free to make proposals about the uses of words, though not free by decree to alter English usage.

Ryle's dicta about "use" and "usage" in his paper 'Ordinary Language' do contain some curious features; and provide us with another example of legislative linguistics. Ryle accuses 'lots of philosophers' (not identified) of perpetrating 'a howler', namely treating "use" and "usage" as synonyms, (p. 174). He tells us, as if it were a commonplace about English usage, that 'A usage is a custom, practice, fashion or vogue'; and that a use is a 'way of operating with something', and (less vaguely) a 'technique, knack or method', and he proceeds to speak as if the use of a word is something which we acquire or master, a know-how (pp. 174–6). Ryle would have done well to consult a dictionary, which Austin commended as the first port of call for a linguistic philosopher.[4] The use which Ryle attributes to "use" is indeed acknowledged by the *OED*: 'the ability to use'. Ryle argues, however, as if "use (of a word)" and "(linguistic) usage" each have only one kind of use. The *OED* lists seven different meanings for "usage" and a score for "use"; and it confirms that there are several different senses in which "use" and "usage" may be used synonymously. Thus "use" may mean 'A custom, practice or habit' or 'usage, wont, habit'; and "usage" may mean 'The action of using something' or 'employment, use'.

I should classify Ryle's statement that it is 'just a howler' to treat "use" and "usage" as synonyms simply as inaccurate linguistics, were it not that it is made in the interests of a philosophical thesis—a thesis about the nature of a philosopher's concern with ordinary language. For Ryle is here trying

[4] The *OED* is an invaluable source for confirming errors made by linguistic philosophers—including Austin, as we shall see later.

to persuade us that philosophers are, or should be, concerned *not* with usage but with the uses and *misuses* of words. He informs us that 'There cannot be misusage' (though, according to the *OED*, "misusage" may be used as a synonym for "misuse"). He adds: 'The methods of discovering linguistic usage are the methods of philologists', which methods he later describes as 'Mass Observation' (pp. 174–5 and 178). Yet Ryle offers us an account of a philosopher's concern with language which is a straight paraphrase of the *relevant OED* definition of "usage", which is 'Established or customary use of words . . .'. What Ryle says is: 'Philosophers often have to describe the stock [i.e. customary] . . . manner of employing [i.e. using] an expression' (p. 177). What then is the howler alleged by Ryle?

He would be entitled to complain that other philosophers had been careless in their uses of "use", had he been more careful. Philosophers who have followed the maxim 'Don't ask for the meaning, ask for the use', have exploited the ambiguities of "use". They have, I think, rarely, if ever, interpreted this word, like Ryle, as meaning knack or know-how. Sometimes they use it to mean function and sometimes to mean purpose—and indeed this is how Ryle seems to be thinking when he says that a philosopher's concern with words is 'Job-analysis' (p. 178). The philosophers in question also use "use" to mean usage, the customary use of words; and this seems to be how Wittgenstein was using "use" when he wrote that philosophers may not interfere with and can in the end only describe 'the actual use of language' (*PI*, § 124). May Ryle complain about this, since he tells us here that philosophers do often have to describe the 'stock' way of 'employing' words? As we shall see, describing English usage is something which Ryle does, not infrequently, in *The Concept of Mind*, though he describes this activity rather less clearly as exploring 'the logic of concepts'. It is indeed desirable not to confuse description of linguistic usage with what Ryle calls 'Job-analysis', meaning, presumably, distinguishing the different kinds of purpose for which we use verbal-tools. If curing this confusion was Ryle's main aim, he obscured this by presenting, as *the* use of "use", a use which is uncommon and is not relevant for this purpose.

It is not always clear whether a statement should count as legislative linguistics, in my sense, or as a mere mistake about usage. For example, in the passage in 'Ordinary Language' following the one which has just been discussed, Ryle makes these false assertions: 'But we cannot ask whether [a person] knows how to use a certain *sentence*' (p. 178), and 'words and phrases can, while sentences cannot be misused' (p. 179). Whether these assertions should count as legislative linguistics depends, according to my definition, on whether they are made in the interests of a philosophical theory or thesis. Is it enough that they are made in the course of presenting a philosophical thesis? I think not. For Ryle introduces these assertions as 'an interesting point', which he then tries to explain. But what he says in this passage does not advance his main arguments; and it reveals the source of his mistake, namely failure to distinguish between sentences and 'sayings of things' (making statements which sentences are used to make) (pp. 178–9). I should not classify the assertions in question as legislative linguistics, but simply as inaccurate linguistics. But clearly there may be borderline cases. We could scarcely incorporate in a definition of "legislative linguistics" a rule for deciding *how* relevant to a philosophical thesis a false statement about language must be.

Here is an example of a borderline case. Mr. J. O. Urmson states that an involuntary groan cannot be described as 'an expression of agony', nor unforced tears as 'an expression of sorrow' (*The Emotive Theory of Ethics*, 1968, p. 31). These surprising statements are presented as reports about English usage, about 'the limits to the use of the word 'express''. Urmson says, more generally, that 'for something to count as an expression of a feeling it must be intentional' (p. 31). His self-imposed restriction on the use of "to express (a feeling)" contributes something to his philosophical purpose; which is to present in a favourable light the account of 'emotive meaning' according to which value-words *express* the speaker's feelings or attitudes. Given Urmson's restriction, we must reject the view that any cry of pain or sigh of boredom has the relevant kind of emotive meaning—a view which Ayer had seemed to adopt in Chapter VI of *Language, Truth and Logic*. Urmson, however, does not draw attention to this point. One is therefore left uncertain whether his inaccurate statements were made *in the interests* of the ethical theory which he was here developing, or whether it was merely a coincidence that they helped his case.

SECTION III

Professor Ayer's Former Practice of *A Priori* Linguistics, and how to Rid Empiricism of "The" Verification Principle

FUTURE historians of ideas may find it difficult to understand how linguistic philosophy so rapidly became dominant in England after World War Two, and why so many philosophers of outstanding ability have spent so much time discussing the uses of English words. I shall not compete with Professor Gellner in offering sociological and psychological explanations, beyond saying that such a historian would need to consider not only what the leaders of the linguistic revolution have said, but the force and persuasiveness with which they said it, their strong personalities. This section will be concerned with one of the main intellectual influences which prepared the way for linguistic philosophy in its post-war forms, namely Professor Ayer's pre-war philosophy. *Language, Truth and Logic* must be discussed here for three reasons. (i) Its contents provide a conspicuous example of *a priori* linguistics. (ii) Its apparent demolition of metaphysics, together with its assumption that all questions of empirical fact belong to the sphere of science and not philosophy, seemed to leave philosophers with nothing left to talk about except language and sense-data. Then "sense-data" went out of fashion, mainly as a result of George Paul's paper 'Is there a Problem about Sense-data?' (*PAS*, Supp. Vol., 1936), and this left only language. (iii) It seems to have led many philosophers to forget what "Empiricism" has traditionally meant, and to equate Empiricism with a rule designed solely to distinguish meaningless from meaningful sentences. I may appear, in the early part of this section, to be playing the familiar and facile game of scoring points against Ayer's brilliant but vulnerable book. Some familiar moves are needed, however, to prepare the way for some which are less familiar.

First we must recognize how explicitly linguistic Ayer's pre-war philosophy was. In Chapter II of *LTL*, he wrote that the philosopher 'must, in fact, confine himself to works of clarification and analysis of a sort which we shall presently describe' (p. 51).[1] His description is given later in the same chapter:

the validity of the analytic method is not dependent on any empirical, much less any metaphysical, presupposition about the nature of things. For the philosopher, as an analyst, is not directly concerned with the physical properties of things. *He is concerned only with the way in which we speak about them.* In other words, *the propositions of philosophy are not factual, but linguistic in character*—that is, they do not describe the behaviour of physical, or even mental, objects; *they express definitions, or the formal consequences of definitions . . . the possibility of philosophical analysis is independent of any empirical assumptions* . . . What has contributed as much as anything to the prevalent misunderstanding of the nature of philosophical analysis is the fact that propositions and questions which are really linguistic are often expressed in such a way that they appear to be factual . . . Thus, to ask what is the nature of a material object is to ask for a definition of "material object" . . . Although it is misleading to write about linguistic questions in "factual" language, it is often convenient for the sake of brevity. And we shall not always avoid doing it ourselves. But it is important that no one should be deceived by this practice into supposing that the philosopher is engaged on an empirical or a metaphysical enquiry. We may speak loosely of him as analysing facts, or notions [or concepts!], or even things. *But we must make it clear that these are simply ways of saying that he is concerned with the definition of the corresponding words* (pp. 57–9. My italics).

How odd that a professing empiricist should dismiss as irrelevant to philosophy all empirical facts; and that he should argue as if giving definitions does not involve making any statements of empirical fact. Did Ayer think that a philosopher should be concerned only with stipulative definitions of his own invention? He says, at the beginning of Chapter III, that the definitions which philosophy provides are not 'explicit definitions' but 'definitions-in-use'; and that the latter show 'how the sentence in which it [the term to be defined] significantly occurs can be translated into *equivalent* sentences' (pp. 59–60. My italics). Since definitions-in-use are to be statements of the form "S_1 is equivalent (in meaning) to S_2", or "S_1 means the

[1] My page-references will refer to the Revised Edition, 1946.

same as S_2", we must ask: means the same *for whom*? Such definitions would be of little interest to others unless they concerned the uses of, the meanings accepted by, some people other than the philosopher who gives them; but in that case they *are* empirical statements about how other people use words. Even when he wrote the 1946 Introduction to *LTL*, Ayer had not apparently recognized the difficulty in maintaining that philosophers should provide definitions but should not make any empirical statements; but he says things which are incompatible with maintaining this. He wrote: 'I wish the principle of verification itself to be regarded, not as an empirical hypothesis, but as a definition'; yet he added: 'it is not supposed to be entirely arbitrary' (p. 16); and he had just claimed that there is 'at least one *proper* use of the word "meaning" in which it would be incorrect to say that a statement was meaningful unless it satisfied the principle of verification' (p. 15. My italics). Now when Ayer spoke of 'one proper use', he cannot have intended "proper" to be purely prescriptive; for he also said that unless a statement satisfies the V P, 'it would not be capable of being understood in the sense in which either scientific statements or common-sense statements *are habitually understood*' (p. 16. My italics). This involves claiming that the 'proper' sense of "meaning", given by the Verification Principle considered as a definition, is the sense in which this word *is habitually used* in scientific and common-sense statements. And this claim is plainly an empirical hypothesis.

There is another reason for saying that Ayer's attempt to exclude empirical statements from his philosophy failed. In *LTL* (as in his later writings) Ayer frequently uses such locutions as "It is logically possible/not logically inconceivable/not self-contradictory/that . . ." In *LTL* it is often not made clear just what is the cash-value of such locutions. Sometimes, however, the context shows that they are used simply to make empirical statements about English usage. This is made explicit, for example, in Chapter VI, in the refutation of naturalistic definitions of moral words. For each such definition that he considers, Ayer uses the same gambit. For example, he demonstrates that "right" does not mean 'generally approved' by saying: 'it is not self-contradictory to assert that some actions which are generally approved of are not right' (p. 104). On the next page, referring to these refutations, he says: 'what we are denying is that the suggested reduction of ethical to non-ethical statements is *consistent with the conventions of our actual language*' (My italics). This makes it clear that, sometimes at least, Ayer used "It is not self-contradictory to say" or "It is logically possible that" as a way of saying that a sentence is good or correct English. I think that this appeal to English usage was inadvertent. Ayer has rarely explicitly treated English usage or ordinary language as a test of philosophical truth. Even in the present passage he says that he is not denying that it is possible or desirable to invent a language in which all ethical symbols are definable in non-ethical terms (p. 105). It is, however, a defect of Ayer's logic-locutions, not only in *LTL*, that it is sometimes unclear whether expressions like "logically possible" mean consistent with English usage, or consistent with his own definitions, or capable of being conceived or imagined. Though Ayer did not always succeed, he did, however, succeed to a remarkable extent in remaining faithful to his own programme of disregarding all empirical facts; as in his demonstration of Phenomenalism described below.

Let us now consider the way in which Ayer practised *a priori* linguistics in *LTL*. In Chapter I, he propounds his own version of the Verification Principle (VP) *as if* it were self-evident. He does not describe it as '*a priori*', which would, on his own account of *a priori* truths, make it a tautology. It never seems to have occurred to him to test his VP by asking whether it fits what, on his own account of philosophy, are the relevant empirical facts, namely what we *do* significantly say, and what we *do* mean thereby. The whole book is a series of deductions from his VP, and many of the conclusions drawn are flagrantly false—that sentences to which we attach meaning are meaningless, or that we *must* mean by sentences things that we do not mean by them.

The first and most influential deduction which Ayer draws is that metaphysical statements are literally meaningless. He wrote:

If a putative proposition [i.e. an utterance which purports to be true or false] fails to satisfy this principle [the VP], and is not a tautology, then *I hold* that it is metaphysical, and that, being metaphysical, it is neither true nor false, but literally senseless (Preface to First Edition, p. 31. My italics).

The reasoning involved here is revealed in Chapter I in an argument of breath-taking brevity:

> We may accordingly define a metaphysical sentence as a sentence which purports to express a genuine proposition, but does, in fact, express neither a tautology nor an empirical hypothesis. And as tautologies and empirical hypotheses form the entire class of significant propositions, we are justified in concluding that all metaphysical assertions are nonsensical (p. 41).

This argument is a deduction from Ayer's eccentric definition of "metaphysical sentence", and from his VP, which he presented, in 1946 though not in 1936, as a definition of "meaning" (p. 16).

A point which Ayer seems to have overlooked is that this deduction from his own definitions implies not only that all metaphysical statements are nonsensical but that all nonsensical statements are metaphysical statements! Presumably he did not really wish to classify as metaphysical such utterances as "potatoes are lazy" or "the mome raths outgrabe". So there is something wrong with Ayer's definition of "metaphysical statement", even for his own polemical purpose. This point does not seem to have been noticed by his early critics; probably because they judged Ayer's conception of metaphysics not by his formal definition, but by the examples and arguments which he used when discussing what he classifies as metaphysical statements; and which suggest that his target was really a more limited one—not any kind of nonsense, but statements which assert or assume the existence of unobservable entities. That this was Ayer's intention seems to be confirmed in the Introduction to the Revised Edition: 'I take it to be characteristic of the metaphysician, in my somewhat pejorative sense of the term, not only that *his statements do not describe anything that is capable, even in principle, of being observed*, but also that no dictionary is provided by means of which they can be transformed into statements that are . . . verifiable' (p. 14. My italics). (The last clause was designed to cover difficulties, more obvious in 1946 than in 1936, in reconciling with the VP scientists' talk about unobservables.)

Is it satisfactory, however, to define "metaphysics" as statements (or theories) about unobservables? Surely not. If we are to do justice to the long tradition of philosophy, any account of metaphysics must acknowledge that it is concerned with ontological questions, questions about what exists, what purported entities are real, fundamental, not analysable into more basic entities; such questions as whether minds exist *as well as* bodies, whether there exist unchanging abstract entities, 'universals', *as well as* spatio-temporal things and events, 'particulars', and so on. If it is granted that metaphysics is, or involves, making claims about what exists, what are the basic entities in the world, and how they are related to each other, Ayer's *LTL* philosophy is metaphysics *par excellence*. Ayer adopts what he describes as 'a thorough-going Phenomenalism'. He claims that both minds and bodies are logical constructions out of 'sense-contents' (his 1936 synonym for "sense-data"). He says that in asserting that a physical object exists one would be asserting only that certain sense-contents *would* occur *if* certain conditions were fulfilled (p. 141). According to Ayer's account, all of the empirical statements that a person makes must be analysed in terms of (and therefore are really *about*) his own sense-data: *his own* sense-data! (See below.) If this is not a bold and bizarre metaphysical theory, in the normal sense of "metaphysical", what is? What Ayer did was to use a persuasive definition. He re-defined "metaphysics" so as to make it applicable only to metaphysical theories other than his own. Not a few philosophers were persuaded to accept this eccentric definition. How odd that they should have failed to recognise immediately as metaphysical a theory which presupposes that nothing (really) exists except sense-data. Ayer did not of course *say* 'Nothing exists except sense-data' or 'Nothing exists which is not observable in principle'. These statements, like their contradictories, are meaningless according to Ayer's VP. But his position involves outlawing as meaningless all ontological theories except the kind of Neutral Monism which is presupposed by Ayer's Phenomenalism and which he had inherited from Hume.

Let us now consider Ayer's three-sentence proof that Phenomenalism *must* be accepted. After he had smuggled in the assumption that sense-contents are private entities, by equating his own use of "sense-content" with 'the word "idea" in this [Locke's] usage' (p. 53), he wrote:

we know that it must be possible to define material things in terms of sense-contents, because it is only by the occurrence of certain sense-contents that the existence of any material thing can be in the least degree verified. And thus we can see that we have not to enquire whether a phenomenalist "theory of perception" or some other sort of theory is correct, but only what form of phenomenalist theory is correct. For the fact that all causal and representative theories of perception treat material things as if they were unobservable entities entitles us, as Berkeley saw, to rule them out *a priori* (p. 53).

This is a paradigm case of *a priori* linguistics. I cannot recall any other professing empiricist[2] claiming to establish by a *purely a priori* argument what we mean by the language in which we talk about material things and our perception of them. Earlier empiricists, in arguing for the privacy of 'ideas of sense', 'impressions' or 'sense-data', appealed to empirical facts concerning our perceptual experience, e.g. the occurrence of illusions, or concerning scientists' discoveries about the causal conditions of perception. Ayer ignores all such empirical considerations in his *LTL* demonstration. Astonishingly, he does not even mention a Realist theory as one of the alternatives which need to be eliminated in establishing Phenomenalism. He just ignores the common-sense assumption that tables, etc., when they are not being perceived, continue to exist and to possess qualities similar to those we perceive them as having. Presumably the reason why Ayer did not mention these beliefs is that unobserved physical objects, as they are conceived by Realists, would be metaphysical objects according to his version of the VP.

We must consider two more examples of Ayer's *a priori* linguistics. These are important for two reasons: (i) the paradoxical conclusions drawn in 1936 were to plague Ayer, and to lead him to jettison his 1936 VP twenty years later; (ii) these examples reveal that in practice Ayer's VP involved assuming that a statement is meaningful *for me* if and only if it is verifiable *by me*. This is not made clear in Chapter I, where Ayer amended the formulation of the VP current among the Vienna Circle, e.g. that the meaning of a proposition is the method of its verification, as Schlick had put it. (See *Gesammelte Aufsätze*, 1938,

[2] Except, of course, Berkeley in his *Principles*.

p. 181.) According to Ayer "verifiable" is to mean, not 'conclusively verifiable', but 'possible for experience to render . . . probable' (p. 37); and it is to mean 'verifiable in principle' and not verifiable in practice (p. 36). In Chapter I, Ayer formulates the VP in the third, and not the first, person: 'a sentence is factually significant *for any given person*, if and only if *he* knows how to verify it' (p. 35. My italics). But consider how Ayer *applied* his VP.

(1) *Ayer's treatment of the problem about knowledge of other minds.* His problem is, given his VP as an axiom, what account can be given of the meaning of statements like 'John has a pain'. Ayer denies that the argument from analogy, 'based on . . . a perceptible resemblance between the behaviour of other bodies and that of my own', could 'justify a belief in the existence of other people whose experiences *I* could not conceivably observe'. His argument is that 'on the view which we are discussing [i.e. the common sense view that other people have private experiences, 'sense-contents', which are like my own], *I* must regard other people as metaphysical objects; for it is assumed that their experiences are completely inaccessible to *my* observation' (p. 129. My italics). This shows that Ayer was using "verifiable" to mean 'verifiable *by me*'.[3] Ayer's solution was to adopt a behaviouristic[4] account of statements about other people's experiences; but it is a queer kind of behaviourism. Behaviourists normally take for granted a Realist theory of perception, though they could adopt a Representative theory. But since, on Ayer's account, a physical object is, for me, a logical construction from my sense-data, any statements that I make about John's body are (are analysable into) statements about *my* sense-data. So Ayer is obliged to conclude that when I say, e.g. 'John has a pain', I am talking about *my* sense-data—those sense-data which I have, or could get, if I do what I would normally describe as watching John grimace, listen to his groans, etc. But although he used the first-person singular in presenting his argument, Ayer reverted to the third person and first person plural in formulating his conclusion: that 'each of

[3] More specifically, this passage shows that Ayer was applying the principle that a statement is verifiable by me only if *I* can observe whatever the statement is *about*.

[4] Ayer describes his account as 'behaviouristic', not in the text, but in his 1946 Introduction, p. 20.

us has to define the content of another man's sense-experience in terms of what he can himself observe' (p. 132); and he speaks of 'this reduction of other people's experiences to one's own' (p. 130).[5] Ayer was not, however, entitled to switch from "I" to "one", i.e. anyone. For he claimed that 'a self... must be held to be a logical construction out of sense-experiences', and that 'for any two sense-experiences to belong to the sense-history of the same self it is necessary and sufficient that they should contain organic sense-contents which are elements of the same body' (p. 125). Thus Ayer had no right to speak of 'other people's experiences', which, on his own account, means: sense-contents other than those which constitute myself and which form series each of which contains organic sense-contents which are elements of some body other than my own. He ought to have concluded that any such series of sense-contents are 'completely inaccessible to my observation' and are, for me, 'metaphysical objects'.

(2) *Ayer's account of the meaning of statements about the past.* This was expressed in *LTL*, with extreme brevity, by saying that statements about the past are 'rules for the prediction of those "historical" experiences which are commonly said to verify them' (p. 102). This thesis was formulated more explicitly, though not then endorsed, in his next book, *Foundations of Empirical Knowledge* (1940): 'I can only attach meaning to propositions which seem to refer to the past if I interpret them as referring to a set of experiences which *I* could obtain now or in the future, these experiences being such as would ordinarily be regarded as indirect evidence for the truth of the propositions in question' (p. 167). I have italicized "I". Its use indicates that Ayer's paradox derives from equating "verifi-

[5] Notice, in passing, the main resemblance and difference between Ayer's application of "the" VP to this problem and that made earlier by Rudolf Carnap ('Psychology in Physical Language', reprinted by Ayer in *Logical Positivism*, 1959, from *Erkenntnis*, 1931). Carnap had concluded that a sentence like "John is in pain" or "John is excited" (as people normally understand it) is 'a metaphysical pseudo-sentence' (p. 174). Carnap's answer to his own question, what does such a sentence mean?, was, in effect, to *define* expressions like "in pain" or "excited" in terms of the 'physical structure (micro-structure) of [a person's] body (especially of his central nervous system) ...' (p. 172). What an odd conclusion for someone who started with the question: how can I (or we) *verify*, e.g., that John is in pain? For nobody is yet in a position to verify such statements by inspecting the micro-structure of John's central nervous system.

able" with 'verifiable-by-me'. Though Ayer did not make this explicit, he was committed to describing historical events and people (e.g. the Battle of Hastings or Julius Caesar) as *metaphysical* entities!

Let us now trace the story of how Ayer wrestled with the paradoxes which he embraced in *LTL*. As early as 1936, Professor Ryle offered Ayer a way of escaping from these paradoxes, in an article 'Unverifiability-by-Me' (*Analysis*, Volume 4). Ryle suggested that the VP be amended to assert, in effect, that a (non-analytic) statement is meaningful, if and only if it is verifiable by someone or other—living or dead, or (presumably) yet unborn. Ryle called his version of the VP 'the principle of verifiability by any verifier you please' (p. 7). He argued that 'The verifiability-principle can contain no reference to me' (p. 11). His way of dealing with statements about other people's experiences is conveyed in these passages:

I want to argue that . . . 'I can only find introspectively my own experiences' is an analytic proposition but one which directly *entails* that it is significant to say 'there are introspectible experiences which are not in me and so not introspectible by me' (pp. 4–5); and My experiences are private certainly. That is a tautology . . . But privacy being a causal notion, it must be significant to say that there are experiences which do not belong to me . . . What then can I understand by the statement 'someone else is having a dream'? Assuming the truth of the principle of verifiability by any verifier you please, it would mean 'someone might wake up and recall having had a dream . . . And I did not dream any such dream' (p. 10).

Twenty years later, in *The Problem of Knowledge* (1956), Ayer finally accepted the version of the VP which Ryle had proposed. His reluctance to do so is revealed by the desperate expedients to which he resorted in the interval. In *Foundations of Empirical Knowledge* (pp. 167–9), he argued that statements about the past are meaningful because it is logically possible[6] that *I* might have existed at any earlier time; and that statements about another person's experiences are meaningful because it is logically possible[6] that *I* should have an experience [e.g. a pain] that is in fact owned by someone else! The arguments which Ayer used in *FEK* to support these conclusions

[6] What can Ayer have meant here by "logically possible"?

were, however, inconsistent with his own premises. His thesis that it is logically possible that *he* might have existed at any other period of history is inconsistent with his thesis that he is (is a logical construction out of) a series of sense-data; for, on Ayer's account, a sense-datum is an occurrence which cannot be identified by reference to something *in* which or *to* which it occurs, so its identity must presumably depend upon the time at which it occurs. His argument to justify his conclusion that it is logically possible that he should have an experience which is in fact owned by someone else, begs his own question. He wrote: 'with regard to any given experience, it is a contingent fact that it belongs to *one series rather than another*. And *for this reason* I have no difficulty in conceiving that there may be experiences which are not related to my experience in the ways that would be required to constitute them elements in my empirical history . . .' (p. 168. My italics). The reason he gives here presupposes that it is meaningful for him to postulate series of experiences other than those which constitute himself; though the meaningfulness of this is precisely what he is here trying to justify, is trying to reconcile with his VP, which he formulates here by saying: '*I* cannot significantly assert the existence of anything that *I* could not conceivably observe' (p. 166. My italics). This is what he here described as the '*a priori* difficulty' which has to be removed before one may appeal to the argument from analogy (p. 169). During the next stage, in his 1946 Introduction to *LTL*, Ayer abandoned his 1940 (*FEK*) position, on the ground (unusual for him) that it does not conform with 'our present usage', and he said that he was 'inclined to revert to a "behaviouristic" interpretation of propositions about other people's experiences' (pp. 19–20).

Before considering what Ayer says in the passage in *The Problem of Knowledge* (1956), where he abandons his original version of the VP, attention will be drawn to Ayer's misinterpretation, indeed caricature, of what he calls 'the older empiricist principle', in his 1946 Introduction to *LTL*. We must consider what Russell had said in his beginners' book *Problems of Philosophy* (1912) in the passage to which Ayer here refers. Ayer criticizes Russell's empiricist principle for 'the defect of imposing too harsh a condition upon the form of scientific theories; for it would seem to imply that it was illegitimate to introduce any term that did not itself designate something observable' (p. 14). Can Ayer really have thought that Russell's account implies that it is illegitimate to introduce terms like "meson", "the force of Gravity", etc.? He makes it appear that Russell might have thought this by quoting from Russell only the italicized part of this admittedly opaque sentence: 'The fundamental principle in the analysis of propositions containing descriptions is this: *every proposition which we can understand must be composed wholly of constituents with which we are acquainted*'. But one need only read Russell's next two paragraphs to see that *of course* Russell's position does not imply what Ayer said it seems to. Russell emphasizes, as the main merit of his theory of descriptions which he is here adumbrating, 'that it enables us to pass beyond the limits of our private experience' (*P of P*, p. 92); that is, that it enables us to do what Ayer's Verifiability-by-Me principle precluded Ayer from doing, leading Ayer to describe another person's pain as a 'metaphysical object'. Russell's opaque sentence should not have been quoted without quoting also some of the passages which explain it, such as: 'it is scarcely conceivable that we can make a judgement or entertain a supposition without knowing what it is that we are judging or supposing about. We must attach *some* meaning to the words we use, if we are to speak significantly and not utter mere noise; and the meaning we attach to our words must be something with which we are acquainted' (p. 91). Admittedly Russell was not here using "acquainted" in its everyday sense. His list of the kinds of thing with which we can be acquainted (in his sense) included so-called sense-data and universals, but excluded material things. This obviously needs amendment to avoid begging questions which acceptance of Empiricism does not require us to beg. Russell's words also need amendment to avoid the suggestion that the meaning of a word is some object to which it refers; as if all words were names, and the meaning of any name were its *nominatum*. The amended version of Russell's last quoted sentence could read: a person can attach meaning to any word only if he can interpret this word in terms of what he himself has experienced. From this principle we can, of course, derive *a* rule for eliminating meaningless sentences, namely that a sentence is meaningless for a person unless he can interpret each of the linguistic expressions which it contains in terms of what he himself has experienced, of the data of his own observation or self-awareness.

I think I understand why Ayer was so slow, so reluctant, to amend his VP by dropping the by-me qualification. Since Locke attempted to formulate Empiricism, the main aim has been to maintain that *each person's* 'ideas', beliefs and knowledge are dependent on *his own* experience. It is a basic tenet of traditional British Empiricism that another person's words can have meaning *for me* only if and insofar as *I* can interpret them in terms of *my* experience. The formulation of Empiricism by Russell, and my suggested alternative, affirm this central tenet, which Ayer *seems* to have abandoned, since he has not rejected the VP, yet has abandoned the by-me qualification. This qualification was rejected emphatically by Ayer in *The Problem of Knowledge* (1956). Here he deals with his problem concerning statements about the past by saying that verifiability does not require 'that any particular person, the author or any other, should in fact be capable of verifying them' (p. 199); he stresses the need to 'distinguish between statements which are unverifiable by anyone and those that are unverifiable by some particular person' (p. 246); and he says: 'Empirical statements may be said to refer to experiences, in the sense that it is only through the occurrence of some experience that they can be shown to be true or false, *but it need not be one's own experience*' (pp. 238–9. My italics). Ayer was here accepting Ryle's 1936 principle of 'verifiability by any verifier you please'. These statements by Ayer occur in the chapter which culminates with a revised account of 'statements about other minds', so one would expect Ayer to make use of his amended version of the VP in arguing that such statements are meaningful. *Yet he does not do so.* The solution he offers is in fact an application of Russell's kind of Empiricism. Ayer writes:

> And if I can know what it would be like to satisfy a certain set of descriptions and to have a certain experience, then I can understand a statement to the effect that someone who satisfies these descriptions is having that experience, independently of whether that person is, or could be, myself (p. 249).

As the context shows, Ayer's if-clause has to be interpreted as meaning: 'if I can understand the description used to refer to a certain person and the description of the kind of experience ascribed to this person'.

There is nothing here about my having to be able to *verify* such a statement; only that, to understand it, I must understand the descriptions which occur in it, i.e., presumably, I must be able to interpret these descriptions in terms of my own experience. Has Ayer recognized that "the" VP, any VP, is redundant? Apparently not. One gets the impression from his later writings that he still feels that *some* form of "the" VP *must* be valid. He ends his paper 'Can there be a Private Language?' by saying: 'No doubt it is a necessary condition for *my* understanding a descriptive statement that it should be, in some way, verifiable. But it need not be directly verifiable ... *it need not be verifiable by me*' (*PAS*, Supp. Vol., 1954. My italics). And he said in his Inaugural Lecture in 1960: 'I have no wish to disown the verification principle, though it suffers from a vagueness which it has not yet been found possible to eradicate' (*The Concept of a Person*, 1963, pp. 20–1). Could Ayer be content with the implications of equating "verifiable" with 'verifiable by someone or other'? He would then have no right to challenge claims that statements about God or Nirvana or the Absolute have been verified by the experiences of mystics and are therefore meaningful for them, if not for others.

I submit that the kind of Positivism which Ayer brought back from Vienna led British empiricists into a blind alley, from which, it seems, they have not yet found an escape—except to suppress "the" VP, while still sometimes using an unidentified version thereof. Philosophers have oscillated between different versions of "the" VP, including the following:

(i) According to Ayer's earlier version, a non-analytic sentence is meaningful *for me* if and only if it is verifiable *by me*.

(ii) According to Ryle's 1936, and Ayer's 1956, version, a non-analytic sentence is meaningful if and only if it is verifiable *by someone, living, dead or yet unborn*. 'Meaningful *for whom*?' we should then ask. If the answer is 'for someone, living, dead or yet unborn', this formula is an uninteresting tautology. If the answer is 'for anyone', or 'for oneself', this formula is obviously false.

(iii) I shall here anticipate something for which I shall argue in Part Two of this book: that a third, and importantly different, version of the VP forms a suppressed premise of some of Wittgenstein's arguments in *Philosophical Investigations*, and in some philosophical writings influenced by his later remarks. This version may be formulated: that a sentence used to make a statement about a person, P, is meaningful *for anyone including P*, if and only if it is verifiable *by people other than P*.

It will be convenient to have labels for referring to these three versions of the VP. I shall refer to them as 'the By-Me version' 'the By-Someone version', and 'the By-Others version'. Acceptance of Ayer's By-Me version commits one to a behaviouristic account of the meanings of statements about the private experiences of others. The By-Someone version does not commit one to any form of behaviourism, and indeed Ryle's purpose in proposing it in 1936 was *inter alia* to avoid the paradoxes involved in Ayer's *LTL* behaviourism. I shall argue later that the By-Others version commits one to conclusions which there are good reasons for classifying as a species of behaviourism. But the question to be pressed now is: why should any empiricist accept or apply, overtly or covertly, *any* version of "the" VP? The central theses of traditional British Empiricism have presumably been these:

(i) that all statements whose truth can be known *a priori* are analytic, their truth being determined by the meanings of the symbols in which they are expressed;

(ii) that *the evidence* for the truth or falsity of any non-analytic statement consists of the data of *some*one's observations and/or self-awareness;

(iii) that *a person's evidence* for the truth or falsity of any non-analytic statement consists of the data of *his own* observations and/or self-awareness, such data including, of course, testimony of other people;

(iv) that all of a person's ideas are derived from *his own* experience. (In this imprecise statement, "ideas" may be interpreted to mean capacities to use certain symbols and/or to recognize certain things.)

Why should anyone have wished to substitute for these theses some *ad hoc* rule designed solely to distinguish meaningless from meaningful sentences?[7] If, or insofar as, empiricists want a rule for eliminating meaningless sentences, they may adopt the rule implicit in the arguments of earlier British empiricists, like Hume and Russell: namely that a sentence is meaningless for a person *unless* he can interpret each of the linguistic expressions which it contains in terms of what *he himself* has experienced. Notice now a feature of Ayer's *application* of his By-Me version on which I have not commented. His paradoxes derive not simply from equating "verifiable" with 'verifiable-by-me', but also (and without making this explicit) from *identifying* meaning and evidence, from identifying what a sentence means to me with my evidence for its truth, i.e., according to Ayer, with the sense-data which I have got or could get which would be my evidence for its truth. As soon as this equation is made explicit, it is obvious that it is indefensible and must be rejected. Correcting this error does not, however, enable us to salvage the By-Me version of the VP. The reason for rejecting this version is that it is a confused conflation of the several theses of traditional Empiricism presented above.

Presumably linguistic philosophers, or at least most of them, *are* still empiricists. Some who take Wittgenstein's instructions most literally would perhaps want to maintain a discreet neutrality, or even dismiss Empiricism because it is a *theory*, and therefore to be banned from philosophy. ('We may not advance any kind of theory.' *PI*, § 98.) And there is an awkwardness about professing Empiricism for those who have been persuaded to equate it with acceptance of some form of the Verification Principle, yet have not managed to formulate this in any way which achieves what they want (i.e. to accommodate their own common-sense beliefs about the world plus respectable scientific statements about unobservable entities, while outlawing as nonsense all other statements about unobservables especially those made by theologians and philosophers). If it is the failure to find a viable formulation of "the" VP which inhibits some philosophers from acknowledging, and many from practising, Empiricism, recognition that Empiricism should not be equated with any VP may do some good. In any case it is incongruous that a philosopher should do what Ayer did in *LTL*, which was

[7] Part of the answer may be a desire not to bore by saying what has been said before.

explicitly presented as a modern and rigorous form of Empiricism: i.e. to lay down a rule, treat it as self-evident and deduce from it many counterfactual conclusions. Ayer showed as little concern with relevant empirical facts as other Rationalist metaphysicians have done in the past—they did not permit mere empirical facts to cast doubt upon what they deduced from what *they* found self-evident. There is a resemblance between Ayer's procedure in *LTL* and Ryle's in *The Concept of Mind*, the book which I shall discuss next. Ryle says things in Chapter I which imply or suggest that he is in possession of some rule which entitles him to dismiss sentences which we do use as 'category-mistakes', as 'improper', 'absurd', 'without sense', etc. I think Ryle would wish to be regarded as an empiricist. How odd that any empiricist should assert or assume in Chapter I a rule about meaning or language, and deduce from it that we cannot or may not say things that we do say! David Hume, in Section I of his *Treatise*, did 'venture to affirm' his rule, designed for much the same purpose—to eliminate talk which he thought to be meaningless. But Hume did at least challenge his readers to falsify his rule, if they could, by finding a counter-example; and he found one himself which he decided was unimportant.[8] So Hume did present his rule, initially, as a hypothesis which needs to be tested by observation, though he concluded too hastily that it is so confirmed. Surely those who profess Empiricism ought to practise Empiricism in their own philosophical writing and thinking, and not only in their lectures on the history of philosophy.

What has been said in this section should not be construed as suggesting that I do not recognize *LTL*, for all its faults, as a classic of condensed and persuasive argument, nor construed as an attack on Professor Ayer, who has so often led the way in revising his pre-war positions.

[8] This is the 'contradictory phenomenon' which Hume describes in the third-last paragraph of Section I: that a person can form an idea of a particular shade of blue which he had never seen.

SECTION IV

Important Ambiguities in Professor Ryle's *The Concept of Mind*

RYLE'S *The Concept of Mind* (1949) is an important book for at least two reasons. It made a generation of philosophers re-think an important family of problems. It showed how over-simplified and inadequate was an assumption made by most earlier philosophers about the words used to describe what may be called loosely 'states of mind': the assumption that such words are simply names of private experiences, or of dispositions to have such experiences. That this view now seems to us naïve is a measure of Ryle's achievement.[1] This book has, however, serious faults. Its arguments oscillate between incompatible theses, and they are presented in jargon which often obscures Ryle's purpose and his methods. He describes his subject-matter as 'the logic of mental-conduct concepts', and his method as correcting mistakes about the 'categories' to which such concepts belong. This vigorous, witty and influential book will doubtless be read for many years to come, and a critique of linguistic philosophy must involve trying to identify its theses and evaluate its methods of argument.

Ryle describes his negative thesis as being to refute what he calls 'the official theory' about minds, meaning Descartes' kind of dualism, according to which a person's mind is an immaterial substance which does not depend for its existence upon his body and in which inhere all of his states of consciousness and mental powers. Ryle dubs this 'the Ghost in the Machine' theory. He claims that it is 'one big mistake and a mistake of a special kind . . . namely a category-mistake' (p. 16), and that it is the source of many other category-mistakes. The most important of these, according to what Ryle says in Chapter I, are:

(i) what he calls 'the doctrine of Privileged Access', i.e. the

[1] The revolt against the traditional philosophy of mind was pioneered by Wittgenstein, but his thoughts on this were not published until 1953 and after.

view that 'only I can take direct cognisance of the states and processes of my own mind' (p. 11), that 'Direct access to the workings of a mind is the privilege of that mind itself' (p. 14);

(ii) the view that the words we use to describe people's characters, mental states, etc., signify 'special episodes in their secret histories', 'modifications' in the 'stream of consciousness' (p. 15);

(iii) what he calls 'the para-mechanical hypothesis', i.e. the view that the mind is 'a field of causes and effects' (p. 18), a 'centre of causal processes' (p. 19). Surprisingly, Ryle speaks as if the view that (some) actions have mental causes were a new hypothesis invented by Descartes (p. 21).

Elucidation of his term "category-mistake" is clearly essential for Ryle's purpose. His method of doing this is to offer examples. He says that a child or a foreigner would be making a category-mistake if he took "the University of Oxford" to refer to an institution of the same kind as does "Christ Church", or took "the division" to refer to a military unit distinct from the battalions, etc., which compose it. He adds that such mistakes are made by people 'who did not know how to wield the concepts *University*, *division* . . . Their puzzles arose from *inability to use certain items in the English vocabulary*' (p. 17). Notice that the clause which I have italicized indicates that Ryle is equating "wielding a concept" with using a word or phrase. In view of this, Ryle's description of his programme—'to rectify the logic of our mental-conduct concepts' (p. 16)—would *seem* to mean: correcting our ways of using the host of English words which, as we say, describe a person's mind. This impression is reinforced by Ryle's claim that all sentences which conjoin or disjoin terms like "body" and "mind", or "mental . . ." and "physical . . ." are category-mistakes, are not 'proper', are 'absurd' and 'make no sense' (p. 22). As examples of such absurd conjunctions he gives: 'there exist both minds and bodies', 'there occur physical processes and mental processes', 'there are mechanical causes . . . and mental causes of corporeal movements'. Ryle certainly appears here to be correcting, and not describing, English usage; for his dicta involve treating as senseless many sentences which are commonly used and understood, like "He is strong (healthy or resilient) in mind and body" or "His behaviour had both mental and physical causes". Chapter I gives one a strong impression that Ryle is doing *a priori* linguistics. He says that his key arguments are 'intended to show why certain sorts of operations with the concepts of mental powers and operations are breaches of logical rules' (p. 8); which suggests that when Ryle brands a sentence as a category-mistake, this is a deduction from some 'logical rule'—from (the reader would assume) the rule or rules for assigning 'concepts' to the proper 'categories'.

Sometimes, however, Ryle describes his programme in ways which suggest that it involves not *a priori* but empirical linguistics. He writes:

> Most of the mental-conduct concepts whose logical behaviour we examine in this book, are familiar and everyday concepts. We all know how to apply them . . . What is in dispute is not how to apply them, but how to classify them, or in what categories to put them (p. 62).

> Many people can talk sense with concepts but cannot talk sense about them... cannot state the logical regulations governing their use (p. 7).

Such statements suggest that Ryle shared Wittgenstein's view that our everyday language is 'in perfect logical order', that what needs to be rectified are the ways in which our everyday locutions have been misconstrued by theorists, notably philosophers, and that Ryle's frequent assertions as to what can or cannot properly be said are intended as reminders about English usage, designed to show theorists that *they* have produced category-mistakes. This interpretation of Ryle's programme fits a good deal of what he does. His thesis that statements using dispositional words have been misinterpreted as reports about private episodes is made out by reminding us how people normally use such words (*and* more important, though much less stressed, how they verify such statements). However, if we interpret Ryle's intentions thus, he cannot justify his branding as category-mistakes the many everyday statements in which we conjoin "mind" and "body", or "mental" and "physical". And sometimes he attributes category-mistakes to 'laymen' as well as to 'theorists (e.g. on p. 50).

What then did Ryle mean by "category-mistake"? According

to him, a category-mistake consists of saying (or asking) about a 'concept' belonging to one 'category' something which can be properly or significantly said (or asked) only about a 'concept' of a different 'category'. This presupposes that we have some criterion (rule) for assigning concepts to the same or to different categories. (When I use "criterion" in this book, I use it to mean 'rule for deciding or judging'. See *OED*.) It is, therefore, a very serious omission in *C of M* that Ryle does not explain and discuss the criterion (criteria?) that he is using for this purpose. His nearest approach to formulating a criterion is when he says: 'When two terms belong to the same category, it is proper to construct conjunctive propositions embodying them' (p. 22). The converse of this would give us the following criterion: that when it is improper to construct a conjunctive proposition embodying two terms, these terms are of different categories. Why did Ryle not formulate this rule? Was it because it would make it obvious that *before* he could apply this criterion he must have some independent way of recognizing when a conjunctive sentence is improper (or absurd or senseless?) And then the obvious question would be: by what rule (criterion) do you decide whether a conjunctive sentence is improper, absurd or senseless?

In fact, Ryle had, in his 1938 paper 'Categories' (*PAS*), formulated explicitly a criterion for assigning terms to different categories. (This is discussed in Section VI.) The 1938 criterion has very different implications from the one suggested in *C of M* (p. 22). Philosophers who had read Ryle's 1938 article usually assumed, when discussing *C of M*, that Ryle was using therein his earlier criterion. Suppose he was; that criterion too depends on our having an independent way of deciding which sentences are absurd or senseless. Thus both of Ryle's criteria for determining category-differences hang unsupported in mid-air, unless he is prepared to endorse some rule(s) for deciding when a sentence is improper or senseless, e.g. "the" V P. Whether some version of the V P is a suppressed premise of Ryle's reasoning in *C of M* is a question which will be postponed until we have considered, in the next section, some samples of his kind of linguistic philosophy. But notice how Ryle uses "not proper" or "improper", and "absurd" or "not significant" or "makes no sense", *as if* they meant the same (e.g. on pp. 22–3). His use of "improper" suggests that his court of appeal is grammatical propriety, English usage; his use of "absurd", "senseless", etc., suggests that he is concerned with epistemological problems and that his court of appeal is "the" V P (or some other rule designed for the same purpose). Presumably Ryle would not have wished his readers to regard his use of "category-mistake" simply as his way of dismissing what *he* feels intuitively to be senseless.

Ryle's main negative thesis seems clear. His positive theses—what he proposes to put in place of Cartesian dualism—are far from clear. My chief concern with *C of M* is to illustrate and explain the many counter-factual statements that Ryle makes about the English language. It is necessary, however, in order to understand what led Ryle to make such statements, to try to identify his positive theses. The source of Ryle's pieces of *a priori* and/or legislative linguistics is the fact that he seeks support from ordinary language for rejecting a theory which is, and for affirming theories which are not, built into the grammar of English (and other European languages). This inconsistency in turn seems to be one source of the ambivalence which we find in Ryle's formulations of his positive theses. The remainder of this section will be concerned with the ambivalence of Ryle's positive theses. Section V will illustrate the inconsistencies in Ryle's attempts to support these theses by appealing to English usage. In Section VI, it will be argued that no theoretical backing can be given for Ryle's use of "category-mistake" and that this 'concept' cannot be salvaged for the purpose of doing *a priori* linguistics.

One of the most puzzling features of *C of M* is that Ryle makes many statements which imply that he is advocating some form of Behaviourism, but also makes many more statements which are incompatible with any form of Behaviourism. Before giving examples, I shall offer a diagnosis of the main source of this ambivalence. Ryle argues as if the rejection of Metaphysical Dualism requires the rejection of what he calls the doctrine of Privileged Access (the DPA). This doctrine could equally well be called 'Epistemological Dualism', for what it claims is that there are two different kinds of access to, ways of knowing about, some of a person's mental states. Other people can ascertain the nature of John's experiences—that he is in pain or is picturing Jane or is longing for a cigarette—only on the evidence of his overt behaviour, including his utterance of what he chooses to tell us; whereas John has direct or 'privileged' access to such states—he does not need to observe his own overt behaviour and interpret or draw inferences from what he observes.

From the start, Ryle makes the DPA one of his chief targets. What he presents as his first main argument against Cartesian Dualism is that it is a corollary of the DPA that one person can only make 'problematic inferences' about the states of mind of another; a conclusion which, according to Ryle, would commit us to conclusions which are absurd: 'Absolute solitude is . . . the ineluctable destiny of the soul. Only our bodies can meet' (pp. 14–15). This argument is repeated in the sequel (e.g. on pp. 51 ff.). Ryle apparently did not recognize, when he wrote *C of M*, that accepting the DPA does not commit one to Metaphysical Dualism; that accepting the DPA leaves it an open question whether a person's sensations, feelings, images or unvoiced thoughts are, as Descartes assumed, modifications of an immaterial mind-substance, or, as many philosophers, including most Materialists, have held, are by-products or 'inner aspects' of physical processes occurring in his brain. Ryle often writes as if we had to choose between Metaphysical Dualism and Behaviourism, and indeed rejecting the DPA does commit one to some form of Behaviourism.

Before going further, however, I must explain how I am using "Behaviourism". Philosophers who assert or deny that Ryle (or Wittgenstein) was a behaviourist, without explaining what they themselves understand by "Behaviourism", have forgotten Socrates' first lesson. The psychologists who have called themselves 'behaviourists' have used this word in some very different ways. For J. B. Watson, who introduced the term, Behaviourism is primarily a methodological principle or policy: that the data of scientific psychology should comprise only observed and publicly observable behaviour of living organisms;[2] that 'introspective data' should never be 'sought during the experimentation, or published in the results'.[3] But Watson also says things which show that he wished to reject Cartesian Dualism in favour of Physicalism. He even spoke of 'the fiction that there is such

[2] See *Behaviourism*, 1925, Ch. I, esp. p. 6.

[3] 'Psychology As The Behaviourist Views It', *Psych. Review*, Vol. XX, 1913, p. 170.

a thing as mental life' (*Behaviourism*, p. 180); and he proposed to drop terms like 'consciousness, mental state, . . . imagery, and the like' (1913 article, op. cit., p. 166), apparently because he thought that there *are* no private states, processes or objects to which such words could be applied. Thus he dismissed mental images as fictitious (*Behaviourism*, p. 213). Compare Watsonian Behaviourism with the kind of theory which Professor C. A. Mace has advocated and presented as a species of Behaviourism: he explicitly rejects Watson's central methodological proposal, for Mace treats introspection as an indispensable source of data, and does not even substitute a synonym for "introspection".[4] The theory which Mace defends, and calls 'Analytical Behaviourism', involves accepting Physicalism without rejecting the DPA.

Psychologists who have called themselves 'behaviourists' and have tried to remain faithful to Watson's methodological policy have usually been inconsistent, at any rate if they have experimented with people as well as rats. They have continued to solicit and to rely upon what others call 'introspective reports',[5] and to interpret such responses as *statements* which give information about what they themselves cannot observe, i.e. their subjects' experiences; and they have sought to make this procedure appear 'objective' and 'scientific' by *re-christening* such responses, e.g. as 'verbal behaviour'.[6] Some of the psychologists who have tried to follow Watson's programme (including Watson) are also inconsistent in another respect: they stretch the meaning of the word "behaviour" to include physical processes within the organism which are not publicly observable. (Compare this with Carnap's kind of physicalism mentioned above, p. 32.) Watson himself initiated this, by using "internal" or "implicit behaviour" to cover, for example, a person's glandular reactions and the movements in his speech organs which, Watson assumed, *constitute* his thinking. Other psychologists have gone further in this direction. Thus Mace stretches "behaviour" to

[4] 'Some Implications of Analytical Behaviourism', *PAS*, 1948–9, p. 7.

[5] When an experimenter says to his subject, e.g.: 'Press the button when this disc looks to you the same colour as that one', the subject's manual response will function as a statement; the subject has to understand such instructions as a request for information about his own perceptual experience, i.e. about something *not* observable by the experimenter.

[6] See, e.g., B. F. Skinner's *Verbal Behaviour* (1957), and Ch. XVII of his *Science and Human Behaviour*, 1953.

include 'bodily states, bodily dispositions, bodily "states of readiness" . . .' (op. cit., p. 4). Psychologists who do this seem (unlike Skinner) to have forgotten the point of Watson's programme—that psychologists' data should be limited to what has been observed and is publicly observable.

When "Behaviourism" is used by philosophers to refer to a philosophical theory or thesis, presumably it is not being used to refer to a methodology for the practice of psychology. This is the psychologists' business. And it would not be useful for us to use "Behaviourism" as a synonym for "Physicalism" or "Materialism". *If* any philosopher has ever held, explicitly and at all consistently, that there are no conscious states or processes or private objects, that the latter are fictitious, it would be appropriate to follow Mace in calling this thesis 'Metaphysical Behaviourism' (op. cit., p. 2). However, the type of philosophical theory or thesis which it is useful for us to label "Behaviourism" is the main claim made by what Mace calls 'Analytical Behaviourism', and which he formulates thus: 'Statements about mind or consciousness just turn out to be, on analysis, statements about the behaviour of material things [i.e. living organisms]' (op. cit., p. 2). This wording is acceptable provided that we do not stretch "behaviour" to cover all physical states and processes, including hypothetical ones, which go on inside organisms.

I shall, however, amend Mace's formulation, using "mind-predicate" to refer to any term which we use to describe a person's mind, mental act or state or process or ability or susceptibility, etc. I shall use "(Philosophical) Behaviourism" to refer to the theses which may then be expressed by saying that the meanings of mind-predicates have to be explained[7] in terms of publicly observable behaviour, *or*, less vaguely, that statements ascribing any mind-predicate to any person can be analysed without remainder into statements about what *other* people can or could observe this person doing. We need a label for this purpose, since such theses have been advocated by not a few philosophers in recent years; sometimes, however, ex-

[7] Notice that, in this definition, "explained in terms of" is ambiguous. It may mean 'taught by reference to', or 'defined in terms of' or 'analyzed in terms of'. That is why I use it. For the philosophers whom I would classify as behaviourists tend to telescope, or oscillate between, these three different claims. I shall explain this statement in Part Two.

pressed in jargon, as a thesis concerning 'the logic of mental conduct concepts' (Ryle), or concerning 'the criteria for saying so and so' (Wittgenstein).

Ryle makes many statements which strongly suggest that he is advocating Behaviourism as I have defined this term; and insofar as he frequently speaks of mental acts or processes as 'supposed', 'occult', 'ghostly', 'mythical', etc., his language suggests that he is also advocating Metaphysical Behaviourism. Here are a few examples:

> Understanding a person's deeds and words is not . . . any kind of problematic divination of occult processes. For this divination does not and cannot occur . . . it is part of my general thesis that the supposed occult processes are themselves mythical; there exists nothing to be the object of the postulated diagnoses (p. 54);

> The sorts of things that I can find out about myself are the same as the sorts of things I can find out about other people, *and the methods of finding them out are much the same* (p. 155. My italics);

> The radical objection to the theory that minds must know what they are about, because mental happenings are by definition conscious, or metaphorically self-luminous, is that there are no such happenings; (p. 161);

> One of the strongest forces making for belief in the doctrine that the mind is a private stage is the ingrained habit of assuming that there must exist . . . "cognitive acts" and "cognitive processes" . . . [like] making judgements or passing from premises to conclusions . . . The imputed episodes seemed to be impenetrably "internal" because they were genuinely unwitnessable. But they were genuinely unwitnessable because they were mythical (p. 318).

Such sweeping claims explain why *C of M* has excited interest among behaviourist psychologists. These claims turn out, however, to be specious. Repeatedly, Ryle unobtrusively re-admits by the back-door the facts which he had ostentatiously kicked out of the front-door. Here are some examples.

(1) In Chapter II, Ryle starts by asserting that 'when we describe people as exercising qualities of mind, we are not referring to occult episodes of which their overt acts and utterances are effects; we are referring to those overt acts and utterances themselves' (p. 25). Yet later in this chapter he says: 'knowing how is a disposition . . . its exercises may be overt *or covert*,

deeds performed *or deeds imagined*, words spoken aloud *or words heard in one's head*, pictures painted on canvas *or pictures in the mind's eye*' (pp. 46–7. My italics).

(2) In the same chapter, Ryle asserts: 'Overt intelligent performances are not clues to the workings of minds; they are those workings'. Yet he adds that Boswell's description of Dr. Johnson's mind 'was, of course, incomplete, since there were notoriously some thoughts which Johnson kept carefully to himself and there must have been many dreams, day-dreams and silent babblings *which only Johnson could have recorded*' (pp. 57–8. My italics).

(3) In Chapter VI, Ryle represents the traditional view of self-knowledge as involving a 'two-fold[8] Privileged Access', namely 'constant awareness' of the contents of one's own mind and introspection, i.e. the occasional deliberate scrutiny of such contents (p. 154). Ryle asserts that 'consciousness and introspection cannot be what they are officially described as being *since their supposed objects are myths*' (p. 155. My italics). And what Ryle is here referring to as 'supposed objects' is shown by his formulation of the traditional view: 'I am conscious of all my feelings, volitions, emotions and thinkings, and I introspectively scrutinize some of them' (p. 155). This bold beginning is cancelled out, however, as the argument proceeds. A person's 'constant awareness' of what he is thinking and doing is reinstated with the aid of homely synonyms like "is *au fait* with" and "eavesdrop on"; for Ryle allows that, when acting intelligently, an agent is '*au fait* both with what he has completed and with what remains to do' (p. 178) and that 'we eavesdrop on our own unvoiced utterances' (p. 184). The deliberate scrutiny of private objects or processes is also reinstated, provided only that they are described as 'objects of retrospection' and not 'objects of introspection' (pp. 167–8). Ryle argues here as if we cannot pay heed to a private occurrence until it has stopped occurring, though this is obviously false of some of his own examples, like having a tune running in one's head. Ryle argues that philosophers who accept the DPA are using "conscious" in a way in which it is not used in ordinary life. Yet his own list of the ordinary uses includes that in which "conscious of" means 'paying

[8] Though no one would say that we have a two-fold access to tables because we may be conscious of them with or without scrutinizing them!

heed to'. And he diverts attention from the other relevant everyday use, in which a person is said to become conscious when he wakens up or comes out of a general anaesthetic; diverts attention by reporting the uncommon usage in which a person under a local anaesthetic 'is said to have lost consciousness from his feet up to his knees' (pp. 156–7).

(4) In Chapter VII, Ryle rejects as spurious 'the hallowed antithesis . . . between things and events which anyone may witness and things and events which only their possessor may witness', and he supports this with the following argument:

> It is true that the cobbler cannot *witness* the tweaks that I feel when the shoe pinches. But it is false that I *witness* them . . . I feel or have the tweaks, but I do not *discover* or *peer at* them; they are not things that I find out by *watching* them, *listening to* them or *savouring* them. In the sense in which a person has had a robin under observation, it would be nonsense to say that he *has had* a twinge *under observation* (p. 205. My italics).

This odd argument hinges on exploiting the obviously inappropriate verbs which I have italicized. The fact that we do not use our eyes, ears or palates to detect pains is scarcely a reason for denying that we have privileged access to them, that we can attend to them and notice facts about them which are not similarly accessible to others. Indeed, on the next page, Ryle's apparently behaviourist claim is cancelled out and transformed into a minor verbal claim. He says: 'the fact that we cannot talk of the observation of sensations by no means precludes us from talking about the notice or heed that people can pay to their sensations' (p. 206). And even the claim that we cannot talk of 'observing sensations', is undermined by Ryle's recognition on the next page that ''observe' . . . is sometimes used as a synonym of 'pay heed to' or 'notice''. In any case, why criticize the DPA as if its supporters spoke of 'witnessing' or 'observing' sensations, when they have usually used other verbs like "to introspect"?

The last two examples illustrate why many of Ryle's linguistic arguments appear to the unsympathetic to be verbal quibbles. However, the point to be stressed here is that Ryle frequently makes dramatic statements which imply that he is advocating some form of Behaviourism, and then proceeds to offer analyses of mental-predicates involving references to private experiences as well as overt behaviour. Yet he never acknowledges that his bold initial claims need to be qualified. This ambivalence remains to the end of the book. In the closing section, Ryle says that 'the early Behaviourists' were in error; but he then says something which implies that his own position is some form of Behaviourism, namely that their practice of behaviourist methods 'quickly made it apparent to psychologists how *shadowy* were the *supposed* 'inner-life' occurrences which the Behaviourists were at first reproached for ignoring or denying' (p. 328. My italics).

Ryle nowhere acknowledges that he gives back with one hand what he has taken away with the other. Consider this passage:

> The technical trick of conducting our thinking in auditory word-images, instead of in spoken words, does indeed secure secrecy for our thinking . . . But this secrecy is not the secrecy ascribed to the postulated episodes of the ghostly shadow-world. It is merely the convenient privacy which characterizes the tunes which run in my head and the things that I see in my mind's eye (P. 35).

It is indeed convenient that others cannot inspect one's unspoken thoughts, imaginings, etc., and cannot *know* anything about these processes which one does not choose to divulge. But the DPA does not imply that such processes are *private* or *secret* except in the sense which Ryle here calls 'convenient'. As Ryle formulates it, the DPA merely claims that 'only I can take direct cognisance of the states and processes of my own mind' (p. 11). Yet Ryle argues as if conceding this commits one to Cartesian dualism; and he habitually caricatures the latter theory by presenting it in spatial metaphors—describing the mind as a 'world' or 'place' or 'stage' or 'theatre' or 'repository' in which inner occurrences are 'located' or 'housed'.

If we discount Ryle's more sweeping claims, which are cancelled out by his own arguments, and look for the most moderate interpretation, his main theses seem to be these:

(a) that minds are not substances;

(b) that most mind-predicates, including all the important ones, describe dispositions which are manifested predominantly in overt behaviour, predominantly but not exclusively, for they are also manifested in private occurrences;

(c) that a person's actions are never caused by private occurrences, acts or processes.

The last of these theses seems, however, to be indefensible. Ryle's arguments for it, in Chapter III, are very weak. This is not surprising, for we *do* talk about actions being caused by resolutions, decisions, etc., which Ryle acknowledges as 'authentic processes' (p. 68). Ryle defends thesis (c) by arguing as if "cause" has to mean 'sufficient condition'; by claiming that resolutions, etc., cannot be called 'causes' of actions, since they are sometimes not executed. Ryle has no right to this argument, since he himself uses "cause" in the vague everyday senses in which it does not mean 'sufficient condition'. He also supports thesis (c) by arguing that to describe a person's motive is to describe his character, to describe some disposition, which involves a law-like proposition about how the person always or usually acts in circumstances of a certain kind (pp. 89 and 110–14). Ryle completely ignores the very different sense in which to ask about a person's *motive* or *reason* for acting is to ask what was his conscious goal in performing, or deciding to perform, the particular action.

I find it very odd that Ryle should have attacked Cartesian dualism by appealing to English usage, which, like other European languages, has dualist assumptions built into its grammar; and that he should neglect the formidable arguments which are available for his purpose. Such as citing the now extensive experimental evidence that our various mental powers are causally dependent upon more or less specific regions of the brain. Or identifying the errors in Descartes' would-be demonstration that he (his mind) was a substance which was not dependent for his (its) existence on his body.

SECTION V

Ryle's Practice of *A Priori* and/or Legislative Linguistics

THIS section will sample the kinds of inconsistency that we find in Ryle's appeals to English usage. But first it must be stressed that Ryle's account of his own method early in *C of M* implies that the subject-matter which is assignable to categories is linguistic expressions, symbols. Some logicians, including Russell in his earlier writings, have talked as if what is assignable to categories (types) is the contents of a Platonic other world. Philosophers more often talk as if, and sometimes say that, what is assignable to categories are the contents of this world, the familiar things that we use words to talk about. *C of M* is sometimes interpreted as if this is what Ryle intended.[1] But Ryle's position, both in *C of M* and in his earlier paper 'Categories' (*PAS*, 1938), seems to be that the subject-matter of category classification is linguistic expressions. Consider what Ryle says in the 1938 paper in answer to his own question 'what are Types Types of?':

> Only expressions can be affirmed or denied to be absurd. Nature provides no absurdities; nor can we even say that thoughts such as beliefs or supposals *or conceptions* are or are not absurd. For what is absurd is unthinkable (p. 201. My italics).

Ryle seems to be accepting the implications of this when he says that it is 'prudent' to 'formulate our theories and enquiries in such a way as to advertise all the time that we are considering whether such and such expressions may or may not be coupled in such and such ways with other expressions' (p. 201). He anticipates, correctly, that he will then be taken to be 'talking grammar', and proposes a way of *trying* to forestall this: 'We try, then, to say that absurdities result from the improper coupling not of expressions but of what the expressions signify';

[1] See, for example, Ayer's 'Philosophy and Language' (*The Concept of a Person*, 1962, pp. 23–5).

and he introduces the term "proposition-factor" to cover 'whatever is signified by any expression'. But he concedes that 'questions about the types of [proposition-] factors are, in a way, just questions about the possibilities of co-significance of certain classes of expressions' (p. 203). Ryle seems to be acknowledging here that talking about 'proposition-factors' is a rather transparent disguise for talking about linguistic expressions.

In any case, Ryle seems to be committed to this account of his subject-matter by what he says in *C of M*. For he equates the ability to 'wield concepts' with the ability 'to use certain items in the English vocabulary' (p. 17); and he contrasts his subject-matter, described as 'the logic of mental conduct concepts', with 'facts about the mental life of human beings' (p. 16); and he describes his subject-matter both as 'the logic of mental-conduct concepts' and as 'the logical behaviour of some of the cardinal *terms* . . . in which we talk about minds' (p. 126. My italics). Admittedly Ryle often writes as if he had forgotten that, according to his own account, it is concepts *qua* word-uses which are assignable to categories. He often says things like: 'Minds are different sorts of things from bodies' (p. 19), or 'Certainly exhibiting team-spirit is not the same as bowling' (p. 17). Certainly! But these statements are not about the words "mind", "team-spirit", etc., or their uses. Ryle's statements *use* these words, just as I use "chalk" and "cheese" if I say: 'Chalk is very different from cheese'. If, when Ryle says that A and B are of different categories, this had meant only that the *things* called 'A' are very unlike the *things* called 'B', even more dissimilar than chalk and cheese, the contents of *C of M* should after all be catalogued as Psychology, and many of its theses would be truisms.

Let us consider the kind of linguistics contained in Chapter IV of *C of M*. Ryle's target here is a view, ascribed to 'most philosophers and psychologists', that 'emotions are internal or private experiences' (p. 83). What these theorists (unidentified) are alleged to lump together, Ryle divides into different categories. I know of no philosopher who has applied "emotions" to all the kinds of predicates in question, but this is not important, for the interest of this chapter lies in Ryle's classification of these predicates, his arguments for adopting it and the conclusions he uses it to support. Ryle's classification differs not only from those of rival theorists but from English usage. Yet he tries to justify his own classification by appeals to English usage. I list below most of his examples of the predicates he is discussing and the categories to which he assigns them:

Ryle's Categories	*The Predicates*
Inclinations or Motives (These terms are treated as if they were synonyms)	vanity, avarice, patriotism, laziness (p. 85), interest in symbolic logic (p. 87).
Moods	
(a) Agitations	anxious, startled, shocked, excited, convulsed, flabbergasted, in suspense, flurried, irritated (p. 93).
(b) Other Moods	depressed, happy, uncommunicative, restless (p. 98), sullen, hilarious, sad, serene, companionable (p. 99).
Feelings	thrills, twinges, pangs, throbs, wrenches, itches, prickings, chills, glows, loads, qualms, hankerings, curdlings, sinkings, tensions, gnawings and shocks (pp. 83–4).

The inclusion under "Feelings" of words normally used to refer to bodily sensations is made to appear less odd by Ryle's introducing them in phrases like 'a throb of compassion' or 'a twinge of remorse' (p. 84). Later in the chapter one learns that, according to Ryle, it is only the words like "throb" and "twinge" which refer to feelings; that the words which follow "of", like "compassion" and "remorse", are names, not of feelings, but of moods; and that a person's feelings are merely *signs* from which he has problematically to infer what is his own present mood. Ryle's account implies that when I say that I feel happy or sad, bored or angry, what I am reporting is a fallible diagnosis of the mood of which my feelings are signs, and is not something which could be 'a direct intimation of consciousness'.

Consider how Ryle tried to justify this original and interesting thesis. Moods are distinguished from Motives on the ground that the former are short-term dispositions, the latter relatively long-term; and that moods 'monopolize' in a way that motives do not, i.e. that being in a certain mood precludes being in other moods in a way that having a certain motive does not preclude having others (pp. 99–100). Agitations are distinguished from Motives (Inclinations) thus: 'Agitations can be violent or mild. Inclinations can be neither . . . [but] can be strong or weak' (p. 94). This appeal to English usage is based on Ryle's 1938 criterion for category-difference.[2] It is inadequate, since it is perfectly proper to attach "mild" to "inclination", "patriotism" or "interest in logic". Moreover, this rule for distinguishing agitations and inclinations conflicts with another which Ryle offers, i.e. that motives are, whereas moods including agitations are not, 'propensities to act intentionally' (pp. 97 and 111). Then fear and anger would be agitations by the first test, but motives by the second test. The first test would exclude "inclination" from the category Inclinations; and the second test would exclude from Moods some of Ryle's exemplars thereof, e.g. "companionable". Since Ryle is introducing "Agitations" as a (semi-)technical term, a new category, he is free to define it as he sees fit; but no clear definition emerges. He says that agitations are 'not occurrences and therefore do not take place either publicly or privately' (p. 83). Yet he describes agitations as 'commotions' (p. 83), and surely a commotion is an occurrence; and his examples of agitations include being *startled* and *shocked*, which terms are commonly used to refer to datable occurrences.

Ryle's remarks about "agitations" may be read as stipulative definitions, but what he says about "feelings" is presented not thus but as a report about how people do use this word, when they do so 'strictly':

> Mood words are commonly classified as names of feelings. But if the word 'feeling' is used with any strictness, this classification is quite erroneous . . . *Feelings, in any strict sense, are things that come and go, wax and wane, in a few seconds*; they stab and they grumble, *we feel them all over us or in one particular place* (p. 100. My italics).

Ryle supports this by appealing to how we do talk, claiming for example that a person 'may say that he keeps on having

[2] This criterion is described in the next section and labelled 'C1D'.

tweaks', but *not* 'that he keeps on feeling . . . happy or discontented' (p. 100). (Why not?) He also claims that: 'Ordinarily, when people report the occurrence of a feeling, they do so in a phrase like 'a throb of compassion', 'a shock of surprise . . .' (p. 84). (*Do* they?) It seems perverse to assert, in the name of 'strictness', that it is 'quite erroneous' to classify "sad", "happy" or "bored" as words for feelings, to support this by appealing to ordinary usage, and yet ignore the fact that in English usage such words are paradigm cases of names of feelings, of complements for "I feel . . .".

A crucial part of the theory developed in this chapter concerns the relationship between feelings, in Ryle's sense, and moods; the thesis that a person's feelings are merely signs from which he has fallibly to diagnose what mood he is in:

> Some thrills, shocks, glows and ticklings are feelings of delight, surprise, relief and amusement. . . . But the transports, surprises, reliefs and distresses of which such feelings are diagnosed, or misdiagnosed, as signs are not themselves feelings, but are agitations or moods (p. 107).

Notice how Ryle describes what he claims to be doing: 'I am trying to show only that it is part of the logic of *our* descriptions of feelings that they are signs of agitations . . .' (p. 104. My italics). A study of English usage scarcely confirms his theses. Ryle's novel account of the relationship between feelings and agitations depends entirely on his own definitions of "agitations" and "feelings". What Ryle does in this chapter is to offer us a way of classifying certain mind-predicates very different from that of standard English; and to obscure what he is doing by representing it as 'the logic of our descriptions'. His motive is made clear. He is trying to persuade us that all the important words that we use in describing emotions and feelings—all except those like "throb", "itch", etc.—are names of dispositions; and therefore that it does not make sense to claim to have privileged access to one's own emotions, motives, inclinations or moods. The chapter ends thus:

> Motives and moods are not the sorts of things which could be among the direct intimations of consciousness, or among the objects of introspection, as these factitious forms of Privileged Access are

ordinarily described. They are not 'experiences', any more than habits or maladies are 'experiences' (p. 115).

If Ryle had practised the method he professed, a question he could scarcely have avoided asking is this: Does it make sense to say 'I think I feel *x*, but may be mistaken, may have misdiagnosed the signs, have misinterpreted my feelings'?—where *x* may be any of the predicates which Ryle classifies as moods. If we ask such questions the answer would surely be Yes for some such predicates, e.g. "companionable" or "jealous", and No for others, e.g. "happy" or "startled".

I shall now consider briefly how Ryle practises 'logical geography' in Chapter VIII, where he is discussing "to imagine" and kindred verbs. Here Ryle *seems* to be doing linguistics of the *a priori* kind. If this passage was intended as empirical linguistics, its conclusions were not in fact reached by observation, since they are at loggerheads with what observation discloses. If anyone were doing empirical linguistics, he could scarcely fail to notice that, apart from "to imagine", the verbs Ryle discusses fall into two classes: (i) those like "to picture", "to visualize", "to see in the mind's eye", which are complemented by a noun (-phrase) designating a person, place or thing; and (ii) those like "to suppose", "to conjecture", "to make-believe", which are always followed by a that-clause, and "to fancy" which is nearly always complemented thus.

For a linguist this should be strong if not decisive evidence that these two sets of verbs are of different categories, that they perform functions of different kinds. The fact that "to imagine" may deputize for each verb in each class is strong evidence that it is a homonym, is used in different senses in "Imagine an A" and "Imagine that p". Instead of drawing this conclusion, however, Ryle says things which serve only to conceal this difference. He oscillates between the two different uses of "to imagine", and he introduces a new verb of his own, "to 'see'", to deputize for our everyday verbs like "to picture" and "to visualize". And then he equates "'seeing'" with "fancying *that*". *Fancy an ordinary language philosopher doing that.* Having taken in the meaning of this italicized sentence, now consider its grammar. Here "Fancy" is not followed by "that", though it is deputizing, not for "Picture", but for "Isn't it surprising *that*". This shows that we cannot, after all, detect the category (linguistic function) of such verbs *merely* by using the grammatical criterion—whether the complement is a noun (-phrase) or a that-clause. We must pay heed to the use of the verb in its context.

Ryle argues that the phrase "pictures in the mind's eye" is a mis-description (p. 253); and presumably he would say the same about "visual images". Ryle (like J. B. Watson) evidently thought it necessary at all costs to deny that such phrases refer to private objects. He describes his thesis: 'Roughly, imaging occurs, but images are not seen' (p. 247); but his arguments imply that images are not objects of 'seeing' either, that there are no such entities to be seen or 'seen'. He offers a variety of synonyms for "picturing so and so" with the aim of eliminating anything to which "mental picture" or "visual image" could be applied. Picturing Helvellyn, we are told, is really just *seeming* to see Helvellyn itself (p. 248), or is 'imagining *that* we see Helvellyn in front of our noses' (p. 256), or is '*thinking* how it [Helvellyn] *should* look' (p. 270. My italics). Each of these descriptions will seem very inadequate to anyone whose visual images are at all vivid. If Ryle had here taken ordinary language seriously, presumably he would have asked *why* "picturing" is the English verb most commonly used to describe what he calls "'seeing'". The answer presumably is that, for most people, the objects of such picturing are in many respects like the material objects which we call 'pictures'. Francis Galton's famous questionnaire confirmed this. (*Inquiries into Human Faculty*, 1883.) If Ryle had applied the criterion for category-classification which he seems to be using in Chapter I of *C of M*,[3] he would have had to assign "pictures that are seen" and "pictures that are 'seen'" to the same category, because many predicates are applicable to both expressions, e.g. "vivid", "faithful" and "lifelike". A consistent appeal to English usage, here as elsewhere, would yield arguments *for* dualism (for what little such arguments are worth).

Ryle's arguments in this chapter seem to involve *a priori* psychology as well as *a priori* linguistics. He says that in picturing something 'there *is* nothing akin to sensations' (p. 266). What

[3] This criterion is described in the next section and labelled 'C2S+D'.

then could we make of the familiar fact that people sometimes mistake picturing something for seeing it? Or of what psychologists tell us about so-called eidetic imagery, i.e. cases where a person can observe in the image of a recently seen object, features which are possessed by the object but which he had not noticed while seeing it? Ryle informs us: 'People are apt grossly to exaggerate the photographic fidelity of their visual imagery' (p. 275). It would be interesting to know how Ryle discovered this! Indeed it is hard to understand how Ryle could make this statement, which presupposes (what he has been denying) that a visual image is something which can be compared with that of which it is an image.

When Ryle makes such assertions of psychological fact, this suggests that his main thesis in this chapter is not about concepts *qua* word-uses; that it is simply that picturing Helvellyn is very different from seeing Helvellyn. In that case, no one, including Descartes, could disagree, and each of us has a simpler method of verifying this thesis than by surveying the linguistic expressions applicable to such experiences. But in that case, why should Ryle not have been content to assert the complementary truism, that a visual image of Helvellyn is very different from Helvellyn? Since picturing is renamed "'seeing'", why not use the same device to distinguish what we picture in the mind's eye from physical pictures, and call the former "'pictures'"? Since Ryle has acknowledged that imaging ('seeing') is a private process, and that twinges, qualms, etc., are inner episodes to which one can pay heed, what difference could it make to any of his main theses if he acknowledged visual images as private objects (or 'objects') of a fleeting and elusive kind? He seemed to be doing this earlier, when he spoke of the 'convenient privacy' of 'the *things* that I see in my mind's eye' (p. 35. My italics).

Here are some more examples of Ryle's dogmatic assertions that we cannot or do not say things that we do sometimes say.

(a) Ryle says (absurdly?) that in our ordinary use of "voluntary", 'it is absurd to discuss whether satisfactory, correct or admirable performances are voluntary or involuntary' (p. 69).

(b) Ryle asserts that the adjectives "obsessing" and "unacknowledged" are applicable to belief but not to knowledge (p. 134).

(c) Ryle makes the sweeping and false assertion that 'no one, save to endorse the Cartesian theory, ever describes actions as expressions of volitions or acts of will' (p. 64). Ryle's defence of this is devious. He says that "volition" is 'a technical concept' which we do not know how to use 'for we do not use it in daily life' (p. 62). But the philosophers who have used "volitions" use it as an umbrella-term to cover making choices, decisions, resolutions and efforts of will. The word "volition" is semi-technical only in the same sense as terms which Ryle introduces, like "agitations"; which he uses as an umbrella-term to cover qualms of fear, twinges of remorse, etc.

(d) Ryle asserts that

> "Inferring" is not used to denote a slowish or a quickish process. "I began to deduce but had no time to finish" is not the sort of thing that can significantly be said . . . reaching a conclusion . . . is not the sort of thing that can be described as gradual, quick or instantaneous (pp. 301–2).

This is the example which Professor White followed (see Section III above)—deducing a false conclusion about what we cannot say from home-made rules about achievement-words. Ryle's argument here is that verbs like "prove", "infer" and "deduce" (and presumably "solve") are to be classified, along with "score" and "arrive at", as "'got it' verbs', another name that he gives to achievement-verbs. (See the Index of *C of M*) Ryle mistakenly assumes that "infer", "deduce", etc., are used only to record the arrival at a conclusion, ignoring the fact that they are also used to refer to the process of thinking it out. Some people deduce the solutions to (solve) problems, infer what you mean, draw conclusions, etc., more slowly than others.

There is room for debate as to whether Ryle's false conclusions about English usage should be classified as *a priori* linguistics or merely as legislative linguistics. As stated earlier, I do not use "legislative linguistics" to refer to what is explicitly presented as a verbal recommendation, as when Ryle says: 'The phrase 'in the mind' can and always should be dispensed with' (p. 40). Some of Ryle's false conclusions are clearly cases of *a priori* linguistics, e.g. those which he deduces from his own rules about achievement-verbs. All of them seem to qualify as *a priori* linguistics in that, according to the Introduction and Chapter I, they are presented as discoveries about the categories to which concepts really belong, and the reader is given the impression that Ryle has some criterion (rule) for assigning concepts to categories. Moreover, any of them would qualify as *a priori* linguistics if a suppressed premise from which it is derived is some version of the VP. Here I must try to answer a question raised in the last section: does some version of the VP form a suppressed premise of Ryle's reasoning in *C of M*? (If not, as we have seen, his rule or rules for assigning concepts to categories lack(s) any rationale.) There is some evidence supporting an affirmative answer to this question. Professor S. Hampshire recognized this in his penetrating review of *C of M* (*Mind*, 1950); but I think that he went far beyond the evidence when he claimed that, for Ryle, 'To rectify the logic of mental conduct concepts' *is* 'to correct what other philosophers have said about the *methods of verification* of statements involving mental concepts ...' (p. 245. Hampshire's italics). This is clearly *one* of Ryle's aims—notably to dismiss Privileged Access as a method of verification. Hampshire, however, goes on to speak as if Ryle's concern ('really') is with methods of verifying *and not* with elucidating statements by analysing their meanings. Hampshire writes: 'Professor Ryle is not really arguing that all or most statements involving mental concepts are (*or are expressible as*) hypothetical statements about overt behaviour ...' (p. 245. My italics).

Hampshire offers some evidence for what he here asserts, but none for what he here denies. He cites Ryle's statement: 'roughly, the mind is not the topic of *untestable* categorical propositions, but the topic of *testable* hypothetical and semi-hypothetical propositions' (*C of M*, p. 46. Hampshire's italics). And he quotes fragments of three of Ryle's sentences, italicizing the words "test", "establish" and "discover". Consider the first-quoted fragment: "'The *test* of whether you understood it ...'" (p. 245. Hampshire's italics). The whole of this sentence reads:

> In short it is part of the *meaning* of 'you understood it' that you could have done so and so and would have done it, if such and such, and the *test* of whether you understood it is a range of performances

satisfying the apodoses of these general hypothetical statements (p. 170. Ryle's italics).

This scarcely supports Hampshire's view about what Ryle is *not* really doing! Nor does the way in which Ryle habitually presents his claims as elucidations of the meanings of statements: by saying things like 'when we describe people as . . . we are referring to . . .' (p. 25), 'when a person is described by . . . the description imputes to him . . .' (p. 27), and so on throughout the book.

It seems more appropriate when Hampshire charges Ryle with 'confusion which either comes from, or leads to, *identifying* the meaning of a statement with *the* method of its verification' (p. 247. Hampshire's italics). This is more, but not wholly, appropriate; for Hampshire here ascribes to Ryle an early and crude version of the VP; and Ryle is surely not guilty of arguing as if there is *only one* way of verifying any given statement. I share Hampshire's diagnosis of Ryle's reasoning insofar as I think that Ryle was covertly using some unidentified version of the VP. (What else, one might ask, could have led Ryle to try to defend a behaviourist position?) It is, however, a matter for speculation with which version of the VP Ryle was operating. Certainly not the By-Someone version, which Ryle had proposed in 1936, as a way of avoiding Behaviourism. Hampshire presents a variant of the By-Someone version as the correct principle which Ryle ought to have adopted. Hampshire lays it down that: 'A statement only becomes void [i.e. meaningless] if it is logically precluded . . . that *anyone* should *ever* under *any* conditions establish its truth or falsity beyond reasonable doubt' (p. 247. Hampshire's italics). If Ryle had adhered to this principle, *C of M*, if written at all, would have been a *very* different book.

There are hints in *C of M* suggesting that Ryle was using as a suppressed premise the By-Others version of the VP, rather than, or as well as, the By-Me version. Notice the context of Ryle's statement, quoted by Hampshire, that 'the mind is . . . the topic of testable . . . statements' (*C of M*, p. 46). Ryle is here discussing the problem of verifying whether a move by a drunkard at the chess-board was due to cleverness, not luck. Notice that Ryle here considers only the *spectators*' problem, and ignores the agent's viewpoint. Ryle does this quite frequently.[7] (See, for example, his discussion of hypocrisy, pp. 173–4.) This is the procedure usually followed by Wittgenstein in Part I of *Philosophical Investigations*. There are some specific grounds for ascribing to Wittgenstein the By-Others version of the VP, and I shall discuss these in Part Two. Ryle's arguments in *C of M* sometimes suggest that he was thinking on the same lines as Wittgenstein. There I must leave my present question. We shall never *know* the answer—unless Professor Ryle can remember, and will tell us what it is.

I suggest that most of the detailed arguments in *C of M* are (dare I say 'really') exercises in the kind of philosophy which Ryle described at the end of his 1931 article, 'Systematically Misleading Expressions' (*PAS*, 1931–2):

> People do not really talk philosophical nonsense—unless they are philosophizing . . . or . . . being sententious. What they do is to use expressions which from whatever cause . . . disguise instead of exhibiting the forms of the facts recorded . . . Philosophy must then involve the exercise of systematic restatement . . . Its restatements are . . . controlled not by desire for elegance or stylistic correctness but by desire to exhibit the forms of the facts into which philosophy is the inquiry. I conclude, then, that there is . . . a sense in which we can properly inquire and even say 'what it really means to say so and so'. For we can ask what is the real form of the fact recorded when this is concealed or disguised and not duly exhibited by the expression in question . . . and I am for the present inclined to believe that this is what philosophical analysis is and that this is the sole and whole function of philosophy . . . I would rather allot to philosophy a sublimer task than the detection of the sources in linguistic idioms of recurrent misconceptions and absurd theories. But that it is at least this I cannot feel any serious doubt.

If Ryle had written *C of M* explicitly as an application of this kind of philosophical analysis, nothing would have been lost. In that case he would not have been tempted to keep telling us what it is proper or improper to say, to practise *a priori* or

[7] Sometimes Ryle confuses the viewpoints of speaker and hearer. For example, he asks: 'How does a person find out what mood he is in?' His answer is that 'the bored man finds out that he is bored . . . by finding that among other things he glumly says to others and to himself 'I feel bored''. He adds: 'Such a blurted avowal . . . is the first and best index, since . . . it is meant to be understood' (pp. 102–3). Meant to be understood *by whom*?

legislative linguistics. He could have started from the fact that we *do* frequently make statements in which we conjoin "mind" with "body", or a mental with a physical term; and then gone on to argue that such talk has misled Descartes and many others into thinking that minds and bodies are alike in being substances. He could then have developed his own analyses of the uses of mind-words, to reveal the extent to which their applicability (to other people) depends on (their) overt behaviour. And if he had been keeping his eye on 'the forms of the facts' (the natures of the things) which his analyses were supposed to reveal, it is unlikely that he would have left his readers so uncertain about his own positive views. I think students of *C of M* will find it more intelligible if they interpret it as an exercise in the kind of philosophical analysis described by Ryle in 1931. This book will doubtless remain a textbook for students for many years. It deserves to be read not only for its important contributions to the philosophy of mind, but also to warn students against its influential errors.

My account of such errors is not exhaustive. I shall mention two more since they recur in *C of M* and in subsequent works by other philosophers:

(i) Arguing *as if* 'No S's are P' follows from the falsity of 'All S's are P'—as if it follows that *no* intelligent action is preceded and caused by a private process of intelligent thinking or planning, because it is false that *all* intelligent actions are so preceded and caused (Chapters II and IX); as if it follows that *no* voluntary action is preceded and caused by a private act of resolving or willing, because it is false that *all* voluntary actions are so caused (Chapter III);

(ii) Arguing that Cartesian dualism commits one to vicious infinite regresses, as Ryle does in almost every chapter. Such arguments appear plausible, *if* one ascribes to dualists the claim that, for example, "intelligent performance" *means* a performance preceded by 'some anterior internal operation of planning what to do'; for then ascribing intelligence to a private performance implies the occurrence of 'yet another interior process of planning to plan' (*C of M*, p. 31); and so on. But all the dualist need do to evade this line of attack is to reject the *definition* of "intelligent", etc., with which he is being saddled, while insisting that meditations as well as unpremeditated actions can be intelligent, in the same sense of "intelligent".

If a historian of ideas cares to compare the contents of *C of M* with psychologists' expositions of Behaviourism, he will find some obvious resemblances. J. B. Watson, the father of Behaviourism, argued, like Ryle, as if rejecting Cartesian dualism requires one to dispense with, and even deny the possibility of, introspection. (See Watson's first manifesto, 'Psychology As the Behaviourist Views It', *Psych. Review*, 1913, esp. p. 170; and the first chapter of *Behaviourism*, 1925, esp. p. 10.) Yet Watson and his followers went on making, and reporting, what others *call* 'introspective reports', and concealed the inconsistency (from themselves at least) by *re-christening* such reports, e.g. as 'verbal behaviour'. Compare this with Ryle's procedure—replacing "introspection" with "retrospection", "conscious of" with "*au fait* with", etc. Watson's declared purpose in banning 'introspective data' was that psychologists should accept as data only *what has been observed and is publicly observable.* (See *Behaviourism*, p. 6.) Yet he proceeded, inconsistently, to stretch "behaviour" to cover what he called 'internal or implicit behaviour', and included under this label data *not* publicly observable but accessible only to introspection. (See, for example, the footnotes on pages 173–4 of his first manifesto.) Compare this with Ryle's use of "covert behaviour" to cover experiences 'which only Johnson could have recorded', and so on.

SECTION VI

Ryle's Misuse of "Category-Mistake"

THE aim of this section is to show that it is not possible to justify Ryle's use of "That is a category-mistake" as a reason for saying 'You cannot properly or significantly say that'. The argument will be slightly technical in parts, though students who have studied any Logic should find it plain sailing. If any other readers get stuck, they should pass on to section VII. For their benefit we may record here that in 1954 Ryle, in effect, conceded the point at issue. He acknowledged that there is no 'exact, professional way' of using "category", that

> there is an inexact amateurish way of using it in which, like a coal-hammer, it will make a satisfactory knocking noise on doors which we want opened to us. It gives the answers to none of our questions but it can be made to arouse people to the questions in a properly brusque way (*Dilemmas*, p. 9).

If everyone had now recognized this point, this section would have been superfluous. But even Ryle does not seem to have jettisoned the concept of a category-mistake. He refers to 'category-skids' in a later paper ('Use, Usage and Meaning', *PAS*, Supp. Vol., 1961, p. 230).

Since I shall be discussing several criteria (rules) for assigning terms to the same or to different categories, criteria formulated in different idioms, I shall adopt a simple terminology into which they can all be briefly translated. To explain this terminology, I shall take the solitary sentence in *C of M* which *looks* like a criterion, express this in my terminology, and then explain my key-words. Ryle wrote: 'When two terms belong to the same category, it is proper to construct conjunctive propositions embodying them' (p. 22). My translation is: 'If A and B are of the same category, there is some P (predicate) applicable to both A and B.'

Regarding "P (predicate)". For the sake of brevity I am departing from Aristotelian usage. I use "predicate" to refer to whatever is left of a sentence-in-use, when we have subtracted the linguistic component about whose category we want to decide. The latter may be any component we wish. We could retain "subject" and "predicate" as correlative terms and use "subject" to refer to this latter component; but I shall use "A", "B", etc., for this purpose, and when referring to A, B, etc., will call them 'terms'.

Regarding "applicable". Unless otherwise stated, I shall use "applicable" to mean grammatically and significantly and univocally applicable. "Grammatically" is to rule out gibberish or sentences like "Oddly is red". "Significantly" will mean 'truly *or falsely*'. I shall assume that in 'Categories' (*PAS*, 1938–9) Ryle used "absurd" and "significant" as contradictory terms, and was not trading on the emotive or other differences between "absurd" and "non-significant". "Univocally" is to mean 'in the same sense of the word(s)', "equivocally" to mean 'in different senses of the word(s)'. In his 1938 paper, Ryle was explicit about the need for "grammatically" and "significantly", but not about the need for "univocally".

About "A" and "B". As we have seen in the last section, Ryle apparently intended that the subject-matter which is assignable to categories is linguistic expressions. I shall discuss category-classification on this assumption.

Two more preliminary points: I shall assume that Ryle used "of the same category" and "of different categories" as contradictory, and not merely contrary, terms, and that he used "category" and "(logical) type" as synonyms. (He normally used "type" in 1938 and "category" in 1949.) There seems to be no room for doubt about either of these points.

Ryle's 1938 criterion for category-difference was formulated thus:

> Two proposition-factors are of different categories or types, if there are sentence-frames such that when the expressions of those factors are imported as alternative complements to the same gap-signs, the resultant sentences are significant in the one case and absurd in the other ('Categories', op. cit., pp. 77–8).

The translation of this into my terminology is:

C1D: If there is some P applicable to A but not to B
or to B but not to A, (p)
then A and B are of different categories. (q)

The label "C1D" is short for "criterion number one for category-difference". I shall label a criterion with "S" instead of "D" if it is supposed to show that A and B are of the same category. I shall add "W" for weak if a criterion offers only a necessary and not a sufficient condition, and is only a partial test. We cannot derive from C1D a strong criterion for assigning terms to the same category. The equivalent contrapositive of C1D ($\bar{q} \supset \bar{p}$) offers only a necessary condition of category-identity, namely:

C1SW: If A and B are of the same category, ($\bar{q}$)
then there is no P applicable to A but not B or to
B but not A. ($\bar{p}$)

The strong criterion for category-identity which would correspond to C1D, namely ($\bar{p} \supset \bar{q}$), is:

C1S: If there is no P applicable to A but not B or
to B but not A, ($\bar{p}$)
then A and B are of the same category. ($\bar{q}$)

Ryle cautiously refrained from asserting C1S, and gave no criterion for determining that two terms are of the same category; which is rather a big gap in a theory of categories. An even bigger gap in Ryle's theory is that he so formulated his criterion for category-difference that ability to use it depends on ability to recognize whether a sentence is 'significant' or 'absurd'. On this topic Ryle's only contribution is to raise the question, in the last sentence of his paper: 'But what are the tests of absurdity?' (p. 206); though he had chided Aristotle earlier for relying 'solely upon common sense and common parlance' (p. 195).

C1D is useless for all Ryle's purposes. Professor J. J. C. Smart has produced *ad hoc* counter-examples concerning pairs of words which one would want to put into the same category, e.g. "bed" and "chair", "nought" and "one" ('A Note on Categories', *BJPS*, 1953–4.) Thus "The seat of this . . . is hard" is applicable to "chair" but not to "bed". Here is a general formula for providing a counter-example in any such case. Let "r" represent the comparative form of any adjective applicable to both A and B. Then "A is r than B" (e.g. "beds are softer than tables") is significant, and "B is r than B" (e.g. "tables are softer than tables") is not significant. According to

C1D, any two expressions can be shown to be of different categories—except where A and B are exact synonyms; because, in their case, "A is r than B" is *also* meaningless. So the only purpose for which C1D might be of any use is that of a grammarian who wanted to identify exact synonyms.

Before leaving his 1938 paper, it may be worth mentioning one of Ryle's passing remarks. He wrote that 'extracting the type' of an expression 'cannot exclude the operation of revealing the liaisons of propositions embodying it' (p. 80). But he had just defined "liaisons" as 'all the logical relations of a proposition, namely what it implies, what it is implied by, what it is compatible with, and what it is incompatible with' (p. 79). It seems pointless to try to develop from this hint a usable criterion, since its application to a single case would involve examining the logical relations between every sentence embodying A, every sentence embodying B and every other sentence in the English language! For Ryle included 'being compatible with' among the relevant logical relations. As Bertie Wooster would say, the mind boggles.

Turning to *C of M* the only sentence which looks like a criterion, quoted above, translates as:

C2SW: If A and B are of the same category, (r)
then there is some P applicable to both A and B. (s)

The equivalent contrapositive ($\bar{s} \supset \bar{r}$) is:

C2D If there is no P applicable to both A and B, ($\bar{s}$)
then A and B are of different categories. ($\bar{r}$)

C2D purports to provide a sufficient condition of category-difference, but in practice it cannot by itself divide any terms into different categories. Whatever two terms are offered as candidates, it is easy to supply a predicate applicable to both. *If* you think you are obliged to choose between assigning them to the same or to different categories, you would presumably want to say 'different' for such terms as "Love", "a Jaguar", "a peerage", "good salmon-fishing", etc.; but the predicate(s) "Money will (or won't) buy you . . ." are univocally applicable to these and to many other very diverse terms. Indeed, if grammatical propriety were the court of appeal, why should not any two terms be assigned to the same category if "exists" can be predicated of each? Notice how Ryle deals with what is, for him, a crucial case: the conjunctive sentence (a) "Bodies exist and minds exist", or its equivalent (b) "Bodies and minds both exist". On page 22, Ryle says that such sentences make no sense, but on the next page he changes his ground and claims that "exist" is not used in the same sense when it is attached to "bodies" and to "minds". He expresses this picturesquely by saying: 'It is perfectly proper to say, in one logical tone of voice, that there exist minds, and to say, in another logical tone of voice, that there exist bodies'. Well, no doubt one can change the 'logical tone' of one's voice half-way through saying 'Bodies exist and minds exist', but can one simultaneously intone "exist" in two different 'logical tones of voice', when saying 'Bodies and minds both exist'? Ryle boldly meets this difficulty by asserting that the latter sentence could only be used *as a joke* (p. 23). Many philosophers and the average English-speaker do not seem to have seen the joke. Notice that Ryle simply assumes without discussion that "exists" has two different meanings when it is attached to "bodies" and to "minds", and so he is simply begging the question. He concedes on page 23 that it is grammatically proper to say 'Bodies exist and minds exist'. So he cannot, by appealing to linguistic usage and applying C2D, show that "body", and "mind" are of different categories—unless he provides some *independent* criterion for deciding when any P is applied in different senses to A and B, or claims that his intuition will do the trick. This is the problem which Professor Fred Sommers tried to solve later on, and to which I shall return shortly.

Notice that since Ryle's solitary explanatory sentence starts 'When . . .', and not 'When and only when . . .', he has still provided no criterion for determining category-identity. If Ryle's sentence had started 'When and only when' (If and only if), he would have been asserting both C2D ($\bar{s} \supset \bar{r}$) *and* the corresponding criterion for category-identity ($s \supset r$), that is:

C2S: If there is some P applicable to both A and B, (s)
then A and B are of the same category. (r)

If Ryle did not intend to assert C2S, notice the implications: when any critic has refuted a claim that two terms belong to different categories according to C2D, he cannot reverse the argument and say '*therefore* they are of the same category'. Could Ryle have wished to rely on a criterion which leaves our questions undecidable? Ryle's examples of category-mistakes and what he says about them suggest that Ryle *meant* 'When and only when'. Consider his examples of 'category-mistakes' in the light of his professed purpose—to show that conjoining "mind" and "body" is a category-mistake. In nearly all of his examples, A is a name of a part or member of that of which B is a name, e.g. when A names an Oxford College and B the University, A a battalion and B the Division, A the Home Office and B the British Constitution, A a right-hand glove and B the pair of gloves. (Echoes of Russell's theory of types.) But this relation cannot be the one which is relevant to Ryle's purpose. Ryle cannot have thought that Descartes thought that a person's mind is a part (or member) of his body, or vice-versa! Then look at his example concerning team-spirit, which may reveal what he thought is the kind of mistake involved in conjoining "mind" and "body". This example is intended to show that "exhibiting team-spirit" is of a different category from "batting", "bowling" or "catching". Ryle wrote: 'Certainly exhibiting team-spirit is not the same thing as batting or catching, but nor is it a third thing such that we can say that the bowler *first* bowls and *then* exhibits team-spirit . . .' (p. 17. My italics. Ryle italicized "and". Had Ryle omitted "first" and "then", would anyone consider this sentence to be a category-mistake?). What is the point of this example, unless (i) that ". . . is exhibiting team-spirit" and ". . . is batting" are of different categories, because the same predicates are not significantly applicable to both, in which case he is using C2D; *and* (ii) that ". . . is batting" and ". . . is bowling" are of the same category, because the same predicates are significantly applicable to both, in which case he is using C2S. Suppose we interpret Ryle as intending 'When and only when' in his solitary sentence, i.e. as using as his criterion, C2S + D; this, instead of leaving all our questions undecidable, makes it possible to verify something. However, it can then be used to verify much too much; namely that any two terms are of the same category—unless or until someone can provide an independent criterion for deciding whether a predicate is being used univocally or equivocally.

I do not want to give the impression that I regard that solitary sentence in *C of M* as a carefully calculated theory of categories! My concern is to discover whether *any* linguistic criterion can be invented which will serve Ryle's purposes. Notice that it would be glaringly inconsistent to combine the 1938 criterion (C1D) with the one I have read into *C of M* (C2S + D); for, by the former, any two non-synonymous terms can be shown to be of different categories, and, by the latter, any two terms to be of the same category. But let us consider a recent attempt to salvage a Rylean doctrine of categories and category-mistakes. I refer to Professor Fred Sommers' article 'Predicability' (*Philosophy in America*, ed. Max Black, 1965). Sommers pin-points clearly an obvious difficulty in applying any criterion for assigning terms to categories. Note that Sommers uses "type" to mean what Ryle, in *C of M*, means by "category", and uses "category" in an apparently very different sense. His criticism is directed against the criterion which I have read into *C of M* (C2S + D), in the form in which Russell used it. This is:

If and only if there is some P applicable to both A and B, then A and B are of the same type.

Sommers points out that any attempted applications of this criterion are 'viciously circular'; for if we begin by assuming that P is applied univocally to A and B, it follows that A and B are of the same type; but if we begin by assuming that A and B are of different types, it follows that P is applied to them equivocally. Hence 'we need a definition of type difference that does not depend on the question . . . whether predicates are ambiguous or not' (p. 264).

Exactly. Yet despite this excellent start, Sommers proceeds to do *a priori* linguistics. He lays it down without discussion that *the* criterion for type-difference is:

C3S + D If and only if there are two predicates P and Q, such that P is applicable to A but not B and Q to B but not A, then A and B are of different types.

Sommers illustrates this criterion by saying: 'lectures [A] and headaches [B] are of different types since it makes sense to say of a lecture [A] that it was delivered by a speaker [P] while it makes no sense to say this of a headache [B]—and, on the other hand, it makes sense to say of a headache [B] that it was cured

[Q] while it makes no sense to say this of a lecture [A]'. Unfortunately for Sommers it also follows from his criterion that "draught Guinness" and "bottled Guinness" are of different types. Let A = "draught G.", B = "bottled G.", P = "stronger than bottled G.", and Q = "stronger than draught G." Producing such counter-examples seems to be a childish game, but it is a move in a game which others have invented, i.e. presenting, and using as if they were *a priori*, rules whose implications they have not sufficiently investigated in order to test them. Should Sommers add a new clause to his rule to preclude my reply, I expect that I shall be able to think of another reply which he has not legislated against. Or will he now stop producing *a priori* rules? Recall the tricks used to pick holes, plug holes and pick more holes in the Verification Principle.

Sommers offers another *a priori* rule on the same page (p. 265). He calls it 'the rule for enforcing ambiguity', i.e. for deciding whether a predicate is being applied in different senses to different terms. In my terminology this rule is:

Given three terms A, B and C and two predicates P and Q, if and only if P is significantly applicable to A and B but not to C, and Q is significantly applicable to B and C but not to A, then *either* P is ambiguous *or* Q is ambiguous.

This complicated criterion is given a single illustration: that "five feet tall" [P] applies to fences [A] and to men [B] but not to statements [C], while "thoughtful" [Q] applies to men [B] and to statements [C] but not to fences [A]; so *either* "tall" is ambiguous when applied to fences and men, *or* "thoughtful" is ambiguous when applied to men and to statements. But the criterion does not tell us which of these conclusions we should draw. Unless we knew in advance of applying the criterion that "thoughtful" is, and "tall" is not, ambiguous in these contexts, the criterion would not even *appear* to be helpful. Sommers then proceeds to apply his home-made rule, but not in a let's-see-if-it-works spirit. He *deduces* from his rule an ontological conclusion 'that there can be no such three things' as those included in 'Strawson's ontology', namely 'spirits, persons and rocks' (p. 267). If this is intended as a discovery about the world, one should ask if Sommers really wishes to reject Hume's thesis that we cannot deduce Matters of Fact from Relations of Ideas. But perhaps Sommers really intended his conclusion to be about whether we can significantly use the terms "spirit" or "former person". This is suggested by his statement: 'It is clear that the type rule leaves us only two reasonable alternatives: either to adopt a spiritless *language* or to accept Cartesian dualism' (p. 269. My italics). Well, if anyone deduces that we cannot significantly use the terms in question, we may refer him to many examples in addition to Strawson's *Individuals*.

The point to which I most want to draw attention, however, is that in the course of applying the rule for detecting ambiguity, Sommers discovers (p. 268) that there is a third alternative: that his rule leaves it open that the ambiguity which it reveals may belong to neither of the predicates, P and Q, but to one of the terms, B. So we need another rule (or intuition?) to decide between the *three* alternatives left open by this rule. Then why call this rule '*the* rule', if that's all the help it can give? In fact, *any* of the three terms might be ambiguous, so the rule leaves us with *five* alternatives to choose between. I think enough has been said to show that Sommers has failed in his attempt to escape from the vicious circle that he so clearly describes, and thereby to salvage a Rylean theory of categories or types. I know of no other attempt to do this which appears, as Sommers' might at first glance, to offer hope of providing rules to rationalize Ryle's use of "category-mistake".

Since writing the above, a neat critique of Sommers' criterion for detecting ambiguity has been published by Miss Susan Haak (*Analysis*, April, 1968). She too complains that this criterion yields no determinate verdict, and she adds two further objections. She gives the following example as one which fulfils Sommers' criterion but where all of the predicates and terms seem, intuitively, to be used univocally: a headache (A) and a lecture (B) but not a book (C) may be said to last an hour (P), and a lecture (B) and a book (C) but not a headache (A) can be said to be detailed (Q). Actually there seems to be more than one sense in which a book could be said to last an hour; but Miss Haak could meet this by substituting, as P, 'to go on for an hour', or 'to stop an hour after it started'. Miss Haak's third criticism is that in order to use Sommers' criterion, we must *already* have decided whether certain predicates are applicable to certain terms, but that this decision depends on whether the predicates or terms are equivocal. This is another way of saying that Sommers has not escaped from the vicious circle which provided his own starting point.

I am not, of course, suggesting that philosophers need expel "category" from their vocabulary. In Section XVIII, I shall indicate one purpose for which it may still be useful. And I am not denying that there are many statements which may be called 'category-mistakes', if we are using "category" in one of the *relatively* clear traditional senses adumbrated by Aristotle, or by Kant, or by Russell (if we equate his "type" with "category"). There is some point in calling it 'a category-mistake' to say about times what can only be said about places or things, or about a class what can only be said about its members. But Ryle has not improved the notion of a category as a philosophical tool. As he uses it, categories are liable to proliferate without limit, for he multiplies category-differences to mark newly noticed, or newly drawn, distinctions between the usages or the functions of words. And though he evidently conceived category-mistakes as ways in which human beings may exceed the bounds of sense, in whichever language they do their thinking, what in fact he discusses is the grammar and the functions of *English* words. Yet many of the statements which he classifies as category-mistakes are neither absurd nor improper in the English in which they are expressed. One of my students, Mr. P. A. Flattery, has suggested that the criterion for determining category-differences should read:

If and only if there is some P applicable to A but not B or to B but not A, then A and B are of different categories *with respect to the P in question.*

This is a legitimate move, but it is of no use for Ryle's 1949 purposes. This criterion would imply that "body" and "mind" are of the same category with respect to each of the many predicates applicable to both, and of different categories with respect to each of the many predicates applicable to one but not the other. If anyone wishes to redescribe the findings of empirical linguistics in this terminology, he is welcome to do so.

SECTION VII

Professor Austin's Contributions to Linguistics

J. L. AUSTIN cannot be charged with practising *a priori* linguistics, though he has had considerable influence on those who do. He did not deduce from rules what people cannot or may not say, nor assert that people cannot significantly say things they do say. Indeed he once wrote that 'sometimes we must allow a usage to be, though appalling, yet actual' and that 'a genuinely loose or eccentric talker is a rare specimen to be prized' (*Philosophical Papers*,[1] p. 132). His accounts of language were, however, often normative and not merely descriptive; or, if descriptive, they describe how English is spoken by the few people who are as fastidious as himself and as sensitive to the nuances and etymology of its words. Austin sometimes conveys his shudders at 'vulgarisms' as well as at the slipshod talk of philosophers and lawyers (p. 145).

Austin made important contributions to linguistics, added a new dimension to grammar, without however representing what he was doing as something more sublime than grammar (pp. 179–80). It looks as if he was influenced by Wittgenstein's simile between language and a tool-kit. In any case, he brought this simile to life and showed how it may be applied in detail to selected areas of English usage. He discriminated and classified many of the varieties of jobs that we do with words, of different uses of the same and different tools, revealing the niceties of adaptation of our mother-tongue to some of our everyday purposes. He introduced new ways of classifying the functions of language. For example, he distinguishes a class of verbs which play an important rôle in ceremonial and legal transactions: 'performative verbs', those like "to promise" and "to christen" which, when used in the first person present indicative, do not describe, but constitute, the performance of an action. (See his papers 'Other Minds' and 'Performative Utterances'.) This was a contribution to grammar of the same

[1] Unless otherwise stated all page references in this section will be to J. L. Austin: *Philosophical Papers*, ed. J. O. Urmson and G. J. Warnock, 1961.

kind as Ryle's classification of the functions of certain verbs, distinguishing 'process-verbs' (like "to run"), 'task-verbs' (like "to pursue") and 'achievement-verbs' (like "to catch up with"). Austin, however, did not represent his classifications of word-uses as an exercise in logic or as the discovery of categories. A theory of categories or types was for him superfluous. He seems to have played his language-game by ear—and by the dictionary, which he says should be a philosopher's first source-book when tackling a problem (pp. 134–5).

Austin's writings are distinguished for their originality, subtlety and wit. He asked many questions which no one had thought of asking before, e.g. 'why care*less*ly but *in*attentively?' (p. 141), and 'why are false teeth called 'false' rather than, say, 'artificial?' (*Sense and Sensibilia*, p. 72). Some of his questions and answers have thrown light on philosophical problems. In describing as a contribution to grammar Austin's classification of certain utterances as 'performatives', I do not wish to imply that this move had no importance for philosophy. Austin was rightly concerned to correct a widespread tendency for philosophers to treat the making of statements as the only or all-important function of indicative sentences. We ignore at our peril Austin's insights concerning grammar, though since these are often concerned with features peculiar to the English language, they may have no importance for philosophers who do their thinking in other languages. Austin has shown that philosophers need to be sensitive to the language in which they develop and try to communicate their thought. This need is not, however, peculiar to philosophers.

What determined the areas of English to which Austin directed his sensitive ears was often the dicta of other philosophers. He was sometimes devastatingly successful in criticising such dicta—when interpreted as pieces of ordinary language. He did not seem to notice, or did not mind, statements by scientists which are silly when similarly interpreted—like using "light" to refer to the whole spectrum of electro-magnetic waves. Sometimes when Austin attempts to show that philosophers' statements are silly, by taking them out of their context and treating them as ordinary language, he misses the point, as he often does in *Sense and Sensibilia*, when criticizing the dicta of Ayer and H. H. Price. When philosophers' statements are not his target, his purpose is sometimes far from clear. His paper 'How to Talk' (pp. 181 ff.) is devoted to describing the differences in our uses of "describing X as Y", "calling X, Y" and "stating that X is Y", without, however, making any attempt to connect his conclusions with any philosophical problem. Quite often Austin seems to be practising his new art for its own sake, sometimes to be doing what he describes as 'drawing the coverts of the microglot . . . hounding down the minutiae' [of English usage] (p. 123).

Let us consider what Austin says in 'A Plea for Excuses' by way of justifying his own method, namely 'to proceed from 'ordinary language'' (p. 129). He writes:

our common stock of words embodies all the distinctions men have found worth drawing, and the connections they have found worth making, in the lifetimes of many generations: these surely are likely to be more numerous, more sound, since they have stood up to the long test of the survival of the fittest, and more subtle, at least in all ordinary and reasonably practical matters, than any that you or I are likely to think up in our arm-chairs of an afternoon—the most favoured alternative method (p. 130).

In the next paragraph, in order to 'counter misunderstandings', he recommends a new label to replace "'linguistic' or 'analytic' philosophy or 'the analysis of language'". He writes:

When we examine what we should say when, what words we should use in what situations, we are looking again not *merely* at words (or 'meanings' whatever they may be) but also at the realities we use words to talk about: we are using a sharpened awareness of words to sharpen our perception of, though not as the final arbiter of, the phenomena. For this reason I think it might be better to use, for this way of doing philosophy, some less misleading name than those given above—for instance 'linguistic phenomenology' (p. 130).

Austin then anticipates some objections to his view that philosophers should put their trust in 'the inherited experience and acumen of many generations of men'. He says: 'that acumen has been concentrated upon the practical business of life. If a distinction works well for practical purposes in ordinary life . . . then there is sure to be something in it . . . yet this is likely enough not to be the best way of arranging things if our interests are more extensive or intellectual than the ordinary'.

He adds that 'superstition and error and fantasy of all kinds do become incorporated in ordinary language and even sometimes stand up to the survival test'. He sums up: 'Certainly, then, ordinary language is *not* the last word: in principle it can everywhere be supplemented and improved upon and superseded. Only remember, it *is* the *first* word' (p. 133).

My main complaint is that, apart from his earliest papers,[2] Austin rarely got beyond the first-word stage. Before documenting this criticism, however, I shall comment on Austin's surprising proposal to call his own method 'linguistic phenomenology'. Let us examine this phrase as Austin examined those coined by other philosophers. Since "phenomenology" means the study or description of phenomena (appearances) and "linguistic" means pertaining to the study of language, one might expect "linguistic phenomenology" to mean the study or description of *apparent* facts about language; might conclude that Austin was modestly disclaiming *knowledge* of how English is spoken, and was taking as his subject-matter what English-speakers *seemed to him* to say. But Austin rarely showed any lack of confidence about his knowledge of English usage. "Phenomenology" has also a more specific meaning—the introspective study of states of consciousness 'in the raw', the attempt to give descriptions of such states purged of all interpretations, judgements or preconceptions. So "linguistic phenomenology" could mean paying heed to the words which spontaneously spring to one's own lips or inner ear in various situations, the investigation of what *I* feel inclined to say, when . . . Though I suspect that Austin and others who appeal to ordinary language do often use this method, I doubt if they would wish to endorse it as their main method, or an important one. Linguistic phenomenology, on this interpretation, would be a science altogether too solitary and subjective.

What led Austin to coin this misleading technical term, as a 'less misleading name' for "linguistic philosophy", was that when we examine what we should say when, we are looking 'not merely at words . . . but also at the *realities* which we use words to talk about, we are using a sharpened awareness of words to sharpen our perception of . . . the *phenomena*' (My

2 'Are There *A Priori* Concepts?' (1939) and 'The Meaning of a Word' (1940).

italics). It is not easy to explain why Austin slipped here from "realities" to "phenomena", for he rarely uses the latter word, and he makes it plain elsewhere that, in his view, what we perceive are pigs, tables, rainbows, etc., and not appearances thereof. Should we accept Austin's claim that examining 'what we should say when' has value as a means of sharpening our perception of the things we talk about? No one would deny that a person's perception of something may be sharpened, may become more discriminating, through his learning or inventing some *new* way of describing it (or may be blunted if the new description is obscure and misleading, like "linguistic phenomenology" as a description of Austin's practice). But the method by which Austin seeks to sharpen our perception of things is reminding ourselves of the familiar ways in which we *do*, normally, describe them, of the everyday uses of English that we learnt as children. This seems to be one of the least promising ways of sharpening, or indeed altering, our perception of anything. Austin did introduce new descriptions, like "performative utterance", "stipulative *if*" and "illocutionary forces"; but these were descriptions of *word*-uses and *not* of 'the realities we use words to talk about'. What Austin sharpened our perception of is grammar.

Notice an ambiguity in Austin's wording: 'what we *should* say when.' If he had written 'what we do say' or 'what people would say', it would have been clear that his linguistic enquiries were intended to be empirical, descriptive. In asking 'what we should say', the "should" may be taken as an "ought", and the answers may be prescriptive, corrective. Indeed Austin not infrequently makes statements about English usage which could not be justified by appealing to dictionaries or to everyday talk. Here are two examples from 'A Plea for Excuses':

(a) 'It is bedtime, I am alone, I yawn: but I do not yawn involuntarily (or voluntarily!), nor yet deliberately. To yawn in any such peculiar way is just not to just yawn' (p. 138). And on the next page, Austin even expresses 'doubt whether there is *any* verb with which both adverbs ["voluntarily" and "involuntarily"] are equally in place'. It looks as if Austin has here made the error of interpreting "involuntary" as the contrary instead of the contradictory of "voluntary", i.e. as meaning 'contrary to one's wishes'. The *OED* is surely correct in reporting our normal usage; in defining "involuntary" as the contradictory of "voluntary", i.e. as meaning 'not voluntary', 'not done willingly or by choice'. Admittedly there are situations, like that of Austin's yawn, where the question 'was it voluntary? would not be likely to be asked, or if asked might be difficult to answer. But there is no doubt that there are hosts of English verbs, including "to yawn", with which 'both adverbs are equally in place.'

(b) In a passage concerning 'the combinations . . . of *adverbs* that are possible', Austin says that 'we can do an action intentionally yet for all that not deliberately, *still less on purpose*' (p. 143. My italics). But surely, in everyday talk, "done intentionally and "done on purpose" are used synonymously.[3] Austin does not try to describe a situation where "(done) intentionally" could not be replaced by "(done) on purpose". All he does is to describe a situation where "intentionally" is appropriate and "deliberately" is not. Austin sometimes speaks of 'the natural economy of language' (e.g. on p. 143). He argues as if he believed that English is so frugal as never to provide us with exact synonyms, with different tools for doing just the same job. If English were perfectly adapted for its functions, it would not contain so many homonyms; some requiring an Austin to distinguish their different roles, e.g. "if". (See below.)

[3] I received from Professor Woozley a challenge concerning this statement. He wrote: 'Aren't you committing the very sin you are preaching against? Doing armchair rather than . . . empirical linguistics'. I had indeed relied only upon my own fallible sense of linguistic propriety. It became clear, however, when I consulted the *OED*, that it does not support Austin's thesis; for it defines "intentional" as 'done on purpose, intended', and "on purpose" as 'by design, purposely, intentionally'. And my attempts to get a non-philosopher to think of a case where he would say '. . . done intentionally, but not on purpose' failed. I lost interest in this, however, on discovering the error underlying Austin's claim, revealed in 'Three Ways of Spilling Ink' (*Phil. Review*, 1966). Consider *his* example:

I needed money to play the ponies, so I dipped into the till. Of course I *intended* (all the time) to put it back as soon as I had collected my winnings. That was my *intention* . . . But was that *my purpose* in taking it? Did I take it for the purpose of, or, on purpose to, put it back? Plainly not (pp. 429–31).

Here Austin *changes the subject*. No one, presumably, would dispute that *as nouns* "intention" and "purpose" are not always interchangeable; but no conclusions can be drawn from this about the *adverbs* "intentionally" and "on purpose". Whether the latter are, in everyday talk, used interchangeably can be checked by the questionnaire method. But can anyone think of any philosophical purpose which this would serve? Austin's kind of language-game is fun when played by ear, but is a bore when done by questionnaire.

These examples illustrate the kind of task to which Austin devotes his investigation of "excuses". He urges the importance of distinguishing the correct uses of the different words belonging to this family; between those of "inadvertence", "mistake", "accident", "aberration" and "absence of mind" (p. 145), between "by mistake", "owing to a mistake", "mistakenly", etc. (p. 146). This sort of investigation, he says, 'is not so much a *lesson* from the study of excuses as the very object of it' (p. 146). For what purpose? Many of the questions he raises are important for lexicographers, but it is only in a few short asides and a footnote on page 146 that he suggests any possible relevance to philosophical problems.

Austin's writings sometimes give the impression that his occasional application of a linguistic finding to a philosophical problem was done from duty rather than interest. This seems to be true of his celebrated paper 'Ifs and Cans'. He discusses here sentences used by G. E. Moore and Professor P. H. Nowell-Smith. He mentions very briefly the philosophical problem which provided their context, i.e. an attempt to reconcile belief in freedom of choice and Determinism. To hold a person morally responsible for an action is commonly (and I think rightly) held to presuppose that his action was freely chosen in a sense which implies that he could have acted otherwise. Determinism, as normally defined, implies that it is never true to say that a person could have acted otherwise, unless this is understood to mean that *if* the relevant cause-factors, in the agent or the situation, had been different, the agent would (necessarily) have acted differently. Both Moore and Nowell-Smith had argued that 'I could have acted otherwise' is to be analyzed as a hypothetical statement, Moore's proposed paraphrase being 'I could have . . .' or alternatively 'I should have . . ., if I had chosen'. At the outset, Austin disavows concern with the bearings of Moore's thesis 'upon the meaning of *right* and *wrong* or upon the problem of Free Will' (p. 154). His discussion concerns the meaning and propriety of the hypothetical sentences used by Moore and Nowell-Smith. His critique is subtle and sometimes penetrating.

What most excites Austin's interest seems to be the curiosity of 'these curious expressions 'I can if I choose' and 'I shall if I choose''. (p. 159). Perhaps this is because it provides a cue for distinguishing and christening two different 'kinds of *if*' (functions of "if"), other than the familiar 'conditional *if*'. He points out that the function of "I can if I choose" is 'the assertion, positive and complete, that 'I can' . . . linked to the raising of the question whether I choose' (p. 160); and he describes this use of "if" as 'the *if* of doubt or hesitation, not the *if* of condition' (p. 161). He lapses, I think, in his account of "I shall if I choose". In the interests of generating another class of ifs, '*ifs* of stipulation', he allocates to this class the "if" in each of these sentences:

(i) I shall marry him if I choose,
(ii) I intend to marry him if I choose,
(iii) I promise to marry him if he will have me.

Austin says that (i) is 'a categorical expression of intention, in which 'I shall' verges towards the giving of an undertaking' (pp. 161–2). This is unsatisfactory. (iii) is an undertaking, whereas (i) and (ii) are obviously not. Using (iii) involves undertaking to do something if a condition is fulfilled whose fulfilment does not depend on the speaker; so the "if" in (iii) is the 'if of condition'. If Austin had considered the sort of context in which (i) or (ii) would be used, he would presumably have recognized that their function would be to express determination to have one's own way, to do whatever one chooses, with no indication of what one will choose and a strong suggestion that one has not yet chosen. If anyone wishes to distinguish the use of "if" in (i) and (ii) from Austin's 'ifs of doubt or hesitation', he is welcome to do so, but let us hope that his account of the former will be more apt than Austin's.

What emerges from Austin's discussion of the function of "I shall if I choose" is that it contributes nothing to settling the philosophical problem which concerned Moore and Nowell-Smith. Austin does, however, make a linguistic point which is relevant to their proposed solutions, i.e. that "could have" is not always equivalent to "should have if . . .". He writes: 'Sometimes 'I could have' is equivalent to the Latin 'Potui' and means 'I *was* in a position to': sometimes it is equivalent to the Latin 'Potuissem' and means 'I should have been in a position to [if . . .]' (p. 163). However, it is, apparently, only as an afterthought that he connects this point with the philosophical problem. His last paragraph starts: 'It is not unusual for an audience at a lecture to include some who prefer things to be important'. For the benefit of such members of his audience, he claims that the arguments he has used go some way to show that Determinism is not true, because 'it appears not consistent with what we ordinarily say and presumably think' (p. 179). This point is made more explicit in a footnote added before publication. Having referred to 'a modern belief in science, in there being an explanation for everything', he says: 'But such a belief is not in line with the traditional beliefs enshrined in the word *can*' (p. 166). So what? Austin's conclusion should surely be the start and not the end of a philosophical discussion. As Ayer has said: 'it is no answer to the denier of free-will merely to pin-point ways of using language in which the falsity of his position is already presupposed' (*The Concept of a Person*, p. 17).

As another example of Austin's failure to advance beyond the 'first-word' stage, let us consider the contents of Chapter VII of *Sense and Sensibilia*.[4] This chapter does contain what is potentially an important contribution to the philosophical debate. Austin mentions what we may call the conventionalist definition of "the real colour", as opposed to "the apparent colours", of a thing, namely that 'the *real* colour of the thing is the colour that it looks to a normal observer in conditions of normal or standard illumination' (p. 65). Austin then asks a series of questions which show that in some cases this definition will not work, e.g. what is the real colour of the moon, or of the sun, or of a fish which looks vividly multi-coloured 'at a depth of a thousand feet', but looks greyish-white when lying on the deck? (pp. 65–6). He thus undermines a gambit popular among ordinary language philosophers for defending a common sense account of perception. Austin undermines this kind of definition and puts nothing in its place. What his questions should bring home to us is that when we contrast the *real* and the *apparent* colours of a thing, we are not using "real" in an existential sense; that "apparent" does not here mean unreal *qua* non-existent. The

[4] Austin was not responsible for this posthumous publication in 1962. It is a reconstruction by Mr. G. J. Warnock from the manuscript notes for a series of lectures which Austin gave many times. Referring *inter alia* to Chapter VII, Warnock writes: 'though there is no room for serious doubt as to what Austin's argument was, it was considerably less easy to tell from his notes exactly how, and in what order, the argument should be deployed' (p. vii).

chocolate-brown colour that I see when I look at a British pillar-box lit by sodium lamps is neither more real nor less real, in the existential sense, than the red colour I see when I look at it in daylight. Did Austin recognize this? Perhaps not. The function of the chapter seems to be to divert our attention from one of the most everyday uses of "real", the existential use, by dwelling in loving detail on another of its uses, i.e. when "real" is contrasted with "fake", or "imitation", or "toy" or "decoy". Could his sensitive ears have failed to detect the familiar Hyde Park Corner and Pulpit use of "Is A real?", to ask 'Does A exist?'? One of Austin's main claims is that the word "real" is 'substantive-hungry', that 'we must have an answer to the question 'A real *what*?', if the question 'Real or not?' is to have a definite sense' (p. 69). But in the familiar existential use, "real" is not substantive-hungry; though of course we can always add a redundant and empty substantive like "being", "thing" or "entity". ('Is God a real being?', 'Are sub-atomic particles real entities?', 'Are numbers real things?')

Could Austin have failed to notice this, despite his knowledge of the logicians' use of the existential quantifier, his knowledge that one of the main problems about perception which has preoccupied philosophers and scientists is whether colours are real, whether things are really coloured, meaning: are *any* of the colours we see, the 'real' or the 'apparent' colours of things, qualities which things have independently of being seen, qualities which things had before evolution produced creatures with eyes relevantly like ours? It seems hard to believe that Austin could have failed to notice this question, and the everyday existential use of "real" (and "really" and "reality").[5] But perhaps he did. We all fail to notice things that don't interest us or don't suit our book (or our lectures). But surely Austin could not have thought that his survey of *one* of our uses of "real" has any relevance to the problems about Primary and Secondary Qualities which have been posed by Democritus, Galileo, Locke, etc. In any case, judged by his own programme, to survey the everyday uses of "real" in the interests of assessing

[5] The footnote on p. 68 suggests that Austin's conscience pricked him: ''Exist', of course, is itself extremely tricky. The word is a verb, but it does not describe something that things do all the time, like breathing only quieter—ticking over, as it were in a metaphysical sort of way.' This joke is all we get about existence.

what philosophers have said about perception, what Austin says is surprisingly off the point.

Austin seems to have been deaf to scientists' talk. Fancy a philosopher in the middle of the twentieth century giving courses of lectures on perception without ever mentioning the languages, the 'conceptual schemes', whereby physicists, physiologists and psychologists describe *and explain* the relevant facts! The most intractable problems about perception stem from the difficulties in reconciling scientists' explanations with the realist beliefs enshrined in the language which we learnt at our mothers' knees, when we learnt to speak of light *revealing* and darkness *concealing* the colours, as well as the shapes, of things. Austin, however, was content to describe to us how we all talk when oblivious to, or not discussing, the philosophers' problems; how we talk in the ordinary language which we use to refer, describe, classify, etc., but which does not and cannot explain many anomalous empirical facts about perception; to some of which his own unanswered questions on pages 65–6 draw attention. It looks as if Austin accepted Wittgenstein's view that philosophers should never theorize or try to explain, should only describe language-games and leave everything as it is. Even so, why ignore scientists' language-games? Many linguistic philosophers discuss religious language, including some who no longer use it. Why then do so few discuss scientific languages, since all, presumably, learned to make beginners' moves in these? It would be disastrous to identify the boundaries of philosophy with the limits of Austin's very limited interests. Socrates, who started it all, is said to have said that in the end philosophers must accept the best hypothesis, the one which conforms best with all the known facts. Presumably Socrates *meant* all the known facts; not just facts about how certain non-technical Greek words were most frequently being used in the Agora.

I have postponed a question which must be faced: is it fair to say that Austin's work fulfils my definition of "linguistic philosophy"? Did he treat language as the subject-matter of philosophy? Though he never went so far as Wittgenstein did in saying 'Grammar tells what kind of object anything is', Austin did once say: '*Knowing what a thing is* is, to an important extent, knowing what the name for it, and the right name for it, is' (p. 51). Some of his remarks, however, indicate that he thought that philosophy involves more than a study of ordinary language; for example, 'ordinary language is *not* the last word' (p. 133); and his description of his own method as being 'to proceed *from* 'ordinary language'' (p. 129. My italics). *Towards what*? Apparently only towards getting philosophers to accept the beliefs 'enshrined' in ordinary language. The declared purpose of his 'linguistic phenomenology' *sounds* more exciting: 'to sharpen our perception of . . . the phenomena' (p. 130). But his recipe for achieving this makes it rather like trying to improve one's vision by donning spectacles which lack lenses; for his method is to ask us to describe the phenomena, *very* carefully, with words we learnt to use before we read any philosophy. Is this not to treat ordinary language as the subject-matter of philosophy, and discriminating attention to everyday usage as our professional function? Austin's dominant motive seems, from his writings, to have been sheer love of language. Ryle's preoccupation with language seems, like Wittgenstein's, to have been motivated by a desire to dispel perplexities. Did Austin ever suffer from doubts or puzzlement about the world and our place in it? If so, he did not betray them in cold print.

When Austin went astray in his descriptions of English usage, he cannot be charged with doing legislative linguistics. His errors were just errors of fact, rather than special pleading in the interests of some philosophical theory or thesis. This is not to say that they were unmotivated. When Austin goes wrong, his motive seems to have been a desire to reveal subtle points about English usage which no one else had or would have noticed. Though Austin did not commit the sins of *a priori* or legislative linguistics, his work is partly responsible for their being committed by others. It has fostered a preoccupation with classifying word uses for its own sake (what White calls 'categorizing concepts'); and it has blurred the difference between descriptions of and prescriptions about English usage, for Austin tended to interpret "what we should say" as what he thought we ought to say rather than as what ordinary people do say.

In the name of *ordinary* language, he demanded standards of purity and precision of speech which are extraordinarily rare except among men who got a First in Classical Greats.

Consider what is properly called 'ordinary language'. Could anyone seriously maintain that it is philosophically fertile to proceed from (or back to) this? Consider for example a recently conceived compartment of philosophy, 'the philosophy of action'. Can we really clarify any 'concepts' by noting the happy-go-lucky way in which most non-philosophers, even well-educated ones, use interchangeably words like "intention", "purpose', "aim", "goal", "object", "objective", "end", etc.? Austin's terminological hyperaesthesia (Heath's phrase) could have been put to better use: for example, paying heed to, and reminding his colleagues about, the everyday uses of their jargon-words—"concept" and "category", "logic" and "criterion"—and making them realize the need to explain their technical uses of these terms. These uses are the topics of the next two sections.

SECTION VIII

The Use of "Concept" in Linguistic Philosophy

PROFESSOR P. L. Heath has said, with his tongue in his cheek, that although "concept" is 'one of the most equivocal terms in the philosophical vocabulary', it 'remains useful precisely because of its ambiguity, as a sort of pass-key through the labyrinths represented by the theory of meaning, the theory of thinking and the theory of being' ('Concept', *The Encyclopaedia of Philosophy*, 1967). English-speaking philosophers have been making much use of this word, and many have claimed that concepts, or conceptual problems, form the subject-matter of philosophy. No doubt such philosophers are perfectly clear as to what they are doing with this word, but they rarely explain this. What then is their subject-matter when they make statements about 'the concept of A' or 'the logic of the concept'? If they are empiricists, presumably they do not think of a concept as Plato thought of an Idea, as a non-sensible entity which was there waiting to be discovered before we mortals did discover it. Nor, presumably, do they think of a concept in the way that Berkeley interpreted Locke as doing, as a particular object housed in a person's mind. Presumably most contemporary philosophers are using "the concept of A" as a way of *mentioning* "A", of talking about the use of the expression "A"—and of other expressions which have the same use, *if there are any*. This way of using "the concept of A" is legitimate, though somewhat cryptic if it is not explained. If, however, a philosopher used "the concept of A" to talk about the *things* called 'As' or about the *properties* of these things on account of which they are called 'As', this would be a very cryptic and misleading way of *using* the expression "A".

We need not so define "concept" that to say that a person has, or lacks, the concept of A implies that *he* has, or lacks, the ability to use the expression "A" or any synonym. If we speak of someone acquiring or possessing, say, 'the concept of a kestrel', we *may* be using this phrase to refer to his ability to use the word "kestrel"; and since "kestrel" is a class-name, the full ability to use it involves the ability to recognize kestrels, to apply "kestrel" correctly. We may, however, use "concept" more liberally and allow that a human deaf-mute or a blackbird may have the concept of a kestrel; in which case having a name for kestrels must not be made necessary, by definition, to having this concept. In this case, we should define "the concept of A" as 'the ability to use "A" *or* the ability to recognize As'. Whichever definition we choose, obviously we should not use "the concept of a kestrel" as a way of referring to kestrels; which are not abilities of men to talk about them, nor of songbirds to recognize and try to avoid them. Nobody is tempted to make this sort of mistake in the case of a class-name like "kestrel". But philosophers are liable to make this error, or at least to give the impression of doing so, when "the concept of" is followed by more abstract or less precise words whose uses they discuss, e.g. "mind" or "imagination" or "person". In this respect, Professor Ryle set a bad example in *The Concept of Mind.*

As we have seen at the beginning of section V, Ryle says things in *C of M* which imply that he intended to use "the concept of A" in the permissible though slightly cryptic sense. This interpretation is supported by what Ryle says in his later paper 'Ordinary Language', where he acknowledges "concept" as a jargon-word, and says: 'It is then salutory to keep on reminding ourselves . . . that what we are after is accounts of how certain words work' (*Phil. Review*, 1953, p. 185). Yet in *C of M*, where he claimed to be discussing 'the logic of concepts' and not 'facts about the mental life of human beings', Ryle oscillated between statements about English usage or the functions of English words and, on the other hand, statements about the things we use words to talk about. His chapter on 'Imagination', for example, contains many statements which seem to be asserting psychological facts rather than giving 'accounts of how certain words work', like:

Roughly, imaging occurs, but images are not seen (p. 247),

In short, there are no such objects as mental pictures, . . . (p. 254),

People are apt grossly to exaggerate the photographic fidelity of their visual imagery (pp. 275–6).

Presumably it is the frequency of such apparently non-linguistic statements in *C of M* that led Ayer to describe Ryle's method as being 'simply to take a new look at the facts . . . to make us fix our attention on the actual phenomena of what is supposed to be our mental life' (*The Concept of a Person*, p. 23). Ayer goes on to say that Ryle's emphasis 'is apparently made to fall upon our verbal habits. But this appearance is delusive . . . the emphasis is not on our verbal habits themselves, but on the situations to which they are adapted' (op. cit., pp. 24–5). This interpretation of Ryle's method does not match Ryle's description of it. (Were Ayer's statements perhaps a tactful way of advocating a method of which he had come to approve?) It is of interest here that Ayer himself sometimes gives the impression that he is using "the concept of A" as a way of talking about the things called 'As'. Thus, he presents Descartes' dualism, correctly, as the thesis 'that a person is a combination of two separate entities' (op. cit., p. 82); yet he also presents it as the thesis that '*the concept* of a person is derivative, in the sense that *it* is capable of being analyzed into simpler elements' (op. cit., p. 85. My italics). If Ayer used the latter sentence to say what is said by the former, "the concept of a person" was being used to refer to people. Strawson, whose views Ayer is discussing in this paper, also speaks sometimes as if Descartes' theory were about 'the concept of a person'. Strawson rejects 'the Cartesian error' by claiming that 'the concept of a person' is 'logically primitive'; which means, he says, that this concept is not to be analyzed in certain ways, notably in terms of 'a particular consciousness and a particular human body' (*Individuals*, pp. 104–5). But Descartes' thesis was about *people*, *us*, and not about uses of words. Presumably no philosophers would wish to speak of the *concept* of an omelette being analyzable into eggs, butter, etc. If concepts have constituents, these must surely be concepts, not things like eggs.

In addition to obscuring the difference between using and mentioning words, the current concept-idiom has another disadvantage. "The Concept of Mind" was an unfortunate title for Ryle's book. In view of Ryle's equation between wielding concepts and using items of the English vocabulary, this title should mean 'The Use of "Mind" and synonymous words, *if any*'. So "*The* Concept" suggests "*The* Use"—as if there is only one use of "mind". Anyone who takes Austin's methods seriously should consider how "concept" is used in everyday talk. Then he could scarcely fail to notice that the commonest use of "concept of A" is to *contrast* the use of "A" by one person or group with that of oneself or of another group. '*Your* concept of Sin' (because I don't use this word, don't share the religious beliefs enshrined therein); 'the *Conservatives*' concept of social justice' (contrasted with the Socialists' more egalitarian definition or use); '*Freud's* concept of the mind' (said by a behaviourist); 'A *man's* concept of fidelity' (said by a woman in a recent television play); and so on. The whole point of using "concept" in such contexts hinges on there being importantly different uses of the same word or phrase; as is conspicuously true of "mind". And *its* uses are not just grammatically different, but are also different in presupposing incompatible metaphysical theories, theories which often cannot be detected simply by considering the ways in which people use mind-words when not stating these theories. For example, the strange theory about the mind which Hume propounded—that it is 'nothing but a bundle or collection of perceptions, which succeed each other with inconceivable rapidity' (*Treatise* I, IV, VI)—did not require him, or lead him, to use mind-words differently from others when he was not philosophizing.

In the case of "mind", it is so obvious that this word has many different uses that Ryle's title should not mislead any but a child or a foreigner. Apart from the host of different things which may be said in testimonials about a person's mind, consider such uses of "mind", the noun, as in saying: 'His mind is not on his job'; 'He is out of his mind'; 'He has lost his mind'; 'He has a mind of his own'; 'He has changed his mind'; and so on. Now that so many philosophers have followed Ryle's example, and preface almost any word whose use they are discussing with "*the* concept of", there are obvious dangers that their hearers, if not they themselves, will sometimes forget the multiplicity of uses of the words in question. One philosopher of my acquaintance did this. A student had responded to 'Write an essay on Obligation and Choice' by discussing the familiar thesis that 'ought' implies 'can'. This philosopher asserted that this was 'the wrong answer', that 'the right answer' was to discuss the thesis that 'I am obliged to do so and so' entails 'I have no choice but to do so and so". He could see only one philosophical interpretation of the phrase "Obligation and Choice", because he interpreted the "the" in "the concept of A" as meaning *the one and only correct* use of "A"; and equated this with what he took to be the standard, the most frequent, use of "A" in the market-place. A conception of philosophy which produces such symptoms should not be allowed to become endemic.

There is an implication of the permissible, though slightly cryptic, use of "the concept of A", which is unacceptable to its users as well as to others. This is that it makes a linguistic philosophers' conclusions about the concept relative to the language to which "A" belongs, and that what linguistic philosophers are really doing is Anglo-linguistics; or, at any rate, that *if* their conclusions are applicable to some other languages, this is coincidential. This important issue needs, and gets, further discussion in Section X. Here we may simply note that it would be a remarkable coincidence if English mind-predicates (a very large class) each had exact synonyms, each of which had the same 'logic' (parallel functions in the linguistic network), in *any* other natural language. How often did the translator of *C of M* into Italian have to do the sort of thing that those translating jokes commonly have to do, i.e. invent a new but similar joke because the joke hangs on a specific double-meaning of a word in language 1 which is not possessed by any word in language 2? Fortunately for the translator, Ryle's Chapter One examples of 'category-mistakes' nearly all hung on A being a member or part of B, and these examples are easily translatable; but what about Ryle's later statements of the form 'You cannot (properly, strictly, significantly) say this about that'?

"Concept" was originally a philosophers' technical term, but during the last fifty years or so it has become such an every-day word that it does not occur to students to ask for an explanation of its use by philosophers. Few philosophers volunteer an explanation of the connection between talk about 'concepts' and talk about words, and those who do are liable to leave room for misunderstandings. I shall give four examples to illustrate this point.

(i) Professor Antony Flew has written:

But insofar as philosophy is a conceptual enquiry, such concern [with the ordinary uses of words] is surely essential. For how else could we investigate the concept of knowledge than by studying the various correct uses of the word 'know' (*Essays in Logic and Language*, Second Series, 1953, p. 9).

It would have been better had he added that the reason is that "the concept of knowledge" is being used to *mean* 'the uses of "knowledge" and of any synonymous words'. Failure to explain this might suggest to the uninitiated that "conceptual enquiry" means something more specialized or profound.

(ii) Professor A. R. White's book *The Philosophy of Mind* (1967) starts with a section on 'Conceptual Analysis', designed to explain to beginners the kind of philosophy practised by 'most contemporary English-speaking philosophers'. This section does end by indicating the connection between 'concepts' and words:

To employ a concept is ordinarily to use a verbal expression in a certain way; to indicate a concept is to mention a word or phrase (p. 11).

But the preceding passage contains many statements which a reflective beginner might find puzzling, for example:

Very much as physical positions are spatially related, so positions of thought—that is, concepts—are "logically" related. While physical points include or exclude one another, the uses of concepts imply or contradict one another (pp. 7–8);

For concepts are in this respect like mathematical points: *they have no qualities other than their relations to other concepts* (p. 8. My italics);

A philosophical examination of the concepts we use . . . consists, therefore, in an attempt . . . to discover how the uses of these concepts are *logically related* to each other and *to their subject-matter* (p. 10. My italics).[1]

(iii) In his book *The Diversity of Meaning* (1962), Mr. L. J. Cohen distinguishes two 'planes of discourse about meaning', 'the verbal and the conceptual planes' (p. 14). On the verbal

[1] Is it implied that the relation between "dogs" and dogs is a *logical* relation? And how can we reconcile the last two quotations?

plane, he says, 'statements about specific meanings cannot be translated into another language or paraphrased in their own'; and his example of such a statement is 'The German word "Katze" means a cat' (p. 14). From this it would appear that Cohen's 'verbal plane' consists of statements about the meaning of a term which is therefore being mentioned and not used. This would pose no problems if his characterization of the conceptual plane were not so puzzling. He starts by saying: 'On the conceptual plane almost all statements about meanings . . . can at least in principle be translated from one language into another' (p. 15). He goes on to speak as if what distinguishes the two 'planes of discourse' is that they are concerned, respectively, with 'language-words' and 'culture-words'. He says that a culture-word is 'individuated by meaning, not by form . . . and its meaning is discussed on the conceptual plane, whereas a language-word is identified by its form and its meaning is normally discussed on the verbal plane' (p. 21). And sometimes Cohen equates 'a concept' with 'the meaning of a culture-word' (e.g. on p. 83) Everything depends then on the explanation of his distinction between culture-words and language-words. What are we to make of the criterion we are offered: 'Quoted culture-words are translatable; quoted language-words which exemplify them are not' (p. 15)? Cohen says things which suggest that culture-words and language-words are two distinct species of words. Thus he offers as examples of culture-words "mass" as used in Physics (p. 15), "time" (p. 17) and "nature" (p. 21). He nowhere acknowledges that these words are like "cat" in that they may not be translated in translating any statement which *mentions* them, and that "cat" is like them in that it should be translated in translating any statement in which it is *used*! When Cohen says that 'quoted language-words which exemplify them [culture-words] are not [translatable]', what can we make of "which exemplify them"? If "physis", "natura", "nature" and all of their synonyms are *exemplifications* of a culture-word, what *is* the latter? At one point Cohen says that the notion of a culture-word 'might be defined as a family of intertranslatable language-words' (p. 22). In that case a so-called culture-word is not, after all, *a word* and is not the sort of thing to which "(un)translatable" could be applied. Had Cohen paid any critical attention to his use of "concept", he could scarcely have given so obscure an account of his distinction between the verbal and conceptual planes of discourse.

(iv) Consider how Professor S. Körner explains his subject-matter in the first four chapters of his book *Conceptual Thinking* (1955). We are told on page 1 that the meaning of "conceptual thinking" must ultimately be conveyed by giving examples, that there are other kinds of thinking, and that there are borderline cases since conceptual and non-conceptual thinking shade into each other. We are offered examples of conceptual thinking *but no examples of non-conceptual thinking*. In Chapter 2, we get a definition of "concept" according to which conceptual thinking must involve the use of signs (p. 14). Yet the chapter ends with this statement: 'How far non-verbal signs including possibly incommunicable signs (for example, private bodily feelings which can be produced at will) can be used in conceptual thinking *is a matter for empirical enquiry*' (p. 15. My italics). This leaves the reader unnecessarily uncertain *what Körner wished to choose* as his subject-matter. Conceptual thinking, by his definition, involves the use of signs, yet we are told that it is an empirical question what is to count as a sign: perhaps a bodily feeling, or, more plausibly, a so-called mental image, is to count as a sign—depending on what? Agreement among psychologists? A forlorn hope! A question which needs to be answered is whether an as yet speechless infant or a squirrel classifying nuts as keepers and rejects is doing conceptual thinking. Empirical enquiries will never suffice to answer such a question, until those who ask it make a decision and give a more explicit definition of their own use of "concept" and "conceptual thinking". Körner does offer a definition of "concept", but it is seriously misleading. He distinguishes between a 'statement-sign' (i.e. presumably, an indicative sentence), a 'statement' and a 'proposition'. His first move is: 'In order to identify a particular statement, it is necessary to mention the sign (the statement sign) . . .'. His next move, in order to distinguish a statement and a proposition, is:

Let us call any rule which permits the arbitrary replacement of a sign by any one of its synonyms, a "synonymity rule". If we add to the rules for *the use of a sign as a statement* a synonymity rule, we shall say that *it* (*the statement sign*) *is now being used not as a statement but as a proposition* (p. 13. My italics).

This is very misleading in implying that an indicative sentence can be used to do two different things—to make a statement *or* to assert a proposition. There is no room for this distinction. To use the sentence "The earth is flat" to state that the earth is flat *is* to assert the proposition that the earth is flat. If "asserting the proposition that p" does not mean 'stating that p', what can it mean? Körner proceeds to define "concept" by means of a parallel distinction where no difference exists:

In order to identify a particular predicate it is necessary to mention the sign (the predicate sign) [e.g. "green", his only example] which is used as the predicate ... By adding a synonymity rule to the rules which govern the use of a sign as a predicate we again change its use. *The sign is then being used no longer as a predicate but as a concept* (p. 14. My italics).

Sophisticated readers might guess that this is a way of saying that "the concept of green" means 'the use of the word "green" and of any synonymous words' (which is, I presume, what Körner wanted to say); but I should expect students to be either puzzled or seriously misled by the claim that "green" can be used in two different ways, *either* as a predicate *or* as a concept. If one *uses* "green", e.g. in saying 'Her dress was green', one is *not* mentioning, saying anything about, the English word "green"; one is using "green" to refer to one (or more) of the shades connoted by this word *and therefore* connoted also by any other word which is synonymous with "green". It is of course a tautology to say that a person who *uses* a descriptive word, e.g. "green", to talk about what it describes, is thereby talking about what is described by any synonymous word; for "any synonymous word" here *means* 'any word which described what "green" describes'. Körner's definition gives the impression that he has not recognized this tautology. Once the tautology is recognized as such, it is obvious that there is no room for a distinction between using "green" *as* a predicate and *as* a concept. Whatever the merits of the ensuing arguments in Körner's book, students who read it are likely to be left confused as to what this book is about.

It is not only practitioners of linguistic philosophy (as I am using this term) who have been obscuring their thoughts by using the concept-idiom. Mr. Cohen and Professor Körner have both published criticisms of linguistic philosophy.[2] One of the factors which led me to write this book was the discovery that the concept-idiom is cryptic to students. I presented a questionnaire to my first-year students. It was drafted in haste, as the idea was conceived on the evening before the last meeting for the session of this class. Such an experiment needs more careful planning, but mine showed at least that it needed to be done. The sheet said: 'Suppose a philosopher started a lecture by saying "I shall discuss the concept of Man", which of the following would you think he was most probably going to talk about?', and then seven phrases followed. Multiple choice was permitted. I told the students to give their first reactions, and not to try to work out what the imaginary lecturer *should* be talking about. The results were very embarrassing. Almost 50 per cent of the responses were for one of three phrases which used "idea", which was fair enough since "idea" has much the same uses as "concept". Only 3 per cent of the responses were for one of the two phrases which made the lecturer's subject-matter the definition or the uses of the word "man". The real shock was that nearly half of the responses were for phrases implying that "the concept of Man" is used to talk about men: the phrases they chose being "the individuals we call 'men'" or "human beings, people, us". These students had had a year of formal logic by a lecturer who quite frequently uses "concept"; one term on ethics by a colleague who also uses the concept-idiom; and two terms of epistemology from me, without the use of "concept", except when briefly expounding Conceptualism as one of the traditional theories of universals. So this was what they had been making of it!

The results of this enquiry led me to write a polemical essay which I sent to colleagues in a number of other Universities, inviting them to repeat my experiment. For this purpose I drafted a similar but more careful questionnaire. Details of this questionnaire and of the results obtained elsewhere are given in an appendix to this section. Five philosophy departments in

[2] See Cohen's *The Diversity of Meaning*, Ch. III, and Körner's papers 'Are All Philosophical Questions, Questions of Language?' (*PAS*, Supp. Vol., 1948), 'Some Remarks on Philosophical Analysis' (*J. of Phil.*, 1957), and 'Transcendental Tendencies in Recent Philosophy' (*J. of Phil.*, 1966).

British Universities used this questionnaire and kindly sent me their results. I must mention these if only because the worst feature of my own results was not repeated. The results elsewhere cannot, however, fairly be compared with mine, since four phrases added to my original seven got more than half of the votes elsewhere. I have pooled the results for the five departments, and distinguished two classes of students: 'beginners', and 'more advanced' meaning those who had studied philosophy for more than one year. The main features of the results are these:

(i) Relatively few students chose one of the three phrases which involve interpreting "the concept of man" as a way of referring to the uses of the word "man", i.e. only 14 per cent of the beginners and 32 per cent of the others.
(ii) The phrase which presumably corresponds most closely to what most philosophers mean by "the concept of man" was "The uses of "man" and of any synonymous words". This was chosen by only 7½ per cent of the beginners and 13 per cent of the others.
(iii) Few chose either of the two phrases which involve interpreting "the concept of man" as a way of *using* "man", i.e. only 10 per cent of the beginners and 6 per cent of the others. But here any is too many, for presumably all would agree that such an interpretation is definitely mistaken, which cannot be said of any of the other choices that were offered.

The last feature of these results increases my embarrassment that so many of my students made this error. I think the explanation is this: that my students associated the questionnaire, coming from me, with theories of universals; for I had used "concept" only in that context, and had defended a resemblance theory, arguing (roughly) that the function of general words, e.g. "man", is to talk about resemblances between individual things, e.g. human beings. However, to explain is not to excuse. As teachers we are not doing our job adequately if we use terms which are interpreted vaguely and variously by our students. I hope that others will not simply dismiss this exploratory experiment by saying 'It could not happen here', without finding out what does happen there if their students are taken by surprise with some such test.

It is not, of course, being suggested that any firm general conclusions can be drawn from the results just described. A critic may retort (one did) that all that has been shown is that some students are ineducable. However, I followed up the questionnaire for students by addressing two questions to four professional philosophers who had recently completed their training at six of the best British Universities. The questions were:

(i) Did any of your philosophy teachers ever acknowledge that their use of "concept" needs an explanation and give one?
(ii) Did you ever ask any of your teachers what he meant by "the concept of so and so"?

To question (i), three said No and the fourth, cautiously, that he could not remember this happening. To question (ii), two said No; one that he *may* have done this when discussing Frege's 'The Concept of a Concept'; the fourth that he did once ask this question and got a short and unsatisfactory reply. I checked these answers by repeating the questions next day. One of the answers was then amended. One of those who had said No to question (i), said now that one of his lecturers had drawn attention to difficulties in defining "concept", and had added, in effect: you will learn how to use it by noticing how I do; which sounds alarmingly like saying 'Sorry I can't tell you what this word means, but copy my way of using it'! If anyone needs further confirmation that philosophers have not realized the need to explain their technical use(s) of "concept", they should have no difficulty in getting it. Is it not surprising that philosophers who have told us that concepts constitute the subject-matter of philosophy, should omit to explain what *they* mean by "concept"? Surely they cannot intend the subject-matter of philosophy to be the many, mostly woolly, ways in which *other* people are now using this word.

Apart from the results of the experiment in other Universities, the foregoing contents of this section were contained in the polemical essay in which I suggested that my questionnaire be tried elsewhere. I received several criticisms which will now be discussed. First a criticism which seemed to imply that I had wasted time in using the questionnaire with my students. Referring to the first sentence in the questionnaire ("Suppose a philosopher started a lecture by saying 'I shall discuss the concept of Man'"), this critic wrote:

> What an odd example. It would fox me. Abstract nouns are the expected sequels to 'the concept of . . .'. 'Randomness', 'Sin', 'Consumer Preference' [are] O.K.; 'Mind' dubious; 'London' out; 'Carburettor' out; 'Kestrel' out; 'Vegetable' out; yet 'Weed' is I think *in* or marginal.

What had led me to use "Man" in my questionnaire was this. I wanted a phrase as close as possible to Ryle's familiar "the concept of mind" and to Strawson's familiar "the concept of a person"; but not *these* phrases, for the students might have read Ryle's or Strawson's books, and I did not wish them to rack their memories of what they had read therein. The purpose of my experiment was to get the students' spontaneous interpretation of the concept-talk of their teachers. I picked "the concept of Man", dropping the "a" as Ryle did in *C of M*, though perhaps it would have been better to leave it in, and I chose "man" because this seems to be an exact synonym of "person", as this word is used, and its meaning analyzed, by Strawson in *Individuals*. If I am correct that, for Strawson, "person", "human being" and "man" (in the sense in which "man" includes woman) are synonymous, I am entitled to ask this critic, and anyone else who professes puzzlement about "the concept of Man", why he was not foxed or even surprised by Strawson's now well-worn phrase. Nobody seems to have questioned the propriety of Strawson's "the concept of a person", though on Strawson's account a person is just as concrete, non-abstract, as a carburettor, and is something whose boundaries are more easily recognized than are those of London. Philosophers who have not felt any qualms about using "the concept of a person" scarcely seem entitled to protest about "the concept of man".

This critic may be correct, apart from the tense of his verb, in saying 'Abstract nouns are the expected sequels of 'the concept of . . .'.' I think this used to be the case. However, under the influence of philosophers, and largely of *C of M*, the educated public have grown accustomed to prefacing almost any noun or noun-phrase with "the concept of". I had used "the concept of a kestrel", as a way of being provocative; of asking where philosophers are going to draw the line. I had not thought of the still more provocative device of complementing "the concept of ..." with a proper name, like "London", or "Fido". But I should be surprised if "the concept of London" has not yet been used seriously in debates by members of the London County Council. A philosopher who legislates regarding the permissible uses of "the concept of", is under an obligation to answer the following question: How did he discover which words may, and which may not, be prefaced by "the concept of"?[4] By intuition, or his own sense of style? By asking himself 'Would *I* ever say that?' A philosopher might confess to using the latter method, but he could scarcely leave it at that. If he presents his claim as a piece of empirical linguistics, we may ask him about the sample of English speakers whose linguistic behaviour he has observed, what methods of observation he employed, and how he managed to complete his observations so quickly. And we should press the question: how he derives 'may not be said' from 'is not (normally, or even, ever) being said'.

Two distinguished philosophers challenged my statements 'that the commonest use of "concept of A" is to contrast the use of "A" by one person or group with that of oneself or of another group. '*Your* concept of Sin' (because I don't use this word); 'the *Conservatives*' concept of social justice' (contrasted with the Socialists' more egalitarian definition or use) . . . The whole point of using "concept" in such contexts hinges on there being importantly different uses of the same word(s).' The first critic wrote, referring to my examples:

> "Conception" seems to me to fit better . . . Roughly a conception tends to be a theory or prejudice, etc. Its exposition would be a proposition, or a complex of propositions. Of course the jargon-word "concept" is sometimes so used too. But where we have a need for "misconception", we haven't and don't need "misconcept".

Well, in my examples, I too would be more inclined to use

[4] I am assuming, I think correctly, that when this critic said that "London", "carburettor," etc., are *out* as sequels to "the concept of . . .", he meant more by "out" than 'not in fact so used'.

"conception" rather than "concept", to speak of 'your conception of sin', as I speak sometimes of the linguistic philosophers' conception of philosophy. But as a matter of fact, it is now very common for speakers of English to use "concept" as I did in my examples. A survey of recent book-titles suffices to show this. "Conception" is rarely used therein except in the biological sense. "The concept of A" is quite often used to refer to the theories or beliefs about A of a certain person or group, e.g. 'The Concept of Freedom *in Anthropology*', 'The Concept of *Jacksonian* Democracy' (i.e. Jackson's concept of democracy), 'The Concept of Property *in Modern Christian Thought*', 'The Concept of Conscience *according to John Henry Newman*', and so on. Judging by book-titles and the testimony of my own ears, "concept" is now being used more often than "conception" for the purposes for which, according to this critic, we *ought* to use "conception". It is not only the vulgar who use "concept" thus. Philosophers sometimes do so too. For example, Ayer speaks of 'such a concept as possession by evil spirits' (*Metaphysics, Reality and Reappraisal*, ed. Kennick and Lazerowitz, 1966, p. 326), and few readers will need to be told that Ayer considers this concept to be a misconcept. (Has anyone the right to veto my use of "misconcept" here?)

A second critic of my statements quoted in the last paragraph, fastened on to the last sentence: 'The whole point of using "concept" in such contexts hinges on there being importantly different uses of the same word(s)'. He wrote:

> No. It is to enable us to distinguish between *conceptions* that can be true, false, hideous, dangerous, mistaken, etc., and *concepts* that can be none of these e.g. of Force, Space, Knowledge. Your example of *man* falls more naturally under conception. Compare "Was ist der Mensch?".

So we should speak of 'the conception', not 'the concept of Man', because we are referring to something which can be true, false, mistaken, etc.; and should talk of 'the concept', not 'the conception of Space', or presumably of Time, because what we then are talking about cannot be false or mistaken! But for the last twenty years, philosophers have been discussing 'the concept of mind', and yet arguing that a certain concept is correct and that others are mistaken. And which is *the* concept of Space which cannot be mistaken—that of Newton or of Leibniz or of Bradley or of Einstein? If you accept one of these you must judge at least some of the others to be mistaken. This critic frequently wrote in the margin of my essay "Was ist der Mensch?"; apparently to convey what ought to be understood by the question I had addressed to my students about the meaning of "the concept of Man". Which implies that I had failed to convey to him why it is important to distinguish the *use* and *mention* of a word; which the question 'Was ist der Mensch?' (What is Man?) fails to do, and leaves us uncertain whether the questioner seeks information about the use of the German word "Mensch", or information about the nature of human beings, or both.

"Concept" became common in philosophers' English during the nineteenth century as a translation of the German "begriff". It is only during the twentieth century that it has become popular in everyday talk. As long ago as 1926, Fowler advised his readers that "concept" should be left to the philosophers, that the 'substituting of it for the ordinary word *conception* is due to Novelty-Hunting' (*A Dictionary of Modern English Usage*, p. 88). His advice was not heeded. As is acknowledged in the 1965 edition:

> the philosophers have not been allowed to keep it to themselves . . . The fate of such words is often to be put to menial tasks . . . as in the advertisement "A new concept in make-up, blessing your skin with its incredible beauty benefits" (p. 102).[5]

The fact that a word *originated* as a philosophers' technical term—and this is true of "logic" and "category" as well as of "concept"—does not give philosophers the right, in Austin's phrase, to fool around with it *ad lib*. It is essential for philosophers to explain their own uses of such words when these have become part of Everyman's vocabulary. In Northern America, the concept-idiom seems to be even more popular than in Britain. I am told that 'What is your concept on so and so?'

[5] Here are some examples of such menial tasks. 'Lytton . . . still thought him exquisite as an ideal human concept, but it was now easier to picture him as such if he forgot . . . certain . . . corpulent developments' (M. Holroyd's *Lytton Strachey*, 1967). 'If you are sitting behind the desk, you do not ask the salesman, "Well, what are you hawking today?" You say, "What is the Concept?"' (George Goodman's *The Money Game*, 1968). 'CONCEPT—the journal for creative ideas for cemeteries' (referred to in Jessica Mitford's *The American Way of Death*, 1967).

is a possible way of asking 'What is your opinion about so and so?' And that "conceptualize" is sometimes used there as a synonym for "explain". So might I perhaps ask an American philosopher whether he can conceptualize his use of "concept"? On the other hand, an American student visiting a British University might have been puzzled to hear a lecturer recommend some 'conceptual hoovering'. The teacher who used this phrase meant presumably 'let's remove the dust from our concepts'. If I used it, I should be more likely to mean 'let's extract "concept" from our talk'. Not that I wish to debar philosophers from using any technical term, including "concept", provided that its technical use is useful and is clearly explained.

APPENDIX TO SECTION VIII

The questionnaire concerning "concept" which was used with students

The questionnaire and the comments thereon, which I sent in 1967 to some colleagues in other Universities, are reproduced below:

'Suppose a philosopher started a lecture by saying that he was going to discuss "the concept of Man", which of the following do you think he'd most probably be going to talk about:

1. The dictionary definition of "man";
2. The uses of the word "man";
3. The uses of the word "man" and of any synonymous words;
4. An idea of Man which is the same for all people;
5. Ideas of Man which may vary between one person and another;
6. An idea of the Ideal Man (à la Plato);
7. The individuals called "men";
8. Human beings, people, us;
9. A way of thinking about Man;
10. Theories about Man;
11. His own theory about Man;

12.}
13.} Add more, according to taste, but leave the last line blank.

Instructions [to the student guinea-pigs]:

(i) Put a cross against the phrase which seems to you most probable, OR

(ii) If several seem about equally probable, put crosses against each.

(iii) Do not waste time trying to work out what a philosopher *ought* to mean by "the concept of Man". What we want to know is your first reaction—what you would think the lecturer's subject is most likely to be on hearing his announcement.

(iv) If you are not happy about any of the phrases suggested, and can think, straight off, of a better paraphrase of the lecturer's probable subject-matter, please write this in the empty space.

My comments on, and explanations of, the suggestion questionnaire:

1. This questionnaire differs from the one I used on my first-year students only in two respects:
   (a) I have offered more options, i.e. 2, 9, 10 and 11 are new. (Perhaps too many now?)
   (b) I have simplified the students' choice. In my questionnaire, I asked the students *either* to mark as 1, 2 and 3 their first three choices in order of preference, *or* to mark 1 against each that they thought equiprobable. Most did the latter. The method I now suggest makes quantitative assessment of the results simpler.
2. If you use such a questionnaire, the options should be randomized. (E.g. Mix them in a hat, and get someone else to pick them out one by one.) My eleven suggestions are obviously not in a random order.
3. I suggest that the two classes of students on whom it would be most valuable to try this experiment are (i) those who have just completed a first-year course (for in many Universities, most such students will not do any more philosophy, and if they do not understand the 'concept' lingo now, they never will); (ii) advanced students who have studied, and been lectured to about, Ryle's *The Concept of Mind*.'

The above questionnaire was used in the Philosophy departments of five British Universities.[6] The results which are given below have been pooled, since otherwise the samples would

[6] These were the departments of Logic at Glasgow and St. Andrews and of Philosophy at Exeter, Leicester and Liverpool.

have been too small. 'Beginners' include some who had studied philosophy for only one term, though most had done so for a full session. 'More advanced students' include those who had studied philosophy for two, three or four years.

DISTRIBUTION OF RESPONSES

Items	*Beginners* (76 *subjects*)		*More Advanced Students* (50 *subjects*)	
1	1	14%	2	32%
2	9		20	
3	12		15	
4	13		7	
5	20		14	
6	11		1	
7	6	10%	3	6%
8	10		4	
9	28		11	
10	31		22	
11	13		10	
Others	6		7	
Total responses	160		116	

SECTION IX

The Misuses of "Logic" in Linguistic Philosophy

LINGUISTIC philosophers have used "logic" and its derivatives in ways which are obscure to the uninitiated. There is, for example, no everyday use of "the logic of the concept of A", and it does not seem possible to give this phrase a usage which is of much use to anyone. I have asked students what they could make of this phrase, but they soon got stuck. They tried, of course, to interpret "logic" in its native, traditional sense; the one which they had learned in studying Formal Logic, and which is employed, though less precisely, in our everyday talk about reasoning or arguments or inferences being logical or illogical. Naturally they got stuck when they tried to apply this to "the logic of the concept of A". For if we try to interpret this phrase, using "logic" as it is used by others, A would have to be a propositional sentence or statement, the kind of thing which could have to other such things logical relations like *implying*, *contradicting*, *being logically independent of*. In that case, you could indeed investigate the logic of the concept of A, could ask which other sentences or statements imply A, are implied by A, etc. But this route is blocked. As used by linguistic philosophers, in "the logic of the concept of A", A is a word or phrase, a subject or predicate as I defined these terms in Section VI, and thus is not something to which "true" or "false" is applicable. In view of this, what should presumably be meant by "describing the logic of the concept of A" is this: producing the (indefinite number of) significant English sentences which embody "A" and exploring the (indefinite number of) English sentences which imply, or are implied by, or contradict or are compatible with *each* of the latter. Perhaps this would not be an incompletable task for any one word, e.g. "mind", though it might take a lifetime. It is obvious, however, that this task is incompletable, if the subject-matter is, not *one* word, but the professed subject-matter of Ryle's *C of M*—all 'mental-conduct concepts', all English mind-predicates. (Does any other language provide as many such expressions as English?) This is the kind of endless task at which I suggested, in Section VI, that Bertie Wooster's mind would boggle.

A critic may retort that "describing the logic of the concept of A" need not be construed as an *unending* task; that the task may be restricted thus: take a few typical sentences-in-use of the form '*x* is A' or 'A is *Φ*', and determine what other sentences are logically implied by each of these, by virtue of the definition or meaning of "A". This makes the task finite, and indeed very limited. It is, of course, important to know that "p is known" does, and that "p is believed" does not, imply that p is true. But if the theory of knowledge were to be confined to drawing up the short list of the analytic propositions entailed by the definition or use of words like "know" and "believe", this branch of philosophy has long since been completed. Admittedly there are many words whose logic (in the present sense) takes more time to discuss, because their definitions or uses are indeterminate; but then the problem becomes not one of *discovering* their so-called logic, but discussion of the ways in which their meanings could or should be made determinate; and why should anyone call this 'logic'? When you have *given* a vague word a determinate meaning, or have replaced it with several terms each given a determinate meaning, you can then return to logic, i.e. to listing the implications of your definitions, the consequences of your decisions.

"The logic of" is often used nowadays to preface not "the concept of A", but just "A", as in the titles of several books, e.g. Mr. B. Mayo's *The Logic of Personality* (1952). Fortunately Mayo does not confine himself to enumerating analytic statements which follow from the meaning of "personality". Indeed it is hard to find any of this, and his choice of the title is not explained. "Logic" occurs in the title of only one of the ten chapters (Ch. VI, 'Personality and Logic'). Let us consider the point at which Mayo appeals to 'logic'. He starts by dismissing the expression "the self" as 'bad grammar'. His argument is that 'the concept of an entity called the self is based on bad grammar, *because there is no precedent for the use of the word 'self' as an independent noun*' (p. 93). Yet he has just referred to 'the notion of the self' as one which is '*held by most ordinary people* and by some philosophers', on the evidence of '*the way in which many people* and some philosophers *talk about the self*'. How could the claims which I have italicized be reconciled? And what are the criteria which Mayo would use to try to show that something is bad grammar? Mayo's next section, headed '"The Self" as Bad Logic', opens by saying that 'it will hardly do to brush aside all talk of the self as bad grammar' (p. 95). Yet the only point at which Mayo appeals to 'logic' to support his grammatical findings is when he dismisses as a blunder 'the elementary logical mistake of hypostatization—of elevating a grammatical expression into a subsistent entity' (p. 97). But why should hypostatization—e.g. a realist interpretation of talk about electrons or minds or unconscious desires—be called a *logical* mistake? If and when hypostatization is mistaken, surely it should be called an *onto*logical mistake. It can only cause confusion to treat answers to the question 'What exists?' as part of the subject-matter of logic. When logicians ask *that* question they are returning to metaphysics. Or if they wish to follow Hegel's example, and treat metaphysics as a branch of logic, they should at least make this clear.

It is often difficult to discover what is the cash-value of "logic" for philosophers who are using it so liberally; for example, to find what *they* think is the difference between 'logical grammar' and *grammar*. Sometimes it is easy to see what is being done with "logic", as in Professor Antony Flew's Introduction to *Essays on Logic and Language* (1951). *Prima facie*, some of Flew's statements are somewhat opaque; for example, when discussing John Wisdom's article 'Gods', he writes:

> though 'invisible and intangible gardener' is grammatically very similar to 'irritable and irascible gardener', it seems that logically the expressions are very different indeed; while the latter refers to a particular and not uncommon kind of gardener, the former expression seems logically to be embarrassingly similar to 'no gardener at all' (p. 8).

But Flew makes it clear what he is doing with "logic". He describes it as 'the fundamental discovery' from which 'modern British philosophy has been developed', that 'expressions may be grammatically similar and yet logically different'. He illustrates this: 'We might say 'This is past' and 'This is red' . . . 'Nobody came' and 'Somebody came' are pairs of grammatically similar expressions. But the members of all these pairs of grammatically similar expressions are logically very different.' (p. 7). Which makes it plain that "logically very different' merely means very different in meaning, use or function. The now popular contrast between 'depth grammar' and 'surface grammar' was introduced by Wittgenstein (*PI*, § 664). It is just a new way of expressing Russell's point that grammatically similar sentences may be very different in meaning. "Doing depth grammar" sounds more profound than what is so described, i.e. paraphrasing sentences in order to make explicit what we do or could mean when we use them.

It is hard to resist the conclusion that philosophers who contrast "logic" and "grammar" in the ways that Mayo and Flew have done are operating with a very narrow and out-dated conception of grammar, based presumably upon such schoolday tasks as parsing, and memorizing Thou Shall/Shalt Not Rules prescribed by language (especially Latin) masters. There is at present considerable disagreement within linguistics about how grammar should be delimited. But some things are clear. The days have gone when linguistic authorities outlawed as 'bad grammar' expressions which are used in some circles, even if this circle comprises only philosophers or other eccentrics. To quote Otto Jespersen's article on "Grammar" in the *Encyclopaedia Brittanica* (1929 to 1959 editions):

> to the scientific grammarian . . . the rules are not what he has to observe [i.e. obey] but what he observes . . . when he examines the way in which speakers and writers belonging to a particular community . . . actually use their mother-tongue.

When Professor J. Watmough revised this article for the 1964 edition, he omitted the quoted sentence as too obvious to need saying, and conveyed the point in passing thus: '. . . a language, its regularities of pattern ("rules")'. Those who write or talk about 'the self' or 'a self' are a minority, but their use of "self" as a noun is not random—it follows 'rules' (i.e. conventions); and description of their usage is, for a modern grammarian, part of his subject-matter. According to his conception of grammar, to say: 'You cannot (may not, must not) say so and so, because it is bad grammar' is unjustifiable, if so and so *is* habitually said and understood by *some* people. Philosophers who practise *a priori* or legislative linguistics seem to confuse the two senses of "rule" distinguished so neatly in Jespersen's Encyclopaedia article: prescriptive and descriptive rules. It seems to be a failure to recognize this distinction and its implications which has led so many philosophers to deduce a '. . . cannot properly be said' from an '. . . is not (normally, commonly) said'. This fashionable fallacy deserves a name. It is very like the one which Moore called 'the Naturalistic Fallacy', and which is most neatly expressed by saying that one cannot derive an "ought" from an "is". We might call it 'the Language Police Fallacy'. There is evidence that Ryle conceives of grammatical rules as commands. He has written:

to know what an expression means involves knowing what can (logically) be said with it and what cannot (logically) be said with it. It involves knowing a set of bans, fiats, and obligations, or, in a word, it is to know the rules of the employment of an expression (*British Philosophy in Mid-century*, ed. C. A. Mace, 1957, p. 254).

Even a Latin master could scarcely be more prescriptive than that. It is not surprising that Ryle found illuminating Wittgenstein's analogy between rules of grammar and rules of chess (op. cit., p. 255). The rules of a game like chess are prescriptive—they specify precisely all of the types of move which are *forbidden.*

A conception of grammar as being so restricted that it takes no cognisance of differences in meaning or use, even between "Somebody came" and "Nobody came", is hopelessly out of date. Otto Jespersen's conception of grammar (*The Philosophy of Grammar*, 1924) is now, I believe, out-moded. In his view, grammar has two main sub-divisions: Morphology which proceeds from the form of linguistic expressions to their meaning, and Syntax which proceeds from meanings or notions to their linguistic expressions. This account of grammar provokes obvious problems for philosophers. It is not our prerogative to veto the discussion of meanings or notions in grammar, but most contemporary linguists have spontaneously recognized the pitfalls in following Jespersen and making meanings and notions so central in grammar, since this seems to put too much emphasis on subjective factors.

Flew, however, argues as if grammar is a purely anatomical study of linguistic expressions divorced from consideration of their meanings or functions; as if grammar comprises only Accidence (word-inflexions, etc.) plus a Syntax restricted to word-order, word-formation, etc. Even if the study of grammar *could* be so restricted, it would be absurd to suggest that linguists need, should or could leave it to philosophers to investigate differences of meaning between anatomically similar sentences; for one of the branches of linguistics is Semantics, 'the theory of meaning'. Semantics must clearly remain common ground for linguistics and philosophy. But linguists have found ways of describing and investigating Syntax other than Jesperson's, but which still take cognisance of the differences which Flew calls 'logical differences between grammatically similar expressions'. We need not go into the complicated and controversial details of either of Professor N. Chomsky's accounts of syntax (*Syntactical Structures*, 1957 and *Aspects of the Theory of Syntax*, 1965). It is enough to stress the importance he attributed to 'transformational rules' (1957) and 'the transformational component' (1965). In explaining the latter term, Chomsky contrasts 'the deep structure' and 'the surface structure' of a sentence. The surface structure *is* that of a given every-day sentence S, and its deep structure is that of a more complex *paraphrase* of S.

It ought not to surprise anyone that students of syntax should pay heed to the meaning, or function, of a sentence,[1] and should elucidate this by offering some paraphrase. The sort of paraphrases which Chomsky offers are not of the sorts that either Russell or Moore offered, but obviously Chomsky is engaged in what is generically the same kind of task that Russell and many other philosophers have pursued under the name of 'logical analysis'. Paraphrasing everyday or literary sentences is a task we all practised at school. We did not then describe it as 'logic'. Why have philosophers used "logic(al)" in describing their paraphrasing performances or the products thereof? Presumably because those who pioneered the view that analysis is *the* (or a very important) function of philosophy operated with the

[1] Admittedly many contemporary linguists *profess* to be studying syntax in isolation from meaning, but this surely is self-deception. If anyone, with the help of a drug or a brain-surgeon, achieved amnesia concerning the meanings of words, he would be incapable of doing any grammar. In form, "he" and "me" are more alike than "he" and "him" or "I" and "me". It is on account of their meanings/uses that "I" goes with "me" and "he" with "him".

now discredited[2] assumption that, for each everyday sentence, there is some *one* paraphrase which is IT, is basic; and that this paraphrase must be expressed in the logical symbolism developed by Russell and Whitehead in their attempt to derive the whole of mathematics from a minimum of axioms and definitions; and so it came to be thought, by Russell, and the early Wittgenstein, that the philosopher has reached his Mecca, *the* logic or logical form of a sentence, when and only when he has found a paraphrase expressed in that logical notation. Since the assumptions which led to the use of "logic" in describing such analyses and their products are now discredited, it is surely time that we stopped using "logic(al)" in such contexts.

Apparently the myth which underlay the pursuit via analysis of 'the logical form' of everyday sentences lives on in contemporary linguistics. In a review of Chomsky's 1965 book, Mr. P. H. Matthews criticises Chomsky's 'new model of transformational syntax' by saying:

> Ideally the form of grammar should itself permit only one TYPE OF SOLUTION for any given description problem; but failing this the theory should at least provide a decisive and well-motivated evaluation-procedure (cf. Chomsky, 1957) (*Journal of Linguistics*, April, 1967, p. 141. His capitals).

In other words, in the Ideal Grammar each sentence would have one and only one correct type of paraphrase, and the Laws of Syntax would in each case uniquely determine what this paraphrase is (provided the motive is good—though it is not clear why Matthews brings this in). Notice the parallel between this ideal and that of philosophers who considered the notation of *Principia Mathematica* to be the Ideal Logical Language, the essential structure of all our thought and talk. Philosophers and linguists seem to share a tendency to ignore what is surely obvious: that for very many sentences it is possible to give several paraphrases which are equivalent in meaning; and that there are no grounds for assuming that there must be one Privileged Paraphrase, which provides unique insight into

[2] See J. O. Urmson, *Philosophical Analysis*. Many of the misuses of "logic" are hangovers from the metaphysical doctrine of 'Logical Atomism', dissected in Part One of Urmson's book.

the meaning ('*the* logical form') or the grammar ('*the* syntactical structure') of the sentence under discussion.

In assimilating so-called logical analyses, linguists' transformational operations and the more humble tasks of schoolchildren, as *paraphrasing*, I am again applying Austin's methods: I am applying the *OED* definition of "paraphrase", i.e. 'An expression in other words of the sense of any passage or text'. Different kinds of paraphrase are involved, but these differences should not blind us to the generic resemblance connoted by this worthy and well-established English word. It seems to be time that other Universities should follow the example of Reading in introducing joint degree courses in Philosophy and Linguistics, to train people who can pursue problems which are of common concern, and who will not think, for example, that grammarians leave it to philosophers to explain the difference in meaning between, e.g. "Somebody came" and "Nobody came" (i.e. it is false that somebody came). Austin, at the end of 'Ifs and Cans', envisaged that co-operation between philosophers, grammarians and other students of language might give birth to a 'comprehensive science of language' which would be independent of philosophy.

When philosophers use words as technical terms, this ought to be to clarify thought, to distinguish meanings which are blurred or telescoped by everyday language. What linguistic philosophers have done with "logic" is precisely the opposite. They have taken a word which had a clear meaning in everyday speech and in traditional philosophy, and they have messed around with it almost without limit. And some of them claim to be following in Austin's footsteps. The onus is upon those who use "logic" so vaguely and variously to explain and try to justify their uses. As the Kneales have said, commenting on those who talk about 'the logic of 'God' and so forth':

> Such an enormous extension of the meaning of a technical term makes it useless for any but the coarsest classification, and it is therefore fortunate that the fashion is still confined to a relatively small school (*Development of Logic*, 1962, p. 740).

Unfortunately this school has waxed rather than waned, since these words were written. A study of logic is probably the best antidote to abuses of "logic".

I shall end this section with a warning about another hard-worked item in the current philosophical jargon, "criterion". The jargon-uses of "criterion" have their origin in the writings of Wittgenstein, and we shall need to consider them in Part Two. Here I shall simply distinguish the everyday uses of "criterion" and certain other uses which philosophers have recently fused or confused with each other and with an everyday use. The *OED* gives two definitions (apart from the archaic 'An organ or faculty . . .'), namely:

(i) 'A canon or standard by which anything is judged or estimated'. (This is very close to my way of defining "criterion", given earlier, as 'a rule for deciding or judging'.)
(ii) 'A characteristic attaching to a thing by which it can be judged or estimated.' (In other words, a property of a thing whereby we can judge or decide whether it is a so and so.)

These uses are closely related. If having a concave tail-end is a criterion, in sense (ii), whereby I distinguish a salmon from a sea-trout, then my criterion, in sense (i), is the corresponding rule or 'canon'.

The everyday use of "criterion" in sense (ii) has been amalgamated by many philosophers with one or other of two different uses, (iii) and (iv) below, and by some philosophers with yet another use, (v) below. In formulating these jargon-uses, I shall not explore alternative ways of wording them. They are:

(iii) The criterion of something being A is identified with the (perhaps complex) property, P, in terms of which "A" is defined, so that 'if *x* has P, *x* is A' is analytic.
(iv) The criterion of something being A is identified with some property, P, whose presence, we are told, *logically* guarantees that the thing is A, but where 'if *x* has P, then *x* is A' is *not* analytic, *not* entailed by the meanings of the expressions "P" and "A".
(v) The criterion of something being A is identified with the sort of thing that has to be pointed at in the process of ostensively teaching or learning the meaning of "A".

Philosophers very rarely explain how they are using "criterion". They often seem to be oscillating between sense (ii) and one (or more) of the jargon-uses. The uninitiated can hardly be expected to guess how a philosopher is using this word. Nor sometimes can the initiated. The everyday uses of "criterion" may change, may already be changing as a result of philosophers' innovations, but will such changes be for the better? We do not need "criterion" to convey sense (iii), for we already have "defining property" to do this job. Jargon-use (iv), which is now common among philosophers, deviates from everyday usage by, in effect, substituting "known or proved" for "judged or estimated" in the *OED* definition. And since the philosophers in question usually speak of *the*, rather than *a*, criterion of being A (or for applying "A"), they give the impression that some single property is both necessary and sufficient for applying an expression; and this is another respect in which they are deviating from everyday usage. The use of "criterion" in sense (iv) is not only unnecessary; it is incoherent—unless or until those who employ it thus explain what can be meant by "*logically* guarantees" where this cannot be replaced by "(logically) entails". Regarding jargon-use (v), this seems to be a by-product of Wittgenstein's telescoping of the very different questions: 'How *do* we use a word?' and 'How did we *learn* to use it?' This error will be discussed at length in Part Two. The fact that Wittgenstein used "criterion" in very different ways has not escaped notice,[3] but noticing this has not noticeably deterred philosophers from following his example.

[3] See, for example, Mr. Rogers Albritton's paper 'On Wittgenstein's Use of the Term "Criterion"', *J. of Phil.*, 1959, and Dr. Anthony Kenny's article on 'Criterion' in *The Encyclopedia of Philosophy*, 1967

SECTION X

How much Linguistic Philosophy is *Anglo*-Linguistics?

MUCH linguistic philosophy consists of descriptions of features of the English language. To what extent do its findings concern features *peculiar* to the English language? This question needs to be pressed, but I am much too ignorant of languages other than English to answer it. To do so would require a series of books by philosophers who were accomplished linguists or by comparative linguists interested in philosophy. I shall, however, offer reasons for being sceptical about the view which linguistic philosophers seem more often to take for granted than to affirm: that what they discuss are universal features of human thought. No one would claim, of course, that all the contributions which they have made to grammar are applicable only to English. It would be surprising if any natural language failed to provide devices for doing the jobs done by what Austin has called 'performative verbs'. And we should expect any developed language to provide different verbs belonging to the types which Ryle has called 'process-verbs', 'task-verbs' and 'achievement-verbs'. Indeed we might make it one of our rules for calling a language 'developed' that it makes such distinctions. On the other hand, Ryle, Austin and many others have spent much of their time describing, and sometimes misdescribing, peculiarities of English grammar, e.g. the English idioms for expressing what, in English, we call 'emotions' or 'feelings', the nuances of English excuse-making expressions, the English adverbs which we should be prepared to attach to different English verbs, and so on. Yet, apart from Austin, linguistic philosophers have usually presented their findings as if they believed that they were describing universal features of human thought; using such headlines as 'the concept of ...', 'the logic of the concept of ...'.

Let us start by considering some statements made by Professor Strawson in Chapter I of his *Introduction to Logical Theory*

(1952). He presents, as a problem which some have found puzzling, to see 'how a linguistic rule for expressions in a particular language can lead to a general statement of logical appraisal which transcends individual languages altogether' (p. 10). Strawson's example of a linguistic rule is: 'In English the words "son-in-law" mean the same as "married to the daughter of"'. He points out that if we translate this statement into French, the phrases mentioned within double quotation marks would not be translated. His example of 'a logical appraisal which transcends individual languages' is: 'A statement to the effect that a certain person is someone's son-in-law is inconsistent with the statement that he has never been married'. Such a statement would, of course, be translated throughout. Strawson goes on to argue, however, that, although we are not *inclined* to do so, we *might* accept, as an alternative translation of the sentence which starts "In English the words "son-in-law" . . .", the sentence "En français les mots "gendre de" veulent dire la même chose que les mots "marié avec la fille de""; and more generally, that we 'might say . . . that in laying down inconsistency-rules in one language, we were implicitly laying down inconsistency rules for the corresponding expressions in all languages' (p. 11). Strawson draws the following conclusions:

> The important thing is to see that when *you draw* the boundaries of the applicability of words in one language and *then connect* the words of that language with those of another by means of translation-rules, *there is no need to draw the boundaries again for the second language. They are already drawn* . . . This is why (or partly why) logical statements framed in one language are not *just* about that language. (p. 12. My italics.)

This last passage is misleading in more than one respect.[1] To start with, in its last sentence the word "just" is misleading in suggesting that a so-called logical statement is *partly* about either the language, e.g. English, or the specific words, in which it is expressed. In either case, a logical statement would not, after all, 'transcend individual languages altogether'. If a logical statement is in part about a certain language, e.g. English, we are stuck with a statement in which 'in English' is included or has to be understood. Alternatively, if a logical

[1]Perhaps, in what follows, I make too much of this passage.

statement is in part about the very words in which it is expressed, this part is untranslatable. Now consider Strawson's statement: 'They are already drawn'; as if the same boundaries of word-meanings which are drawn in the language in which one is speaking are already drawn in the second language, whichever that may be It looks as if Strawson has forgotten the vital hypothetical clause which is needed when we pass from a linguistic rule to a statement which transcends individual languages. I have stressed in discussing "the concept of A" that an adequate paraphrase must incorporate an if-clause: 'the use of the word "A" and its synonyms in other languages, *if there are any*'. The sort of statement that Strawson calls 'a logical appraisal' is not, surely, *about* the language, or the particular words, in which it is expressed; but whether it is translatable into one, never mind all, other languages, is an empirical question, not one which can be settled *a priori*, which can be answered by Logic. (As Professor Woozley has pointed out to me, Strawson would no doubt wish to answer this criticism by saying that the second clause in my quotation from him can and should be read as an if-clause: 'when . . . you connect (i.e. *if* you *can* connect) . . . by means of translation-rules'. But what Strawson wrote, especially 'They are already drawn', seems adapted to conceal rather than reveal the vital if-clause.)

Notice the active verbs used by Strawson, when he says that we 'draw the boundaries' of word-uses in, e.g., English, 'and then connect' these with words of another language by translation-rules. Drawing the boundaries of application of English words is something which, as Austin would stress, we have had done for us; though we retain some freedom to *re*-do this for limited sectors of English, by getting agreement among a group which shares some common purpose. French-speakers have had the task done for them officially, by the French Academy, though they sometimes kick against the pricks and adopt vulgar English and American words. Many pairs of languages have developed wholly independently, and even the languages of Western Europe have evolved to some extent independently. There has been much two-way interaction between, e.g., French and English, through the influence on both of Latin, the interchange of dry goods including books and tourists, and so on. As expected of two such languages there is more or less exact matching of meaning for large areas of their vocabularies; including words used to name objects made by man and by nature and practical activities performed by members of both communities, and including technical terms used in the sciences. But with regard to abstract nouns and adjectives which are not used as technical terms, and whose connection with ostensively specifiable objects or processes is more or less remote, it would be a fortunate coincidence if such a word in one language had an exact synonym in the other; and it would be a *miracle* if this were true for each such word in each language. The failure of other closely-related and highly-developed languages to provide exact, or even close, synonyms for many of the English words which preoccupy linguistic philosophers is far from being rare. German has no exact synonym for "attention". French has no close synonym for "mind". This should surprise none of us unless we have forgotten the shock of learning at school that French is so poverty-stricken as to use "aimer" to embrace attitudes as different as loving and liking. (Though the French are not noted for indifference to this difference.) I have been labouring the obvious to correct the misleading impression, given by Strawson's words, that the verbal boundaries drawn in one's own language are 'already drawn' in 'the second language'. To what extent this is true and to what extent it is false for any pair of languages is, of course, an empirical question. All that can be asserted *a priori* is the tautology: that if a person *uses* a sentence to make a statement, *what* he says is translatable into any language into which it can be translated.

The Kneales seem to have been unhappy about the passage by Strawson which I have been criticizing, for they quote it and then comment:

> If this means that logical rules are rules for all possible languages, it amounts in effect to an admission that they are not conventional and therefore not linguistic in any ordinary sense of that word, but rather requirements to be satisfied in the making of what we ordinarily call linguistic rules (*D of L*, p. 639).

The Kneales' suggested interpretation of Strawson's words is not, perhaps, uninfluenced by their own view that there are synthetic *a priori* truths, Laws of Logic, which would have to be obeyed in all possible languages. It seems clear, however, that this thesis is not what Strawson intended in the passage in question. He warns the reader against 'the illusion of an independent realm of logical facts, of which linguistic rules are merely adventitious verbal clothing', and he ends this section by saying: 'rules about words lie behind all statements of logical appraisal' (p. 12). But has he recognized that a rule about a word is about *its use in some particular language to which it belongs*?

Strawson's words suggest, no doubt inadvertently, that any statement can in principle be translated into any other language. This is something which commonly seems to be presupposed in the writings of linguistic philosophers. At any rate they deny, sometimes with indignation, that what they are philosophizing about is the English language. But I think that this charge is very often justified; for when they are not engaged in their usual occupation of discussing the meaning(s) or use(s) of English words, phrases or sentences, when they do discuss *logic* in the traditional sense, i.e. discuss the logical relationships between statements, they nearly always confine themselves to consideration of relations between statements made in English; without acknowledging and sometimes seeming to deny that some such statements can only be made in English and that many such statements cannot be made in many other languages. Indeed, Strawson seems to be guilty of doing this in some of his later writings. In *Individuals* (1959), Strawson describes his method as being 'up to a point, the reliance upon a close examination of the actual use of words' (p. 9), yet he describes his subject-matter as:

'a massive central core of human thinking which has no history or none recorded in the histories of thought; there are categories and concepts which, in their most fundamental character, change not at all' (p. 10).

Strawson proceeds to argue as if the, 'our', concept of a person is one such. I find this as surprising as did Mr. Cohen, who invited Strawson to compare 'the Renaissance conception of an individual human being with the Graeco-Roman one, or . . . the medieval European conception of the soul with the modern one' (*The Diversity of Meaning*, p. 82). More plausibly, though also unjustifiably, Strawson treats the, 'our', concepts (categories?) of subject and predicate as belonging to that changeless central core of human thinking.

Let us consider the grammatical criterion which Strawson offers for distinguishing subject-expressions and predicate-expressions. This provides a warning of the dangers of taking the grammar of English and the other languages that one knows as the map of a realm of concepts or categories which transcends, or permeates, all natural languages, and in which all thought is rooted. I shall quote some of the points made by Professor Tsu-Lin Mei in criticizing what Strawson says in 'Proper Names' (*PAS*, Supp. Vol., 1957) and in Chapter 5 of *Individuals*. Tsu-Lin Mei informs us that Strawson's criterion is not applicable to Mandarin, the official Chinese language, and he protests against Strawson's 'linguistic imperialism' in arguing as if English is 'the paradigm of all languages' ('Subject and Predicate, a Grammatical Preliminary', *Phil. Review*, 1961). Tsu-Lin Mei points out that the rule for English is: once a predicate, always a predicate, and that this 'explains Strawson's observation that the expression "is wise" demands a certain kind of completion, namely, completion into a proposition or propositional clause'; but that this criterion breaks down completely with respect to Chinese, for 'No Chinese expression satisfies his [Strawson's] criterion that it occurs only as a predicate-expression in propositions'; since a typical Chinese word (morpheme) like "tsungming" may be used as a predicate ('is clever'), or as a subject ('Cleverness ...'), or as part of an adverb ('cleverly') (pp. 168–9). Moreover: 'He [Strawson] says that predicate-expressions introduce their terms in ... a style appropriate to assertions and propositions only, [but] Chinese predicates do not introduce their terms in the assertive or propositional style, for the simple reason that no such style can be found in Chinese' (p. 169). And further, Strawson distinguishes subject-expressions on the ground that 'they introduce their terms in a grammatical style (the substantival) which would be appropriate to any kind of remark (command, exhortation, undertaking, assertion) or to none'; but this description applies to predicates as well as subjects in Chinese. Thus the same morpheme "chouyan" may function as 'Smoke?' (an invitation to smoke), as 'Smoke!'

(a command) or as '. . . smokes' (an answer to a question) (p. 171). Tsu-Lin Mei ends with the tart comment: 'discredited is the school of ordinary usage, since one of its prominent representatives, himself a logician of note, is shown to be unaware of what his statements are about' (p. 175).

Linguistic philosophers are sensitive to the criticism that what they are usually doing is, in practice, *Anglo*-linguistics. This is denied, but usually without much argument. Consider Ryle's way of dismissing this criticism with a brusque aside. 'The job done with the English word 'cause' is not an English job, or a continental job' ('Ordinary Language', *Phil. Review*, 1953, p. 171). 'There are no French implications or non-implications' ('Use, Usage and Meaning', *PAS* Supp. Vol., 1961, p. 228). In the latter article, unlike the former, the vital if-clause is, by implication, recognized, when Ryle says that Carroll's story about the smile of the Cheshire cat 'survives translation into any language *into which it can be translated*' (p. 228. My italics). At the International Congress of Philosophy at Vienna in 1968, Ryle's only reply to my paper 'Anglo-linguistic Philosophy' was to assert that what is absurd or nonsensical in one language is absurd or nonsensical in any language. (I did not *hear* him add 'into which it can be translated'.)

Let us examine this curt kind of answer. 'There are no *French* implications'. Well, here is an implication which is invalid in English but valid when translated verbatim into Welsh:

Sian's dress has the colour of a ripe tomato;
Sian's hair has the colour of a ripe chestnut;
Therefore Sian's dress and her hair are of the same colour.

For in Welsh, the same colour-word "coch" is applicable to shades which we call 'red' as well as those which we call 'warm brown'. 'What is absurd in one language is absurd in any language.' Presumably Ryle would judge it absurd, and indeed a category-mistake, to speak of 'hearing a pain', or of 'hearing heat'. Yet such phrases were used by Mr. A. R. Thomas of the Bangor Linguistics department to translate things which are said in our local Welsh dialect, and are used also in the University of Wales Dictionary of Welsh (*Geiriadur y Brifysgol*) to illustrate the uses of "clywed". This verb, whose primary use is to report what one hears, is also used to report that one feels warm or cold, that one smells e.g. tobacco, or that something tastes sweet; yet it is not used to report what one sees. Viewed through our linguistic spectacles, this is a peculiar way of 'drawing boundaries'. We can express roughly what is common to the uses of "clywed" by means of "to experience" or "to perceive", but the boundaries of the latter are less circumscribed, for they include vision. When *Syniad y Meddwl*[1] comes to be written, the 'logic' of some of the 'concepts' which it discusses may present problems not dreamed of in Ryle's philosophy of mind.

Some readers may feel that I am cheating in drawing on second-hand information about a language which they cannot use either. I shall therefore, with some trepidation, challenge linguistic philosophers on their home ground; their second home anyway, for so many of them, unlike myself, are classicists. Incidentally, the features of Plato's Greek on which I shall comment, I hope without howlers, were not mentioned by any of my former teachers who are classicists. I have learned about them by puzzling over translations and questioning colleagues in our Classics department, notably Mr. John Pollard. 'What is absurd in one language is absurd in any'. But surely some of Plato's arguments are absurd when translators try to express them in English. Consider the argument in the *Phaedo* (70–2) by which Plato's Socrates tries to prove that men's souls keep oscillating between Hades and *terra firma*, residing *en route* in a series of different bodies; tries to prove this from the humble premises that anything which becomes hot does so 'from being' cold, that anything which becomes big does so 'from being' small, etc. Translators have struggled to make this argument appear non-absurd in English, but without success. The plausibility of the argument in Ancient Greek hinged upon two deficiencies in that language:

(i) The verb "gignesthai" performed (I am told) two entirely different rôles. It was used to say that a pre-existing thing had changed, acquired a new property, e.g. that the water had become hot; and it was also used to say that a new

[1] This, I am told, is the nearest equivalent in Welsh to "The Concept of Mind".

entity had been made or produced, e.g. a bench by the carpenter. Plato's argument exploits this double use, or is based on failing to recognize it. The best an English translator can do to cover this up is this: to replace the appropriate English verb with a neologism—instead of saying 'So and so is produced or made', saying 'So and so becomes (period)'; perhaps after softening us up by using "comes into being"; hoping, presumably, that the reader will not respond to 'so and so becomes (period)' with 'becomes *what*?'

(ii) Classical Greek (I am told) provided adjectives for opposite qualities corresponding to "hot" and "cold", "big" and "small", "wet" and "dry", etc.; and from each such adjective a noun was formed, literally 'the hot', 'the cold', 'the big', etc. However, the Greek language of Plato's day, was deficient in abstract nouns corresponding to our "temperature", "size", "humidity", etc.; nouns which we use to refer to variables involving a continuous range of degrees, largely as a result of our methods of measurement.

Plato's conclusion—that life is 'produced from' death, so that birth involves a soul returning from Hades joining yet another body—was derived from a generalization which sets a problem for translators (*Phaedo*, 70e. *Cf.* 71b). It is variously translated; for example as: 'all things which have opposites [are] generated out of their opposites' (Jowett); and 'all things which have a contrary [are] produced from nothing else than their contrary' (H. Cary, *Five Dialogues*, Everyman). Presumably Ryle would agree that these sentences used by Jowett and Cary are absurd. It is easy for us to see that the two, so different, meanings of "gignesthai" have got telescoped and confused. (One feels that Plato *ought* to have smelt a rat, for how could such humble premises prove such an ambitious conclusion? Conclusions about life beyond the grave could scarcely be established from the fact that Greek, like most languages, provided pairs of words like "bigger" and "smaller" for describing the *same* two-term relation depending on which term you mention first.) Presumably we are not entitled to say that Plato's argument was absurd *in Ancient Greek*, since it was accepted by such an intelligent Greek.

Another example of an argument which is absurd when expressed in English, but cannot presumably have been absurd in Plato's Greek is one of his chief arguments for his conclusion that the physical world is only half-real (*Republic*, 478d–479e). This argument was a by-product of the fact that the Greeks made do with a single word "einai" to express both what we express by "to be so and so" and what we express by "to exist or be real". Plato's argument involved making the following move. It is correct to say of any physical object, e.g. a house, both 'that is big' and 'that is small'. Both of these statements may, of course, be true, since the speakers are presumably comparing this house with houses of different sizes. But Plato argued as if we may delete "big" and "small", and are committed to saying, as an implication of the former statements: 'that is (exists)' *and* 'that is not (does not exist)'; and therefore that physical things like houses partake of both being and non-being, and so are only half-real, less real than the changeless Ideas or Forms.

Plato's philosophy will be discussed further for two purposes: (i) to show that from the start Western philosophy involved the still prevalent confusion between using and mentioning words; (ii) to show that linguistic philosophers are not justified in claiming, as they sometimes do, that Plato was a member of their club. I leave it to scholars to decide, or guess, whether Plato actually committed himself to the semantic-cum-metaphysical theory known as 'Platonism'; and if so, whether he later abandoned it. He did at least treat this theory as more than a tentative hypothesis. My concern here is with the reasoning which led him to it. To save words, I shall speak of 'Plato', when sometimes I should say 'Plato and/or Socrates'. The critic who advised me to reflect upon the question 'Was ist der Mensch?' (p. 106 above), also advised me to reflect upon Plato's questions 'What is Justice (or Beauty, etc.)?' If Plato often failed to make it clear precisely what he meant by such questions, this is not surprising. But surely philosophers who practise linguistic analysis ought by now to have analyzed the forms of Plato's questions.

Plato was troubled by the fact that people ascribe beauty, for example, to objects which are extremely dissimilar, and indeed seem to have *no* observable properties in common: e.g. to the body of an athlete, something composed of physical organs in certain spatial relationships; to a piece of music, something composed of sounds related in certain temporal patterns; to a poem, something composed of words, where it is relationships of meanings, associations and assonance which are important. Plato argued that since beauty is the same thing when it is ascribed to such different objects, it is necessary to ask 'What is the beautiful?' In Ancient Greek "to kalon" functioned as "beauty" does in English, but their phrase (literally "*the* beautiful") made it tempting to hypostatize the common characteristic or 'thing' presumed to belong to all the objects which they found beautiful. The ambiguity of his initial questions, e.g. 'What is the beautiful?', is revealed by what Plato did when trying to answer them:

(1) Surveying and comparing the different objects that people found beautiful, in an apparently empirical search for some property or resemblance common and peculiar to them, and when Plato was thinking on these lines his favourite answer was the property of being harmonious.

(2) Trying (less frequently) to formulate an acceptable verbal definition of the word in question; what we would express by saying '"Beautiful" means so and so'.

Plato found his questions, 'What is the beautiful (the good, etc.)?', very difficult to answer. His conclusion (hypothesis?) was that the beautiful is a single, changeless, and therefore non-physical, entity, which is apprehended by Reason and not by any of the sense-organs; and the same conclusion was drawn concerning the good, the just, and so on; and even at one stage for *the bed* (*Republic*, Book X). Plato argued *as if* saying that beauty is the same thing when it is ascribed to different objects implies that "Beauty" ("to kalon") is a proper name designating a single, changeless entity. He introduced new locutions for referring to this transcendental entity: "auto to kalon", literally 'the beautiful itself', sometimes translated by Jowett as 'Absolute Beauty'. And sometimes, for emphasis, Plato used "to kalon auto kath' hauto", literally 'the beautiful itself by itself'. Incidentally, Plato performed the remarkable feat of formulating his theory of Forms in a five-word sentence which used only the definite article and a single adjective: "tōi kalōi ta kala kala", literally 'through the beautiful the beautifuls [*sc.* are or become] beautiful' (*Phaedo*, 100e). Plato could be as terse as Ayer when he tried, though he did not often try.

There are still philosophers and mathematicians who accept Plato's theory (though not, I think, for *the bed*). But after 2500 years of debate, surely all philosophers ought to distinguish between these question-forms:

(1) What do we (or should we) mean by, or how do we (or should we) define, *the word "A"*?

(2) What property or properties are common, or common and peculiar, to the *things* which are called 'As'?

(3) What is A, or what are As?

Form (3) may be used to ask either, or both, of questions (1) and (2); *but the latter are different questions.* This is obvious if, for "A", we substitute, say, "human being".

I am not qualified to make generalizations about Plato's locutions. But very often, I am told, Plato presented his questions in form (3), and apparently he did this oftener than is revealed by English translations. For sometimes a translator represents Plato as seeking for the 'definition' of so and so, where Plato was asking: what *is* so and so? Here is an example from the *Meno* (73c). Jowett's translation presents Socrates as seeking for 'one definition of them all' [i.e. of all virtue*s*], and as referring to 'this definition of virtue'. Which makes it sound as if Plato was explicitly discussing verbal definitions. Jowett here used poetic licence in translating as 'definition' the Greek words "hen ti", meaning literally 'one thing' or 'a single something'. Rouse[2] translates these words as 'something which is the same [in all virtues]', which reveals how Plato posed his question. Cary[3] used philosophical licence by translating "hen ti" as 'that which is one and the same thing [in all persons who have virtue]'; which makes it sound as if Plato was plugging his theory of Forms more explicitly than does the Greek "hen ti". (Perhaps Cary was more committed to Platonism than Plato.)

There is, however, at least one dialogue where Plato explicitly and repeatedly presents questions in form (1), the *Cratylus*. Here Plato discusses the nature of language, and the

[2] W. H. D. Rouse, *Great Dialogues of Plato,* Mentor, 1956.

[3] Henry Cary, *Five Dialogues,* Everyman, 1910.

meanings and derivations of various Greek words; and Jowett appropriately presents Plato's subject-matter as 'the word so and so', where so and so is some Greek word which Jowett does not translate. It is of interest and importance that near the end of this dialogue, in which Plato distinguishes question-forms (1), (2) and (3), he asks:

Let us suppose that to any extent you please you can learn things through the medium of names, and suppose also that you can learn them from the things themselves, which is likely to be the nobler and the clearer way . . .?

And he answers:

the knowledge of things is not derived from names. No: they must be studied and investigated in themselves (439a and b. Jowett's translation).

This makes it clear what Plato would have thought of Austin's so-called linguistic phenomenology; and of Wittgenstein's dictum: 'Grammar tells what kind of object anything is' (*PI*, § 373).

Sensitiveness to the criticism that they are doing Anglo-linguistics is, I suspect, the main reason why so many linguistic philosophers have adopted the current jargon, and are reluctant to follow Austin in describing their work as a study of words, whose aim is 'a revised and enlarged *Grammar*' (*PP*, p. 180. His italics). When they present their findings as discoveries about 'the logic of concepts', this suggests that these are revelations of universal principles governing all thought. But they are certainly not doing this when they trace the boundaries of application, the functions and the syntax, of English words like "can", "real", "attention", "mind" or "intentionally". Their study of 'the logic of concepts' usually turns out in practice to be about certain words, and sentences containing these words. Then their conclusions are relative to the language to which these expressions belong, and if their conclusions apply also to some other languages, this is fortuitous. As has been shown by some examples from Welsh and Ancient Greek, different languages generate different so-called conceptual problems; and many such problems need to be resolved by changing the language in question, not simply describing it as

Austin did. Solving such problems is a type of task which has been tackled by almost all philosophers since Socrates. Philosophers can scarcely avoid doing so, since, as Austin says, 'words are our tools . . . and we must use clean tools' (*PP*, p. 129). But solving such problems is not the *goal* of philosophy; only a necessary preliminary, if philosophy is concerned, as it has been traditionally, with trying to understand the world and our place in it. Many philosophers have apparently abandoned the latter goal. They argue as if the idiosyncrasies of their native tongue at the time of writing provide a Court of Appeal for settling philosophical problems and for outlawing or by-passing metaphysical theories. This is indeed a revolution, and one which drastically reduces the scope and importance of philosophy.

SECTION XI

Mr. Warnock's Way of Defending Linguistic Philosophy and Professor Strawson's Way of Doing it

IF ANYONE reads this book but has read little or no recent philosophy, he might wonder if I am not caricaturing what I criticize. Such a reader would do well to consult Mr. Geoffrey Warnock's *English Philosophy Since 1900* (1958). This book has many merits, not least its lucidity. Its later chapters provide a dispassionate defence of what I have been criticizing as an impatient outsider. Warnock's neat assessments of the work of Moore, Russell and the early Wittgenstein seem to me to be fair and sometimes penetrating. I do not agree with his evaluation of recent Oxford philosophy, but I think his description of it is accurate—though sometimes incomplete. For example, in his exposition of Ryle's *C of M* he presents as a problem which needs to be explained the fact that many people have interpreted Ryle's positive thesis as behaviouristic; yet he does not mention Ryle's recurrent attacks on the doctrine of privileged access! However, what will be considered here is Warnock's account of the recent revolution in philosophy.

In his closing chapter, Warnock discusses the questions 'in what this so-called revolution consists' and whether its effects are to be lamented; questions which, he says, have been 'widely discussed and almost inextricably confused'. 'The two observations most commonly made by way of picking out the novelty in contemporary philosophy are probably, first, that it is now 'anti-metaphysical', and second, that it has become entirely 'linguistic'' (p. 160). I shall quote first Warnock's candid comments on the latter point. His quotation from Sir Isaiah Berlin provides some confirmation that the concept and category idioms have been adopted to impress the general public:

Sir Isaiah Berlin has said that contemporary philosophers 'have done themselves unnecessary harm, in the eyes of the uninstructed, by advertising their methods as "linguistic". No doubt this was a tempting and perhaps necessary weapon in the early days, when the current philosophical jargon . . . needed a sharp and immediate antidote . . . But of course what philosophers are talking about is not words *qua* words, but about concepts and categories: the most general and pervasive among them which particular uses of words constitute (for thought is largely a matter of using words). Words are not distinguishable from the concepts they express or involve: but it does not follow that all there is before us is "mere words"—trivial questions of local usage' [*The Twentieth Century*, June, 1950]. However [Warnock comments], this objection to the description of current philosophy as 'linguistic' seems to amount to no more than that 'the uninstructed' may be led . . . to think ill of the subject, through drawing from it a conclusion which in fact 'does not follow'. And a desire to save the uninstructed from the consequences of their own fallacious reasoning seems hardly a sufficient motive for rejecting a description which in some sense at least is quite clearly correct. It may be true that philosophers do not as a rule talk about words '*qua* words'; but they do very often talk about words; and that they do so is certainly the most immediately obvious difference between their work and that of their predecessors. The use of the term 'linguistic' may have been 'unfortunate'; but it is also accurate enough and, one might add, candid (pp. 161–2).

Though Warnock rejects Berlin's argument, he does, however, follow his advice. Warnock habitually uses "concept" and "category" in describing the subject-matter of contemporary philosophy; even when he is defending Austin's work (pp. 157–9), though this was not how Austin described his topics.

Let us now consider how Warnock meets the complaint that contemporary philosophy is 'anti-metaphysical'. Warnock argues that this point could not support the claim that a revolution has occurred:

For one thing, although philosophy at present is for the most part admittedly *un*metaphysical, it is not doctrinally *anti*-metaphysical in the manner of Logical Positivism; and further . . . metaphysical writing in the style of Absolute Idealism has itself no just historical claim to the status of a tradition or an orthodoxy. Russell and Moore were not wholly pursuing revolutionary new paths; they could almost as well be represented as reverting to old ones. The manner of Russell and of Professor Ayer is indeed strikingly unlike that of Bosanquet or Bradley; but it is related nearly enough to that of Mill or Hume (pp. 160–1).

It would appear from this that Warnock is here operating with the arbitrary re-definition of 'metaphysics' which Ayer gave in *LTL*, for on what other definition could the works of Russell, Ayer, Mill and Hume be represented as unmetaphysical? (And even then Russell is miscast.) Indeed, even on the account of metaphysics which Warnock gives in Chapter XI, each of these philosophers ranks as a metaphysician. In this chapter Warnock attempts to explain why linguistic philosophers are uninterested in metaphysics. He says that 'metaphysical fervour . . . depends in large part upon a kind of illusion', that metaphysics 'is impossible perhaps, and certainly unattractive, to the disillusioned'; and he attributes the disillusionment to the fact that it has 'become almost impossible to believe that some *one* way of seeing [the world], some *one* sort of theory, has any exclusive claim to be the *right* way' (pp. 144–5). What Warnock has said earlier in this chapter implies that he is conceiving metaphysics as a purely *a priori* enterprise, for he says: 'It is . . . characteristic of a metaphysical theory that facts should neither be cited in its support nor be brought in evidence against it' (p. 137); and also that he is conceiving a metaphysical theory as 'all-embracing', as 'intended to transform 'the *whole* intellectual scene'' (p. 138). It is not surprising then that philosophers should be disillusioned with metaphysics, if they equate metaphysics with the dogmatic assertion of an *a priori* theory which is designed to explain *everything*. Fortunately we are not obliged to choose between linguistic philosophy and the kind of metaphysics depicted by Warnock. I shall describe a different and more viable kind of metaphysics in the last section of this book.

Another complaint about contemporary philosophy which Warnock discusses in his final chapter concerns its 'ideological neutrality' (pp. 166 ff.). Warnock writes:

It is at any rate certain that questions of 'belief'—questions of a religious, moral, political, or generally a 'cosmic' variety—are seldom if at all directly dealt with in contemporary philosophy. Why is this so? The first part of an answer to this question can easily be given: there is a very large number of questions, not of that variety, which philosophers find themselves to be more interested in discussing. But many would go further. They would wish to say that philosophy has nothing to do with questions of that kind . . . They would say, more generally, *that philosophy is the study of the concepts that we employ, and not of the facts, phenomena, cases, or events to which those concepts might be or are applied.* To investigate the latter is to raise political or moral or religious, but not philosophical, problems or questions (p. 167. My italics).

As Warnock recognizes, this view is closely related to Logical Positivism. Remember Ayer's theses in *LTL* that philosophical analysis is 'independent of any empirical assumptions' (p. 57) and that a book on ethics should 'make no ethical pronouncements' (p. 103). Yet Warnock proceeds to argue that it is right and proper that philosophers should remain ideologically neutral. By way of comment, I shall quote what Warnock says in a more recent book, *Contemporary Moral Philosophy* (1967). In his Introduction he writes: 'the successive orthodoxies of moral philosophy in English in the present century have been, notwithstanding the often admirable acumen of their authors, remarkably barren . . . There seems to have occurred an extraordinary narrowing of the field; moral philosophy has been made to look, if not simple, yet bald and jejune, and, in its fruits, unrewarding' (pp. 1–2). Yet the only remedy that Warnock proposes, at the end of this book, is that ethics should start with a more thorough investigation 'of the sense and scope of 'moral'', because 'it seems prudent that . . . we should decide what we are talking about', and because it is 'also possible that such investigation should show . . . what class or range of considerations, identifying an issue as a moral issue, are consequentially relevant to moral assessment of it' (pp. 75–6). It seems very doubtful, however, whether yet more research into how we apply the word "moral", as opposed to "non-moral", to issues, will help us to decide what is right or good as opposed to wrong or bad; any more than research into how we apply the word "Art" would help us, or has helped us, to *evaluate* what we call 'works of art'.

In Chapter XII, Warnock contrasts two motives for conducting conceptual (linguistic) investigations: the desire to dispel perplexity and the desire to acquire 'systematic conceptual knowledge'. The former motive is attributed to Ryle and Wittgenstein, the latter, newer, interest to Austin. Warnock stresses the value of Austin's interest in language as such, by arguing that just as non-clinical, normal psychology is needed to complement therapeutic, abnormal psychology, so the study of our healthy concepts (our normal word-uses) is needed to complement the study of concepts for the purpose of curing philosophical confusions (p. 159). Warnock evidently considered Austin's method to hold much promise for future development. I think he would regard Strawson's *Individuals* as a fulfilment of this hope for 'systematic conceptual knowledge'. This is one of the most original and influential philosophical works published in Britain during the last decade. It is doubtful, however, whether its merits provide any justification of linguistic philosophy, from which it seems to me to derive its defects and not its merits. In his Introduction, Strawson speaks as if his own programme differs from 'conceptual analysis', not in purpose, but only in 'scope and generality'. He writes:

> Up to a point, the reliance upon a close examination of the actual use of words is the best, and indeed the only sure, way in philosophy. But the discriminations we can make, and the connexions we can establish, in this way, are not general enough and not far-reaching enough to meet the full metaphysical demand for understanding . . . He [the metaphysician] must abandon his only sure guide when the guide will not take him as far as he wishes to go (pp. 9–10).

One would expect from this that Strawson will appeal to and rely upon 'a close examination of the actual use of words' as often and as far as possible. In fact, he rarely does this at all. His arguments are conducted at a very high level of abstraction, and are presented in the concept-idiom which is nowhere explained. It is often difficult to know how he would wish to connect his arguments with 'the actual use of words'. The premises from which he argues, in Chapter 3, against the coherence of solipsism and of Cartesian dualism and for his own concept of a person, are not presented as accounts of our actual uses of words. Is this their intended basis? An affirmative answer is suggested by an occasional statement like this: 'So the facts in question do not explain *the use that we make of the word 'I'*, or how any word has the use that word has. They do not explain *the concept we have of a person*' (p. 94. My italics). However, consider a principle which Strawson more than once affirms:

> that one's states of consciousness, one's thoughts and sensations, are ascribed *to the very same thing* to which these physical characteristics, this physical situation, is ascribed (p. 89).

Is this merely a reminder that "I *am* . . ." and "He *is* . . ." may be completed both by "thin" or "bald" and by "angry" or "in pain"? Then this principle would be too weak to prove anything, since it is also common for "I *have* . . ." to be used with such complements as "a thin body" or "a pain"; and the latter idiom suggests that "I" refers to something distinct from both my body and my pain.

Consider another of Strawson's central principles, which forms the main premise of his arguments against rival theories:

> it is a necessary condition of one's ascribing states of consciousness, experiences, to oneself, in the way one does, that one should also ascribe them, or be prepared to ascribe them, to others who are not oneself (p. 99).

This is produced, like a rabbit out of a hat, as 'a very simple, but in this question, a very central thought'. One discovers in a footnote that Strawson's point is 'a purely logical one: [namely that] the idea of a predicate is correlative with that of a range of distinguishable individuals of which the predicate can be *significantly, though not necessarily truly*, affirmed' (My italics). In other words, he is simply affirming the tautology that a general word (e.g. "pain" or "person") must be significantly applicable in more than one case. But this explanation invalidates Strawson's use of his central thought. On the next page, he offers his main argument against Cartesian dualism. The three premises are: 'One can ascribe states of consciousness to oneself only if one can ascribe them to others. One can ascribe them to others only if one can identify other subjects of experience. And one cannot identify others if one can identify them *only* as subjects of experience, possessors of states of consciousness'. These premises are supposed to show that a Cartesian is committed to the absurd conclusion: 'All private experiences, all states of consciousness will be mine, i.e. no one's' (p. 100). Strawson has here overlooked the clause in his footnote which I have italicized. In view of that forgotten clause, his first premise should have been: 'One can ascribe states of consciousness to oneself only if one can *significantly but not necessarily truly* ascribe them to others'. His second premise should then have been: 'One can ascribe them to others only if one can identify *what one believes to be* other subjects of experience'. A dualist can consistently accept these premises. He need not, of course, accept Strawson's third premise, for he may say, as Strawson goes on to acknowledge, that one can identify another subject of experience as 'the subject that stands to that body in the same special relation as I stand in to this one'. Strawson claims that this reply is incoherent, on the ground that

> it requires me to have noted that *my* experiences stand in a special relation to body M; but it requires me to have noted this as a condition of being able to identify other subjects of experience, i.e. as a condition of my having the idea of myself as a subject of experience; i.e. as a condition of thinking of any experiences as mine (p. 100).

This seems to be simply a reaffirmation of Strawson's 'very central thought', and one which again ignores the crucial qualification given in the footnote. His reasoning is made clearer on page 106, where he writes: 'There is no sense in the idea of ascribing states of consciousness to oneself, or at all, unless the ascriber *already* knows how to ascribe at least some states of consciousness to others' (p. 106. My italics). As his use of "already" reveals, the position he is gratuitously attributing to the dualist is that one *first* forms the concept of oneself as a person, finds a use for "I", and *later infers* that there are other persons, that there are conscious experiences going on in other organisms, by analogy with one's own case, and thus finds uses for "you" and "he". This is gratuitous because it assumes that a dualist is obliged to treat the argument from analogy as providing a historical account of the process by which a person reaches the belief that there are other persons. But a dualist may and surely should treat the argument from analogy as a way of meeting sceptical doubts, of *justifying* the belief which Strawson ought to have mentioned in his second premise. Philosophers who accept Strawson's refutation of dualism as valid do, I think, share his assumption about the rôle of the argument from analogy. For example, in expounding Strawson, Mr. J. M. Shorter writes:

> the argument from analogy requires that one should *first* have a notion of oneself, of one's own case, and *then* discover how to ascribe mental attributes to others by arguing analogically . . . ('Other Minds', *Encyclopaedia of Philosophy*, Vol. 6, p. 8. My italics).

If Strawson's simple central thought had been interpreted by him, not as the very general tautology, but as a reminder about our actual use of pronouns, it could have served *some* purpose; not indeed to provide a refutation of dualism, but as an argument against another of his targets, solipsism. It could have been a reminder that one could not learn to use "I" in the way we do without learning to use "you" and "he" in the ways we do; that our uses of "I", "you" and "he" are interdependent; that one uses "I" to convey *to another person* that one is referring to oneself, "you" to convey *to another person* that one is referring to him, and so on. But if this is the hidden basis of Strawson's simple central thought, he ought to have affirmed its converse—that it is a necessary condition of one's ascribing states of consciousness to others, in the way that one does, that one should also ascribe them to oneself. Strawson never mentions this converse, but it is surely a principle which we should want to affirm on epistemological, and not merely on logical or linguistic, grounds.[1] This principle cannot be derived from Strawson's tautology that a predicate (a general word) must be significantly applicable in more than one case. But it seems that unless one had *experienced* anger (or pain) and had learned to apply "anger" (or "pain") to such a state of consciousness, one would not know what was being ascribed to another person when he was said to be angry or in pain.

There is a fatal flaw in Strawson's own account of 'the concept of a person'; a flaw attributable to his neglecting our actual use of words. Strawson tries to accommodate what Ryle had called 'the doctrine of privileged access' while outlawing the argument from analogy. Ryle had argued that accepting the doctrine of privileged access commits one to relying upon analogical argument as the source (or justification?) of our beliefs about the states of mind of others, and that this pattern of argument is so precarious that it not only provides scope for scepticism but makes scepticism wellnigh inevitable for a consistent thinker (*C of M*, pp. 14–15 and 51–4). In the following passages, Strawson shows that he shares Ryle's opinion that the argument from analogy must be rejected:

[1] Austin acknowledges this principle, in passing and without discussing it, when he says that, in order to know that you are angry, 'It seems that more is demanded than that I shall have learned to discriminate displays of anger in others: I must also have been angry myself' ('Other Minds', *Philosophical Papers*, p. 72).

we should have to think of the ways of telling [that another person is, e.g. depressed, i.e. his depressed behaviour] as *signs* of the presence, in the individual concerned, of this different thing, viz. the state of consciousness. But then we could only know that the way of telling was a sign of the presence of the different thing ascribed by the P-predicate by the observation of correlations between the two. But this observation we could each make only in one case, viz. our own (p. 106);

and Strawson goes on to argue that if we allow

a logical gap . . . to open between the criteria on the strength of which we say that another is depressed, and the actual state of being depressed . . . then depressed behaviour, however much there is of it, is no more than a sign of depression (p. 109);

and that we cannot then consistently stop short of the absurd conclusion:

all states of consciousness will be mine, i.e. no one's (p. 100); or, as he puts it here: if *only* mine, then not *mine* at all (p. 109).

The solution which Strawson proposes is as follows:

(i) to define "person" as 'a type of entity such that *both* predicates ascribing states of consciousness [which he calls 'P-predicates'] *and* predicates ascribing corporeal characteristics, a physical situation, etc. [which he calls 'M-predicates'] are equally applicable to an individual entity of that type' (p. 104);
(ii) to claim that this concept of a person is 'primitive', meaning that it is not analyzable in ways which had been proposed by other philosophers (pp. 104–5);
(iii) to claim, in the cases of 'at least some P-predicates',
  (a) that the 'behaviour-criteria' on the strength of which one ascribes them to others are 'not just signs of the presence of what is meant by the P-predicate, but are criteria of a logically adequate kind for the ascription of the P-predicate' (p. 106),
  (b) that 'one has an entirely adequate basis for ascribing [such] a P-predicate to oneself, and yet . . . this basis is quite distinct from those on which one ascribes the predicate to another' (p. 107),
  (c) that 'the concept must cover both what is felt, but not

> observed, by X, and what may be observed, but not felt, by others than X (for all values of X). But perhaps it is better to say: X's depression *is* something, one and the same thing, which is felt, but not observed, by X, and observed, but not felt, by others than X' (p. 109).

The predicates about which these claims are made are described as 'a crucial class of P-predicates'; but despite their being so crucial from Strawson's standpoint, he indicates which predicates he would assign to this class only by excluding 'those which carry assessments of character and capability' and by giving three examples: 'I feel tired, am depressed, am in pain' (p. 107). In illustrating his theses, however, he uses only one of his examples, the one which makes his claims least implausible; and he minimizes the implausibility by discussing the predicate "am/is depressed" rather than "feel(s) depressed", though it is the latter which is comparable with his other two examples; for "I am in pain" is equivalent to "I feel pain". It is scarcely controversial to claim (1) that John's behaviour may provide others with 'logically adequate criteria' for concluding that John *is* tired or *is* depressed. It is clearly controversial to claim (2) that John's behaviour may provide others with 'logically adequate criteria' that John *feels* tired, *feels* depressed or *feels* pain. And surely it is the predicates involved in claim (2) rather than in claim (1) which Strawson ought to be discussing; since it is only these which *unambiguously* fulfil a condition for membership of Strawson's crucial class, namely that they ascribe states of consciousness. And 'John *is* tired' does not entail, nor is it entailed by, 'John *feels* tired'; and although 'John *feels* depressed' may entail 'John *is* depressed' (depending on how one is using "depressed"), 'John *is* depressed' does not, surely, entail 'John *feels* depressed'. We may believe that John *is* depressed when he goes on moaning about his ill-luck and the ingratitude of others, without disbelieving his statement that he does not *feel* depressed.

If Strawson had not made the claim which I have labelled (iii)(c), we could have assumed that, in making claim (iii)(a), he was using "logically" loosely when he speaks of 'logically adequate criteria'; that he was using "criterion" to mean 'empirical evidence', and "logically adequate criteria" to mean 'empirical evidence which would be considered sufficient or conclusive'; and that his intention was to remind us that, in our everyday language-games, empirical evidence is often considered sufficient to justify a claim to know something which is not, however, *entailed* by a statement of the evidence. In that case, we may complain that it was inappropriate to use "*logically* adequate" for this purpose. For, in its context, Strawson's contrast between "logically adequate criteria" and "signs" suggests that he is using "signs" to mean 'empirical, inductive, evidence', and using "are logically adequate criteria for" to mean 'entails'.

However, Strawson's claim (iii)(c) is incompatible with the foregoing interpretation of claim (iii)(a), for it implies that he intended to use "logically adequate criteria" literally and not loosely. But Strawson's *identification* of the depression or pain which a person feels with what others can observe generates obvious paradoxes. On Strawson's account it is extremely puzzling that my pain, an allegedly single thing, should be so terribly two-faced—should be an ache in the bowels to me, and should be my clenched jaw and trembling hands to you. More important, Strawson ignores the obvious objections to his account of the crucial P-predicates, by just dismissing relevant but awkward empirical facts, *including facts about how we talk*. He does so in a single parenthetical remark: '(of course what can be observed can also be faked or disguised)' (p. 109). This is Strawson's only reference to those actual uses of words which here demand discussion; demand it because, enshrined in our talk about depression, pain or fatigue being 'faked' or 'concealed', are our beliefs that the relevant behaviour is sometimes unaccompanied by the relevant state of consciousness, and *vice versa*. Strawson's method of 'closing the logical gap' involves recommending that we should describe as 'one and the same thing' what, according to our everyday ways of speaking and thinking, are obviously distinct and separable 'things', namely *feeling* pain or depression and exhibiting pain- or depressive-*behaviour*. A and B cannot be 'one and the same thing' if A can exist without B and B without A. If claim (iii)(a) was intended as a reminder concerning our actual use of words in saying things like "I know that, I see that, he is in pain", Strawson should not have suppressed the implications of our actual use of expressions like "faking" and "concealing pain". (My attempt to provide a solution to Strawson's problem will be postponed until Section XVI.)

The samples of Strawson's arguments discussed above illustrate how far removed they seem to be from 'the reliance upon a close examination of the actual use of words'. In appearance, Strawson has almost completely freed himself from the latter method. He presents his subject-matter as 'concepts' and 'categories'. But if we asked him the Strawsonian question: how do we *identify* a particular concept or category?, the answer would presumably have to be: by mentioning some word or phrase whose 'actual use' is supposedly being discussed. However, Strawson does quite often go far beyond an examination of our actual use of words. He displays subtlety and imagination in exploring modes of experience very different from our own, notably in Chapter 2. He does, however, adhere to the tradition of linguistic philosophy in maintaining ideological neutrality, in the form of ontological neutrality. Or at least he professes to do so, though often his aim *seems* to be to justify the ontological commitments of the plain man's mid-morning view of the world. I shall outline enough of Strawson's arguments to explain why I say this. In Chapter 1, Strawson seems to be using "ontology", and its derivatives, in the usual sense, in which ontological questions are questions about what is real, what exists. Presumably this is how most readers would interpret "ontology" when Strawson says, by way of explaining his concern with questions about identifying particulars: 'That it should be possible to identify particulars of a given type seems a necessary condition *of the inclusion of that type in our ontology*' (p. 16. My italics).

Strawson introduces his question about identifying a particular as a communication problem: to ask whether a speaker identifies a particular is, in effect, to ask whether his words make his hearer think of the particular thing to which the speaker is referring. Identification, in this sense, is thus parasitic on identification in a sense which Strawson does not explicitly acknowledge until Chapter 2: 'Each of us can think identifyingly about particulars without talking about them' (p. 61). Strawson asks how we identify particulars which are not perceptible by the speaker or the hearer. His answer is that we do so via a single unified spatio-temporal framework of three spatial and one temporal dimensions, using one's own location within it as one's point of origin. He seems to be claiming that this is necessary not only for 'our conceptual scheme' but for any scheme which we can envisage in which particulars can be talked about in a common language; and that a thing's being locatable in this sense is a condition of saying that this thing '*really* exists' (p. 29. His italics). Again, his words suggest that he is concerned with what are normally called 'ontological questions'.

Strawson's key principle is introduced thus: if there were a type of particulars, β, 'such that particulars of type β cannot be identified without reference to particulars of another type, α, whereas particulars of type α can be identified without reference to particulars of type β', this, he says, may be expressed by saying that, in our scheme, α-particulars are 'ontologically prior to β-particulars, more fundamental or more basic than they' (p. 17). Strawson applies this principle to 'two important general types or categories of particular': (i) to 'private particulars', e.g. 'sensations' and 'mental events', which can only be identified by reference to 'the persons to whose histories they belong' (p. 41); (ii) to 'particulars which might be called 'theoretical constructs'', e.g. 'certain particles of physics', which can only be identified by reference to 'observable bodies' (p. 44). His use here of "theoretical constructs", which is normally used, like "logical constructions", to mean 'fictitious entities', seems to imply that he considers the particles in question to be not 'ontologically basic' in the normal sense, i.e. to be non-existent. But Strawson cannot presumably have intended to claim that the unobservable particles of physics could not exist unless we, and objects detectable by our sense-organs, existed. One cannot rule out *a priori* the possibility that the Universe has gone (or will go) through a stage in which all matter is gaseous.

It seems to me that the basis of Strawson's conclusion that some kinds of particulars are 'ontologically prior' to other kinds is this: that we humans cannot refer to an entity unobservable by us except by making references, usually implicitly and indirectly, to what we now observe. If I have understood his arguments, Strawson's key principles concerning the identification of particulars are based upon a rule which is not made explicit, and which is a relation of "the" verification principle; a rule for drawing *one* of 'the bounds of sense', i.e. for eliminating as meaningless certain members of a certain class of sentences. To render this rule precise, we should need to say something like this: that a sentence which is ostensibly used to refer to a particular is factually meaningful for a person, only if *he* can identify this particular by specifying its spatial and temporal 'directions' and 'distances' from things which *he* is observing at the time of speaking or hearing or thinking. I speak of a reference to a particular being 'factually meaningful' in order to indicate the exclusion of what Strawson calls 'story-relative identification' (pp. 18–23). He contrasts 'identification within history' with 'identification within his [another person's] story' (p. 22). To rule out story-relative identification, he says: 'the known individuating fact must not be such that its statement essentially involves identifying the particular in question by reference to someone else's discourse about it' (p. 23). If my diagnosis of his reasoning is correct, Strawson has to face some awkward questions. How specific need the specification of location be, in order to make meaningful a would-be reference to a particular? If an astronomer starts his story with 'Somewhere, once upon a time . . .', need his story be intended or interpreted as science-fiction? Moreover, we may ask what is the status of the rule which Strawson is using. Synthetic *a priori*? If not, can it be defended except by appealing to some more general version of "the" verification principle? And if so which, and how is *it* to be defended?

Strawson's key principles for identifying particulars have implications concerning the temporal order in which we acquire concepts; but, I want to say, they have no *ontological* implications. We may readily agree that we, with the sense-organs that we possess, cannot acquire the concepts of electrons or light-waves unless we have already acquired concepts of physical objects. A Cartesian could concede that *we* cannot acquire the concept of an immaterial soul unless we have first acquired the concept of a person as a conscious physical organism. Do any ontological conclusions follow? It was perhaps such considerations which led Strawson to start Chapter 2, by disavowing any interest in *ontology* in the normal sense of this word:

Claiming a special status for one class or category of entities as opposed to others is very common in philosophy. It is the philo-

> sophical phenomenon of category-preference. I have been exhibiting category-preference in claiming that material objects are, in a certain sense, basic in relation to other categories of particulars. But I should like to emphasize the point that there are certain ways in which category-preference may be exhibited, in which I am not exhibiting it. Suppose αs are the favoured type of entity. Then sometimes preference is manifested by the declaration that the word 'exist' has a primary sense or meaning, and that only αs exist in this sense . . . sometimes by the declaration that only αs are real; and sometimes by the declaration that other things are reducible to αs . . . I want to emphasize that in saying that material bodies are basic among particulars, at least in our conceptual scheme as it is, I am not saying any of these things. The meaning given to the term 'basic' is strictly in terms of particular-identification . . . It seems to me also unobjectionable to use the expression 'ontologically prior' in such a way that the claim that material bodies are basic particulars in our conceptual scheme is equivalent to the claim that material bodies are ontologically prior, in that scheme, to other types of particular (p. 59).

According to this, Strawson is offering us an arbitrary redefinition of "ontological", according to which "αs are ontologically prior to βs" means *only* '*we* can identify as without reference to βs, but not vice versa'. He does not seem to have always remembered this. At the outset he seemed concerned to decide what sorts of things should or may be included 'in our ontology' (p. 16); and he ends the book by saying that perhaps he might be said 'to have found some reason in the idea that persons and material bodies are *what primarily exists*' (p. 247. My italics). But if the ontological neutrality avowed on page 59 is his considered position, Strawson's kind of descriptive metaphysics will be considered to be a poor substitute by those who conceive of metaphysics as an attempt to understand the world, after taking account *inter alia* of the discoveries of scientists, of the claims made by religions, and of the phenomenological facts which make it so difficult to accept a naïve realist account of perception.

Should Strawson's *Individuals* be classified as linguistic philosophy? Some would describe this book as linguistic philosophy at its best. I should have qualms about classifying it without qualifications as linguistic philosophy, despite what Strawson says in his Introduction. Certainly Strawson is not merely a linguistic philosopher. He has made distinguished contributions to the theory of logic, and has written what I consider the most illuminating and discriminating of the many books on Kant.[2] But if it is not impertinent to say so, I suggest that his thought has been unduly restricted by respect for Wittgenstein. Consider what he said in his review of Wittgenstein's *Investigations*:

it is difficult not to share the conception of philosophy held by the first philosopher of the age. Yet there are at least two very different directions in which it may seem unduly restrictive. First, there is the idea that the *sole* purpose of the . . . descriptions we give of the different ways in which words function, is to dispel particular metaphysical confusions; and associated with this, an extreme aversion from a systematic exhibition of the logic of particular regions of language. Now . . . there can be an investigation of the logic of a set of concepts, which starts with no purpose other than that of unravelling and ordering complexities for the sake of doing so . . . [and, the second direction:] We might make room for a purged kind of metaphysics, with more modest and less disputable claims than the old (*Mind*, 1954, p. 78).

Strawson's later work often appears to be a fulfilment of this 1954 programme for extending Wittgenstein's desperately restrictive conception of philosophy. Moreover Strawson's purged metaphysics, as practised in *Individuals*, corresponds closely with what Austin described as 'linguistic phenomenology', except that Strawson's primary concern, here and elsewhere, has been not with the minutiae but with what he regards as 'categories and concepts which in their fundamental character change not at all'. But why should not a purged metaphysics include speculative metaphysics? Indeed Strawson does a little of the latter while doing what he calls 'descriptive metaphysics', e.g. in his accounts of the 'no-space world' and of Leibniz's monadology. I hope that he will do more such metaphysics.

[2] *The Bounds of Sense*, 1966

PART TWO

LUDWIG WITTGENSTEIN: THE INSTIGATOR OF THE REVOLUTION IN PHILOSOPHY

SECTION XII

The Rôles of G. E. Moore and Wittgenstein Compared

In order to try to bring about its fall, more must be said about the rise of linguistic philosophy. So far, nothing has been said about G. E. Moore, and only a few passing references have been made to Wittgenstein. This part of the book will deal at some length with the works of Wittgenstein and his influence. Moore's contributions will be discussed very briefly, since, in the sense in which I am using "linguistic philosopher", Moore cannot fairly be assigned to this class; and because it is not difficult to see how his philosophical practice, as distinct from his conception of philosophy, encouraged others to conclude that the subject-matter of philosophy is ordinary language. One might say, roughly, that whereas Ayer, in *LTL*, described philosophy as a study of language yet proceeded to do metaphysics, Moore described the primary task of philosophy as metaphysics yet proceeded to do what certainly seems to be linguistic analysis.

Moore's early work (1897–1902), which is commonly ignored by others as it was later by himself, belongs to the Idealist tradition of dogmatic metaphysics. In his first paper, 'In What Sense, if Any, Do Past and Future Time Exist?' (*Mind*, 1897), Moore defended Bradley's view that time is unreal. In 'The Nature of Judgement' (*Mind*, 1899), Moore claimed that everything that exists is wholly composed of what he called 'adjectival concepts', entities which (he assumed) have an objective existence and, like Plato's Forms, are eternal and unchangeable. The views which we associate with Moore emerged in 1903 with the publication of *Principia Ethica* and 'The Refutation of Idealism' (*Mind*). But his continuing concern with metaphysics, in the traditional sense, is made clear in his lecture 'What is Philosophy?' delivered in 1910 (published in *Some Main Problems of Philosophy*, 1953):

I will try to begin by describing those questions which seem to me to be the *most* important . . . it seems to me that the most important and interesting thing which philosophers have tried to do is no less than this; namely: To give a general description of the *whole* of the Universe, mentioning all the most important kinds of things which we know to be in it, considering how far it is likely that there are in it important kinds of things which we do not absolutely *know* to be in it, and also considering the most important ways in which these various kinds of things are related to one another (p. 1).

And in 1942, in 'A Reply to My Critics' (*The Philosophy of G. E. Moore*, ed. P. A. Schilpp), where Moore sometimes admitted uncertainty about what he had meant by his earlier statements, he was very emphatic in rejecting the suggestion made by John Wisdom that he equated philosophy with analysis (pp. 675–6), and equally emphatic in rejecting C. H. Langford's suggestion that, in giving his analyses, the subject of an analysis had been 'a verbal expression' (p. 661).

I make these points because Moore is sometimes retrospectively canonized as an early father of linguistic philosophy. Professor Norman Malcolm gives the most explicit version of this interpretation in 'Moore and Ordinary Language' (*P of GEM*). He is, I think, viewing Moore through spectacles provided by Wittgenstein, when he says that Moore 'takes his stand upon ordinary language and defends it against every attack' (p. 365); and that Moore's 'great historical rôle consists in the fact that he has been perhaps the first philosopher to sense that any philosophical statement which violates ordinary language is false' (p. 368). The feature of Moore's philosophy on which Malcolm concentrates here is his celebrated method of refuting philosophical paradoxes, by simply asserting that he knows, and that we know, with certainty, propositions which philosophers have doubted or denied; for example Moore's proof that external things exist: 'I can prove now . . . that two human hands exist. How? By holding up my two hands and saying, as I make a certain gesture with the right hand, 'Here is one hand' . . .'. Malcolm interprets Moore's proofs, which Moore described as a defence of common sense, as reminders of how we ordinarily use words (p. 355). So interpreted, they are, according to Malcolm, rigorous proofs, for Malcolm adopts it as an axiom that 'it is not possible for an ordinary form of speech to be improper. That is to say ordinary language is correct language' (p. 362). Malcolm much weakens his interpretation of Moore's purpose, however, by what he says at the end of this paper. Acknowledging that Moore's blunt way of dismissing philosophers' paradoxes 'often fails to convince the author' and 'does not get at the sources of the philosophical troubles', he attributes this to Moore's failure to make it at all clear that he had been defending ordinary language and on what grounds he had been doing so. The implication is that Moore (unlike Malcolm) did not understand what he was doing.

It is, however, easy to see why Moore's writings often give the impression that he is appealing to ordinary language, and trying to clarify everyday expressions. Moore took his stand on the principle that for very many sentences, such as "The earth has existed for many years past", we all know for certain what they mean, and that what they mean is true; that the philosophical problem is to give their correct analyses. 'The question what is the correct analysis of the proposition meant . . . by 'The earth has existed for many years past' is a profoundly difficult question, and one to which . . . no one knows the answer' (*Philosophical Papers*, p. 37).

A great deal of Moore's work is presented as a search for 'the correct analysis' of statements whose truth we know. He was forever asking what other philosophers' statements *meant*, what so and so normally *means* or the different things it might *mean*; and he often expressed his analyses in the form '"—" means that . . .'. This suggests that the subject-matter *was* linguistic expressions. Moore acknowledged this in 1942: 'I am afraid it is pretty certain that I have often, in giving analyses, used this word "means" and thus given a false impression' (*P of GEM*, p. 664). This statement is part of the puzzling reply received by Professor C. H. Langford when he sought to clarify Moore's intentions on this point.

Langford starts by presenting what he calls 'the paradox of analysis':

> Let us call what is to be analysed the analysandum, and . . . that which does the analysing the analysans . . . the paradox of analysis is to the effect that, if the verbal expression representing the analysandum has the same meaning as the verbal expression representing

the analysans, the analysis states a bare identity and is trivial; but if the two verbal expressions do not have the same meaning, the analysis is incorrect (p. 323).

Notice that this statement of the dilemma presupposes that the two verbal expressions are both being used, not mentioned. In the sequel, Langford suggests two different analyses of what Moore meant by "analysis" and invites Moore to choose between them. In the first alternative, two expressions representing analysandum and analysans are both being used; in the second both expressions are being mentioned, and an analysis is a statement of the form '"—" means what is meant by "—"'. The latter alternative escapes from the paradox of analysis, at the cost of being explicitly linguistic.

In his reply, Moore says that quite definitely he never intended to use "analysis" in the latter way. But he gives a remarkable reason for denying that, for him, the analysandum is a verbal expression, namely that what he would regard as 'an analysis of a verbal expression' would be *listing the words it contains and describing their order*! Another reason he gives for rejecting the second alternative is that a statement of the form '"—" means what is meant by "—"', 'could be completely understood by a person who had not the least idea what either expression meant'. Oddly enough, Moore does not acknowledge the obvious way of escaping between the horns of Langford's dilemma, namely by saying that in the analysandum an expression is mentioned and in the analysans another expression is used. This third alternative, like the second, would make analyses explicitly linguistic, but Moore's second reason for rejecting the second alternative does not apply to the third. Langford had dismissed the third alternative in a single sentence, saying, mistakenly, that it implies that an analysis is a statement of the form '"A" means A'. He asserts that to say '"X is a small Y" means that X is a Y which is smaller than most Y's' is 'indistinguishable from saying that the expression "X is a small Y" means that X is a small Y'! (p. 336). It is surprising that Moore overlooked this obvious error.

Moore goes on to say that 'in my usage, both *analysandum* and *analysans* must be concepts or propositions, not mere verbal expressions. But of course, in order to *give* an analysis you must *use* verbal expressions'. This strongly suggests that Moore intended to use "the concept of A" not as a way of mentioning "A", but as a way of using "A" to refer to a concept conceived of as something which "A" denotes. Whether he was still thinking of concepts as Platonic objects or was thinking of them as psychological entities is left obscure. Moore recognized that his answer exposes him to Langford's 'paradox of analysis'. He wrestles with this difficulty without success. He says: 'if in making a given statement one is to be properly said to be "giving an analysis" of a *concept*, then . . . both *analysandum* and *analysans* must be *concepts*, and, if the analysis is a *correct* one, must, in some sense, be *the same concept*' (p. 666. His italics). He ends by saying: 'I do not know, at all clearly, *what* I mean by saying that: "*x* is a brother" is *identical* with "*x* is a male sibling", and that "*x* is a cube" is *not identical* with "*x* is a cube which has twelve edges"' (p. 667). Moore insists that any analysis of "*x* is a cube" which mentioned the property of having twelve edges would be an incorrect analysis; on the ground that we can recognize cubes without knowing that they have twelve edges, and that 'as we actually use it' "cube" is not synonymous with "cube with twelve edges". But by these criteria many of what Moore offered as analyses cannot be correct, e.g. his various analyses of perceptual judgements in terms of 'sense-data'; for as we actually use it "I see a hand" is not synonymous with statements about sense-data.

In his reply to Langford, Moore seems to have forgotten how he had thought of analysis earlier, for example in *Principia Ethica* (pp. 5 ff.). There he introduced his question as 'how 'good' is to be defined', but tried, at once, to explain the kind of definition he sought: 'My business is solely with that object or idea which I hold, rightly or wrongly, that the word is generally used to stand for. What I want to discover is the nature of that object or idea'. He adds that 'definitions which describe the real nature of the object or notion denoted by a word . . . are only possible when the object is complex'. Moore concluded that "good" is like "yellow" in denoting a quality which is simple, unanalysable, and therefore not definable, but that it is unlike "yellow" in that the object denoted by "good" is apprehended, not via our sense-organs, but by 'intuition'. Moore may, by 1942, have abandoned his earlier conception of analysis as isolating the simple constituents of complex objects, but he failed to provide any clear substitute. His puzzled and puzzling reply to Langford failed to provide any viable interpretation of his own practice of analysis other than ones which he wished to reject, and which make the analysandum a verbal expression. This strengthens the suspicion that he was really doing what he often seemed to be doing, namely clarifying the meaning of words and sentences by giving paraphrases. Passmore is probably correct in suggesting that 'Dissatisfaction with Moore's uncertainties ... did something to drive his successors in a more 'linguistic' direction' (*A Hundred Years of Philosophy*, p. 215). One might add that Moore's example encouraged other philosophical analysts to use the concept-idiom. Having said that, I would accept Warnock's summing up on Moore's work and influence:

> in theory he did not conceive of philosophy quite differently from his metaphysical predecessors. His practice, however, consisting as it mostly did in the pursuit of analyses, naturally tended to give rise to the idea that the business of philosophy is clarification and not discovery; that its concern is with meaning, not with truth; that its subject-matter is our thought or language, rather than the facts. In its influence the practice was far more important than the theory (*English Philosophy Since 1900*, p. 29).

The importance of Wittgenstein's rôle in inspiring linguistic philosophy is undisputed. Mr. G. J. Warnock has written: 'There can be no serious doubt that the most powerful and pervasive influence upon the practice of philosophy in this country today has been that of Ludwig Wittgenstein' (*English Philosophy Since 1900*, 1958, p. 62). Mr. J. O. Urmson has written: 'It is certain that Wittgenstein had an enormous influence upon, and was indeed the main originator of, the new philosophical methods' (*Philosophical Analysis*, 1956, p. 62). Professor Strawson, in a review of *Philosophical Investigations*, describes Wittgenstein as 'a philosopher of genius' and as 'the first philosopher of the age', and ends by saying of the book: 'It will consolidate the philosophical revolution for which, more than anyone else, its author was responsible' (*Mind*, Jan., 1954). Since, in the sequel, I shall make many criticisms of his writings, I want to start by saying that it seems to me that, in his own very unusual way, Wittgenstein was a genius. He threw out revolutionary ideas, exploring whose far-reaching implications has occupied several generations of philosophers; ideas which have changed the face of philosophy throughout the English-speaking world. For example, his thesis that all necessary truths are tautologies, his early adumbration of "the" Verification Principle, and his simile between using words and using tools. I consider, however, that his restriction of philosophy first to 'the logic of language' and later to 'grammar' was misguided and has diminished the importance of philosophy, in theory and in practice.

Wittgenstein's personality evidently made an immense impact on all who were privileged to know him and especially to listen to him while in intellectual labour. (See the accounts of him given in *Ludwig Wittgenstein*, 1958, containing a Memoir by Professor N. Malcolm and a Biographical Sketch by Professor G. H. von Wright.) Presumably his influence was largely due to his flair for making remarks which jolt the intellect or the imagination and present old problems in a new light. Some such remarks were insights of the first importance. I shall mention some of these in passing, but shall not usually elaborate on their implications since many others have performed this task. My task is one which is more neglected—to exhibit the incoherence of Wittgenstein's attempts to explain, develop or systematize his hunches, and to show that some of his alleged insights illuminate paths which peter out. In fairness, it must be said that he was far from satisfied with what he had written; but I can judge his thought only by his published writings, and I find it impossible to quote, never mind comment on, some of his statements without wondering whether he was being ironical.

Wittgenstein's *Tractatus Logico-Philosophicus* (1922) seems to me to be the prototype of *a priori* linguistics; not Anglo-linguistics of course, for it was intended to apply to all languages. It seems to be an attempt to combine two 'insights', which were treated as *a priori* truths:

(a) that we must explain how a sentence can be used to assert a fact about the world by regarding a sentence as a *picture*;
(b) that the ultimate structure of the world and of our thoughts about the world must be similar to that of the symbolism

> recently invented by Russell and Whitehead in *Principia Mathematica* (1910), as amended by Wittgenstein.

Wittgenstein treated these insights as self-evident in that he did not explain them or try to justify them, but used them to reject rival theories about language and meaning. English and German sentences look very different from the formulae used by Russell and Whitehead. Wittgenstein concluded that the former must be a shorthand way of expressing thoughts whose real structure, whose ultimate 'logical form', is very different indeed from their expression in any natural language. Wittgenstein says things which clearly imply that *every* significant sentence, true or false, is 'a picture of reality'. "England won the World Cup in 1966" does not look at all like a picture of that series of football matches or of the winning goals. However, Wittgenstein's picture theory of meaning is now commonly interpreted as implying not that any sentence which might actually be used is a picture, but rather that the thought expressed by any such sentence comprises a host of so-called atomic propositions, each of which is a picture of a so-called atomic fact. Yet we are never told what could form the subject-matter of an atomic proposition. As the Kneales point out (*D of L*, p. 632), Wittgenstein seems to have regarded it as being beneath the dignity of his book to explain what he had in mind when he spoke of 'atomic facts'. He does not give a single example to indicate how we are to translate an everyday or scientific statement into the language which would reveal its logical form. History records the sources of Wittgenstein's insights. He discovered that a sentence must be a picture of a corresponding fact, through noticing, in a magazine, a picture of some toy cars used in a law-court as a visual aid for depicting a motor-accident. (Malcolm's *Ludwig Wittgenstein*, pp. 7–8). The second insight was due to his studying mathematical logic as a pupil of Russell at Cambridge.

Wittgenstein's practice of *a priori* linguistics inspired others to do likewise. Ayer starts the Preface to the first edition of *LTL* by saying: 'The views which are put forward in this treatise derive from the doctrines of Bertrand Russell and Wittgenstein'. Adoption of "the" Verification Principle by the Vienna Circle may have been inspired by some of Wittgenstein's remarks which have not yet been published in English. Of particular interest here is one of Wittgenstein's contributions to a conversation at the home of Schlick on 22 December, 1929, as recorded in *Friedrich Waismann: Wittgenstein und der Wiener Kreis* (1967). I append a translation by my colleague Mr. L. E. Thomas:

THE MEANING OF A SENTENCE IS ITS VERIFICATION

If I say, for example: "There is a book up there on the case", how do I set about verifying it? Is it enough if I look at it, or if I consider it from various sides, or if I take it in my hand, feel it, open it, turn the pages and so on? There are two views on this matter. One of them says: No matter how I set about it, I can never completely verify the sentence. The sentence always leaves a backdoor open. Whatever we do, we are never certain that we have not made a mistake.

The other view, which I would wish to defend, says: No, if I can never completely verify what the sentence means (*den Sinn des Satzes*), then also I cannot have meant anything by the sentence. Then the sentence also means nothing.

In order to determine the meaning of a sentence I should have to know a quite definite procedure by which the sentence could be regarded as verified. In this respect ordinary language vacillates a lot, much more than scientific language. There is a certain freedom here, and this amounts to saying: The symbols of our ordinary language are not defined unambiguously (p. 47).

Notice that it is a By-Me version of the VP which is here advocated, but one which requires 'complete', i.e. conclusive (what Ayer later called 'strong') verification.

In Wittgenstein's later writings, philosophy is identified with a study of language which is, at least in intention, empirical. His *Philosophical Investigations* was published posthumously in 1953; but some of its contents are very similar to those of *The Blue and Brown Books* (1958), which are based on lecture notes dictated by Wittgenstein to some of his students between 1933 and 1935. These notes, in typescript form, were circulated widely among British philosophers, and seem to have excited considerable interest. They show that Wittgenstein was capable of expressing his thoughts in a relatively clear and consecutive manner.[1] The Brown Book seems to me to be far more illuminating than either of the works which Wittgenstein had fully prepared for publication: the *Tractatus* and Part One, at least, of his *Philosophical Investigations*. The latter is a repudiation of the former; though Wittgenstein often speaks in the *Investigations* as if all earlier philosophers had made the same mistakes as he did in the *Tractatus* and were therefore also targets of his criticisms. His later writings are based on two new insights about language, two similes:

(a) that using language is like, should be thought of as, playing a game,
(b) that using language is like, should be thought of as, using a tool-kit.

We are told that the former insight came to Wittgenstein when, during an afternoon walk, he saw a football game in progress (*Ludwig Wittgenstein*, p. 65). He then recognized, apparently, that language is not, after all, an album of pictures but rather an Olympiad of (usually non-competitive) games. History does not record when he discovered that language is like a tool-kit, but his training as an engineer makes it easy to understand the origin of this idea. These new insights made him so hostile to the assertions made in the *Tractatus* that he went to the opposite extreme, and prescribed an occupation for philosophers which would prevent them from doing again the sort of thing that he had done in the *Tractatus*. Though English was not his native tongue, his proposals involved making it a prison for many English-speaking philosophers.

Although Wittgenstein frequently told us to think of language as a tool-kit, and frequently told us to think of it as a game or family of games, he never analysed his similes. He never got down to details, like asking: in *which* respects is a language like (and unlike) a tool-kit; like (and unlike) a game. However, his similes caught on, and other philosophers recognized some of the likenesses, though not, apparently, the unlikenesses. Anyone analysing the tool-kit simile would surely ask what people make and use tools *for*; and then recognize that although we

[1] And so also do the surviving notes that he made during World War One (*Note-books 1914–1916* (1961)). We are told that he wished all of these notes to be destroyed.

often use tools for making or repairing other tools, at least some of our tools are made and used for satisfying human needs more directly; and that using tools *simply to make records of the uses of other tools* is an unusual use of tools (though not unknown, for a computer may be used for this purpose among countless others). Yet this last use of our verbal tool-kit is the only one, the only language-game, to be permitted in Wittgenstein's prison. For consider Wittgenstein's instructions, in the *Investigations*, for the practice of philosophy:

> And we must not advance any kind of theory. There must not be anything hypothetical in our considerations. We must do away with all *explanation* and description alone must take its place (§ 109).
>
> Philosophy may in no way interfere with the actual use of language; it can in the end only describe it. For it cannot give it any foundation either. It leaves everything as it is (§ 124).
>
> Since everything lies open to view there is nothing to explain. For what is hidden, for example, is of no interest to us [i.e. to us philosophers, us prisoners] (§ 126).

These passages show the aptness of my metaphor—the prison. The prisoners may do their describing, as Wittgenstein did, with words as well as by drawing pictures and by silent gesturing. But they may use the verbal tools only to *describe* how verbal tools are used by free men. Free men are free to play many language-games; they may and do use verbal tools for intellectually exciting tasks, like explaining, theorizing, problem-solving. The prisoners are not permitted to use verbal tools for some of the most important purposes for which such tools were designed. They are permitted only one monotonous game. They are even debarred from sharpening or redesigning a free man's tools, for they 'may in no way interfere with the actual use of language', must 'leave everything as it is'. When a free man does some describing he does not do so as an end-in-itself; he has some goal, like getting the hearer to do something—to see something or buy something or laugh at something. Wittgenstein's goal in prescribing this bread-and-water diet of describing was apparently therapeutic—to enable the prisoners to cure themselves of the habit of asking perplexing questions. Sometimes Wittgenstein seems to be re-defining "philosophy" to mean curing oneself of puzzlement, of the habit of asking the very questions, the attempt to answer which is what had hitherto been meant by "philosophy". As Hume recognized, there are more pleasurable ways of stopping oneself from worrying about such questions, of inducing 'carelessness and inattention', than the ascetic régime required in Wittgenstein's prison.

One of the most striking features of Wittgenstein's work is his propensity to seize upon some simple simile, to see this as a revelation, and then to devote many years struggling to explain everything (or nearly everything) in terms of one or two such similes; yet producing in the end only an album of remarks, as he himself describes *Philosophical Investigations* in the Preface. If this is philosophy, it is certainly a new kind of philosophy. But is it a legitimate kind at all? It is natural to be pleased when one hits upon a new phrase or notices a resemblance that one had not noticed before. The phrase "*a priori* linguistics" gave me some insight-feeling, and still does. But it is not sufficient to leave it to such a phrase to do all the work. Arguments are needed to justify its use, and examples to indicate what is and what is not meant by it. Such 'insights' need to be brought under enough control to enable others to judge whether their author is being consistent. Doing this is surely a necessary part of what has traditionally been called 'philosophy'. Wittgenstein did not do this. If he tried, his failure was almost complete. He would produce a simile and give it a name, e.g. "language-game", and then leave the name to do the work. He left himself free to use and did use such names in vague and unexplained ways, in apparently different ways in different contexts. Interpreters and critics are thus given no controls for the purpose of testing what he said for meaning or for consistency. The imagination of the interpreter is given an almost free reign; which is a virtue in poetry, but not, I think, in philosophy. And so, as Professor Heath once said, *Philosophical Investigations* is 'a gold-mine for commentators', but 'is little better than a salt-mine for the sort of reader who expects a book . . . to begin at the beginning, go on to the end, and then stop' (*Phil. Quarterly*, 1956, p. 66). There is endless scope for searching for truths hidden in Wittgenstein's remarks. If anyone wishes to pursue wisdom by this method he is welcome to do so, though there are many methods which seem to be more promising, and whose practice is less like the tasks of Tantalus. For the remarks published to date fill eight volumes,[2] their contents are arranged in a more or less random order,[3] and the editors did not provide their collections with indexes. So unless you have a photographic memory, it may take the best part of a life-time before you are in a position to compare all his other remarks which contradict, confirm or seem to cast light upon, the remark you wish to make remarks about at the moment.

In the sequel, I shall not compete in the now popular game of affirming what is *the correct interpretation of*, or *what Wittgenstein really meant by*, his earlier or his later remarks. Those who play this game make an assumption which it would be hard to justify: that, for the remarks which he had polished for publication, Wittgenstein would have been willing to accept paraphrases which reduce or remove the ambiguities. There is, however, some evidence suggesting that the ambiguities were deliberate and indeed contrived. Compare the remarks in question with the relatively clear and connected passages which had not been (or not fully) polished for publication, the *Notebooks*, in *The Blue and Brown Books* and in Part Two of the *Investigations*. I sometimes feel that interpreting Part One of the *Investigations* is as subjective as seeing a Rorschach ink-blot *as* this or that. I shall mention how the patterns in Wittgenstein's ink-blots strike me; but only in order to put my cards on the table, lest others should think this relevant to my complaints about his inconsistencies.

[2] In addition to the four already mentioned in this section, there are *Remarks on the Foundations of Mathematics* (1956), *Philosophische Bemerkungen* (1964), *Zettel* (1967), and *On Certainty* (1969).

[3] Professor Max Black reports: 'In later life, Wittgenstein proposed more in earnest than in jest to arrange the sentences of a philosophical book in alphabetical order' (*Companion to Wittgenstein's Tractatus*, p. 2).

SECTION XIII

Wittgenstein's *Tractatus*, the Purest kind of *A Priori* Linguistics

APART from its theses that philosophy is 'a critique of language' and that all necessary propositions are tautologies, the theories implicit in Wittgenstein's *Tractatus* are almost extinct. It seems necessary, however, to consider its contents, if only to make his later remarks intelligible. But readers who lose patience before the end of this section can pass on to the next section with no great loss. What I shall say about the *Tractatus* will not constitute a hermeneutical discourse, of which there is no shortage.[1] What is offered here is *not* a balanced and scholarly assessment of everything in the *Tractatus*. No doubt others have found in it many things that I have missed; but I hope that the converse is not wholly false. My aim is to exhibit some of the main inconsistencies in the *Tractatus* which are relevant to my purposes, especially the inconsistency between Wittgenstein's account of philosophy and his own practice thereof. Although Wittgenstein claims that the proper rôle for philosophy is to be a 'critique of language' (4.0031), and to provide 'elucidations' of what people say (4.112), he ignores almost completely the uses of language by everyone except certain mathematical logicians. Although he complains that most of what philosophers have written is nonsensical (4.003), he ends this book by saying that *its* contents are nonsensical (6.54). Features of the *Tractatus* which will be stressed are (i) that this alleged critique of language contains nothing but *a priori* assertions and deductions therefrom, that it is a voyage in 'logical space' (his phrase) remote from the things we say and talk about here below; (ii) that the use which is made of the picture theory of meaning is to generate mystifi-

[1] See G. E. M. Anscombe, *An Introduction to Wittgenstein's Tractatus*, 1959; Eric Stenius, *Wittgenstein's Tractatus*, 1960; Alexander Maslow, *A Study in Wittgenstein's Tractatus*, 1961; Max Black, *A Companion to Wittgenstein's Tractatus*, 1964; James Griffin, *Wittgenstein's Logical Atomism*, 1964; David Favrholdt, *An Interpretation and Critique of Wittgenstein's Tractatus*, 1964; George Pitcher, *The Philosophy of Wittgenstein*, Part 1, 1964.

cation, by arguing that there are facts which cannot be stated, notably facts concerning the logical form of statements (4.12), and then equating such facts, 'the inexpressible', with 'the mystical' (6.522).

I must inflict many quotations on the reader, since any summary or paraphrase would be judged a misinterpretation by someone. Except when otherwise stated I shall follow the translation by D. F. Pears and B. F. MacGuinness, published in 1961. I shall start by quoting the main assertions made about philosophy:

Most of the propositions and questions to be found in philosophical works are not false but nonsensical. Consequently we cannot give any answer to questions of this kind, but can only establish that they are nonsensical. Most of the propositions and questions of philosophers arise from our failure to understand the logic of our language . . . And it is not surprising that the deepest problems are in fact *not* problems at all. All philosophy[2] is a 'critique of language' . . . It was Russell who performed the service of showing that the apparent logical form of a proposition need not be its real one (4.003–4.0031).

A philosophical work consists essentially of elucidations. Philosophy does not result in 'philosophical propositions', but rather in the clarification of propositions. Without philosophy thoughts are, as it were, cloudy and indistinct: its task is to make them clear and give them sharp boundaries (4.112).

The correct method in philosophy would really be the following: to say nothing except what can be said, i.e.[3] propositions of natural science—i.e. something which has nothing to do with philosophy—and then, whenever someone else wanted to say something metaphysical, to demonstrate to him that he had failed to give a meaning to certain signs in his propositions. Although it would not be satisfying to the other person—he would not have the feeling that we were teaching him philosophy—*this* method would be the only strictly correct one (6.53).

These iconoclastic claims later met with approval among members of the Vienna Circle, but attempts to get Wittgenstein to join this group proved unsuccessful.

[2] When Wittgenstein speaks of 'philosophy', he is sometimes referring to erroneous philosophy, other people's, sometimes to enlightened philosophy, which here includes that of Russell.

[3] Presumably he meant 'e.g.' rather than 'i.e.'.

The *Tractatus* is normally regarded as a classical statement of the theory known as 'Logical Atomism'. There is however a very important difference between Wittgenstein's apparent position and the theory which Russell devised and christened 'Logical Atomism'.[4] For Russell this was an epistemological as well as metaphysical theory, for it claims that the only ultimate realities are sense-data, the immediate data of sense-perception and introspection, and that all the other things that we talk and think about are 'logical constructions'. Russell's theory was presented as a form of Empiricism, a development of Hume's version. Wittgenstein seems to have taken it for granted (i) that Russell was correct in thinking that our everyday and scientific statements must be analyzable into elementary statements, (ii) that elementary statements must be expressible in an amended version of the logical notation of *Principia Mathematica*. Wittgenstein, however, presented these theses as if it were irrelevant to discuss what is the subject-matter of elementary propositions. His presentation of his truncated version of Logical Atomism is extremely unsystematic. The relevant assertions are scattered throughout the first 45 pages of the *Tractatus*. I shall list what seem to be the most important of these assertions, putting them into some sort of order:

Man possesses the ability to construct languages capable of expressing every sense, *without having any idea how each word has meaning or what its meaning is* . . . Language disguises thought. So much so, that from the outward form of the clothing *it is impossible to infer the form of the thought beneath it* . . . The tacit conventions on which the understanding of everyday language depends are enormously complicated (4.002. My italics).

A proposition has one and only one complete analysis (3.25).

In a proposition a thought can be expressed in such a way that elements of the propositional sign correspond to the objects of thought. I call such elements 'simple signs', and such a proposition 'completely analysed'. The simple signs employed in propositions are called names (3.2 to 3.202).

It is obvious[5] that the analysis of propositions must bring us to ele-

[4] See 'The Philosophy of Logical Atomism', *Monist*, 1918 and 1919, reprinted in *Logic and Knowledge*, ed. R. C. Marsh, 1956.

[5] When Wittgenstein starts with "It is obvious (or clear) that", what follows is usually paradoxical. See also 4.012, 5.542 and 6.42.

mentary propositions which consist of names in immediate combination (4.221).

The simplest proposition, the elementary proposition, asserts the existence of an atomic fact[6] (4.21).

An elementary proposition consists of names. It is a nexus, a concatenation of names (4.22).

An atomic fact is a combination of objects (things) (2.01).

Objects are simple (2.02).

Objects can only be named (3.221).

The name cannot be dissected any further by means of a definition: it is a primitive sign (3.26).

From the existence or non-existence of one atomic fact it is impossible to infer the existence or non-existence of another (2.062).

If all true elementary propositions are listed, the world is completely described (4.26).

A proposition [i.e. a non-elementary proposition] is a truth-function of elementary propositions (5).

All propositions [i.e. non-elementary ones] are results of truth-operations on elementary propositions (5.3).

The italicized clauses in the first of these quotations suggest that Wittgenstein was claiming that when you make a statement, you never have any idea what is meant by the words that you use! His words might be interpreted as making the more moderate claim that you *may* not know the meaning of the words that you use. But the stronger of these claims would seem to be the appropriate interpretation; for, according to the other quoted passages, Wittgenstein was claiming that, whenever you make a statement, your sentence is a shorthand device for asserting the truth or falsity of the members of some collection of elementary propositions, each of which would, *if* anyone could formulate it, have to consist solely of names, each name being a label which uniquely designates a single simple object, an object which can only be named and not described. If this is so, then indeed none of us knows what our statements mean. A

[6] I shall follow Ogden's 1922 translation in rendering "Sachverhalt" as 'atomic fact', rather than 'state of affairs' which Pears and MacGuinness use instead. When Wittgenstein used "Sachverhalt", as he usually did, to refer to a fact corresponding to an elementary proposition, "state of affairs" seems much too vague. The state of the whole universe at a given time could be called 'a state of affairs'.

question which this account would provoke anyone to ask is: what then are these simple objects which form the hidden subject matter of our talk? We are told only that these objects are 'in a manner of speaking . . . colourless' (2.0232), and are 'unalterable' (2.0271); plus a few vague statements such as that the simple objects 'contain the possibility of all situations' (2.014) and '. . . fit into one another like the links of a chain' (2.03). Notice that Wittgenstein gave no indication whether he was thinking of simple objects as particulars or as universals or both. His expositors disagree about how he should be interpreted on this crucial question.

It is not surprising that Russell did not recognize his own theory of Logical Atomism in the *Tractatus*, and wrote in his Introduction: 'Mr. Wittgenstein is concerned with the conditions of a logically perfect language—not that any language is logically perfect'. Presumably Russell drew this conclusion because Wittgenstein showed so little interest in trying to relate his abstruse assertions about language with our actual uses of language, and left his phrase "simple object" an uncashed cheque. Apparently Russell's comment was mistaken, and Wittgenstein's intended subject-matter was *our* languages, German, English, etc. This is indicated by the fact that, in his *Philosophical Investigations* (§§ 90–105), Wittgenstein's description of his *Tractatus* view is incompatible with Russell's interpretation. Thus he criticizes the author of the *Tractatus* for arguing 'as if *our usual forms of expression* were essentially unanalysed; as if there were something hidden in them that had to be brought to light' (§ 91. My italics).

It is not surprising, however, that Russell mistook Wittgenstein's intention, for Wittgenstein says things which make nonsense of his programme of revealing the hidden structure of our everyday and scientific statements; and Russell mentioned some of them in his Introduction, though without comment or criticism. Consider the glaring inconsistency between asserting on the one hand:

It is obvious that the analysis of propositions must bring *us* to elementary propositions which consist of names in immediate combination . . . Even if the world is infinitely complex, so that *every fact consists of infinitely many atomic facts* and *every atomic fact is composed of infinitely many objects*, there would still have to be objects and atomic facts (4.221 and 4.2211. My italics);

and asserting on the other hand: 'The meanings of simple signs (words) must be explained to us if we are to understand them' (4.026). The latter statement shows why the former statements are incompatible with Logical Atomism as an epistemological theory. In the former, Wittgenstein speaks as if it would make no difference to his position if every elementary proposition needed to contain an infinite number of simple signs; though in that case it would be logically impossible for any finite being to formulate any elementary proposition. A critique of 'the logic of our language' could scarely be more cavalier in its logic.

Wittgenstein was not unaware of the difficulties in giving his abstruse theory some possible application. Some of his remarks in the *Notebooks* show that he had worried about this. As candidates for the title of "simple objects" he considered 'points of the visual field' (p. 45) and 'this watch' (p. 60); and he says things like 'presumably the chain of definitions must sometime have an end', and 'the reference of our propositions is not infinitely complicated' (p. 46). Yet in the *Tractatus* he conceals or resolutely dismisses such worries thus:

If we know on purely logical grounds that there must be elementary propositions, then everyone who understands propositions in their unanalysed form must know it. In fact, all the propositions of our everyday language, just as they stand, are in perfect logical order (5.5562).

He thus demonstrates that you and I have always known the truth of his theory, though, according to 4.002, without knowing that we knew it. A philosophical critique of language could scarcely be more *a priori* than that!

There are one or two passages where Wittgenstein, momentarily, takes cognisance of language-uses of people other than mathematical logicians, shows awareness of the difficulties in reconciling these with his deductions, and dismisses the problems with brief and baffling assertions. The problems stem from Wittgenstein's theses that each elementary proposition is logically independent of all other elementary propositions (2.062), and that any non-elementary proposition is a truth-function of elementary propositions (5). What is meant by saying that one proposition, p, is "a truth function of" propositions, x, y and z, is, briefly, that p is a compound proposition which simply asserts the truth or falsity of x and/or y and/or z; so that the truth or falsity of p depends solely upon, and is completely determined by, the truth or falsity of x, y and z.

There are many kinds of everyday statements which cannot be squeezed into the prescribed mould, for example, statements which are expressed in the form "if p, then q". Such statements have been misrepresented by logicians as asserting merely that it is in fact false both that p is true and q is false. This thesis yields absurdities. It implies that any statement of the form "if p, then q" is true, if p is false. Thus 'if the moon is made of cheese, then so and so' would be deemed true whatever we substitute for "so and so", e.g. 'Adolf Hitler will live to be 100' or 'Adolf Hitler is dead'.[7] I shall now consider two short passages where Wittgenstein deals with two other types of statements which cannot be interpreted as truth-functions. First a class of statements which had been discussed by Russell, those which describe the attitude of a person to a proposition, for example that John doubts or believes or hopes or fears that p. Such statements are not truth-functions of p, for their truth or falsity is independent of the truth or falsity of p. Consider how Wittgenstein asserts his way out of the impasse. Referring to 'certain forms of proposition in psychology, such as 'A believes that p is the case' and 'A has the thought that p'', he says:

> if these are considered superficially, it looks as if the proposition p stood in some kind of relation to an object [*sic*] A . . . It is clear [!], however, that 'A believes that p', 'A has the thought that p', and 'A says p' are of the form '"p" says p' (5.541 to 5.542).

The last assertion is supposed not only to solve the problem under discussion, but also to show 'that there is no such thing as the soul—the subject, etc.—as it is conceived in the superficial psychology of the present day' (5.5421).

So far I have followed most translators of the *Tractatus* in rendering "Satz" as 'proposition'. "Satz" is the standard German word for 'sentence' but it may also mean 'statement' or 'proposition', provided that what is stated is expressed in a sentence.

[7] The thesis in question yields other kinds of absurdity; on which I shall not digress, for the one mentioned here is enough to refute it.

As used by Wittgenstein, "Satz" usually needs to be translated as 'proposition' or 'statement', since he ascribes truth or falsity to a 'Satz'. But regarding Wittgenstein's formula ""p" says p", the inverted commas within it indicate that its subject—that which 'says p'—is a sentence which is being mentioned, not a proposition or statement. So what his cryptic solution to his problem amounts to is that "John says or believes that the earth is flat" (a) is used to make a statement of the same form as is ""The earth is flat" says that the earth is flat" (b). Sentence (b) is intelligible if "says that" means 'means that'; but in that case it is an explicit tautology, which no one could ever have occasion to *use*, since it could not convey any information to anyone. In that case it is obvious that (b) is not of the same form as (a); for a statement that John believes or says something is not a tautology. (What Wittgenstein meant here by "of the same form" is not clear, but he could not consistently allow that a tautology and a contingent statement are of the same form.) If, in (b), "says that" is not a synonym for "means that", if it is supposed to have the same function as it does in "John says that . . .", then (b) is surely nonsense. For it is only people who *say things* in the sense of making statements. Sentences do not talk, make statements about the world; they can be *used* to say things only if somebody so uses them.

Wittgenstein's single-sentence solution to Russell's problem involves translating a statement about a person into a statement which makes no reference to that person. Russell was prepared to stomach this when he wrote his Introduction to the *Tractatus*, because he then wished to say that 'persons are fictions', i.e. logical constructions. There is another obvious absurdity in Wittgenstein's proposed solution: that it involves ignoring the many *different* attitudes a person may have to a proposition—the differences between *hoping*, *fearing*, *doubting*, *believing*, etc. Wittgenstein proposed to replace all such verbs with the same verb: ". . . says that . . .", which has to mean '". . ." means that . . .' Yet this would-be solution was treated seriously by many readers of the *Tractatus*, including Russell.

There is another passage where Wittgenstein briefly dismisses difficulties in applying his deductions about the nature of language to an everyday use of language, namely to express value-judgments. His solution is to say:

It [value] must lie outside the world. And so it is impossible for there to be propositions of ethics. Propositions can express nothing of what is higher. It is clear [!] that ethics cannot be put into words. Ethics is transcendental. (Ethics and aesthetics are one and the same.) (6.42 and 6.421.)

These oracular assertions are followed by a few more which are scarcely less mysterious, for example:

If good and bad acts of will do alter the world, it can only be the limits of the world that they alter, not the facts, not what can be expressed by means of language. In short their effect must be that it becomes an altogether different world. It must so to speak wax and wane as a whole (6.43).

We can perhaps grasp what he meant by these statements, in what sense good and bad acts of will make the world wax and wane as a whole. But if ethics, identified with aesthetics, 'cannot be put into words', as Wittgenstein says, presumably he must be using "ethics" in some private sense in which it has nothing to do with the use of words like "ought" or "good" or "wrong"; and since he does not explain this sense, we cannot know what he was talking about. If one took in isolation his statement: 'it is impossible for there to be propositions of ethics', one might interpret this as anticipating the view that moral words have functions other than that of being predicates in true or false statements. But a reader in the early 1920s would have needed a powerful faculty of intuition to see that this was what was meant, in view of the other assertions, especially: 'It is clear that ethics cannot be put into words'.

One of the insights of the *Tractatus*, the theory of Logical Atomism, was derived from Russell. The picture theory of meaning was Wittgenstein's own invention. To indicate how this theory is commonly interpreted, we may consider an account of it by a philosopher whom no one would consider unsympathetic to Wittgenstein, that of Professor Norman Malcolm in his article on Wittgenstein in *The Encyclopedia of Philosophy* (1967, Vol. 8). The italics are mine, to draw attention to things at which the reader should look critically:

What makes it possible for a combination of words to represent a fact in the world? . . . Wittgenstein's explanation consists in the striking idea that a sentence is a picture. *He meant that it is literally a picture, not merely like a picture in certain respects* . . . One would not normally think that a sentence printed on a page is a picture. According to the *Tractatus* it really is a picture, *in the ordinary sense*, of what it represents. Wittgenstein conceived the proof of this to be that although words we have not previously encountered have to be explained to us, when we meet for the first time a sentence that is composed of familiar words, we understand the sentence without further explanation. This can appear to one as a remarkable fact. If it is a fact, the only explanation would be that a sentence shows its sense . . . This is exactly what a picture does . . . Since a *sentence* is held to be a picture there *must* be as many elements to be distinguished *in it* as in the state of affairs it portrays . . . For Wittgenstein meant that our sentences possess a concealed complexity that can be exhibited by analysis . . . A picture can depict reality, but it cannot depict *its own form of representation.* It depicts (represents) its subject from the "outside", but it cannot get outside itself to depict its own form of representation . . . "There must be something identical in a picture and what it depicts, to enable one to be a picture of the other at all" (2.161). *Therefore, logical form*, the form of reality, which all pictures possess, *cannot be depicted by any picture.* This consideration must apply to sentences too . . . *We cannot say how language represents the world* . . . We understand the elements of a sentence and we see how they are combined. *But we cannot say what this combination means.* Yet . . . the sentence shows its meaning.

As described by Malcolm, Wittgenstein's conclusions are surprising and his arguments puzzling; but the puzzles are not of Malcolm's making. On the contrary, his simplified account makes Wittgenstein's arguments appear much less baffling than they are. As Malcolm makes clear, Wittgenstein used his picture simile to derive his cryptic conclusion that language can be used to *show* things which cannot be *said.* Indeed Wittgenstein claimed that 'What *can* be shown *cannot* be said' (4.1212).[8] And this thesis is of crucial importance to him, because it seems to permit his conclusion (6.54) that his own statements in the *Tractatus* are nonsensical, while avoiding the implication that reading the book is a waste of time. He wished us to believe that his book achieves something—showing things which cannot be said about the relationship between language and the world.

[8] This assertion is however contradicted by: 'Propositions show what they say' (4.461). Which illustrates the sort of problems his expositors face when trying to reconcile his assertions.

There is one important feature of Malcolm's exegesis, which would now be rejected by some of Wittgenstein's expositors. Malcolm assumes that the picture theory was meant to apply to all propositions ('sentences'). Some philosophers now accept the interpretation, advocated by Mr. Irving M. Copi, that the picture theory was meant to apply only to elementary propositions (*Mind*, 1958, pp. 145–65). In this respect, Malcolm's interpretation conforms to what Wittgenstein says; Copi's to what Wittgenstein ought to have said to avoid obvious inconsistencies, notably the one to which I drew attention by my italics in quoting Malcolm's statement: 'Since a *sentence* is held to be a picture there *must* be as many elements *in it* as in the state of affairs it portrays'. I shall return to this question after considering what Wittgenstein says.

Wittgenstein misuses his picture simile by means of arguments whose badness is glossed over in Malcolm's exegesis; and indeed in Russell's Introduction, for, surprisingly, Russell refers to these arguments as 'very powerful'. Let us consider what Wittgenstein says in the three relevant passages—2.1 to 2.2; 4.01 to 4.022; 4.12 to 4.1212. In trying to follow Wittgenstein's thought, the primary difficulty is to see what he could have meant by the key phrase "die Form der Abbildung". I shall now quote from Ogden's translation which renders this phrase as 'the form of representation'. Pears and McGuinness translate it as 'pictorial form'. This sounds like an aesthetic term concerned with the Visual Arts, and it seems inappropriate since it is primarily sentences which Wittgenstein refers to as pictures. The phrase "pictorial form" seems to me to camouflage the obscurity of the arguments, and certainly does nothing to illuminate them.

In the passage where Wittgenstein first introduces the picture theory we find a series of assertions about 'the form of representation'. These seem to be irreconcilable.

(i) We are told that the form of representation is the *possibility* that the things depicted are combined with each other as are the elements in the picture (2.151).

(ii) We are told that the form of representation is what is *identical* in both the picture and what it depicts (2.161 and 2.17).

(iii) We are told that a picture's form of representation is 'its standpoint', i.e. a position outside the object depicted (2.173).

(iv) Finally, the form of representation, that which is supposedly identical in the picture and what it depicts, is equated with 'logical form, i.e. the form of reality' (2.18).

Between (ii) and (iii), there is an assertion which is *using*, and not explaining the meaning of, "form of representation": 'The picture, however, cannot depict its form of representation; it shows it forth' (2.172). Although it does not come at the end, this assertion is treated by Wittgenstein as the main conclusion, which the other assertions are presumably supposed to explain and justify. By combining it with (iv), Wittgenstein gets the conclusion which he presents later, that propositions cannot represent logical form.

Is it not astonishing that Wittgenstein should endorse this conclusion in the course of an exposition of Logical Atomism? (I am assuming that the standard interpretation of the *Tractatus* —as, *inter alia*, a version of Logical Atomism—is correct.) This theory claims that the complete analysis of any proposition reveals its logical form. Wittgenstein follows Russell in using "the logical form of a proposition" in this way. (See 4.0031.) For Wittgenstein to deny that it is possible to *say* what is the logical form of a proposition, would be to reject the possibility of achieving the goal of Logical Atomism. And Wittgenstein does deny this. Not in the present passage, where he does not go beyond the innocuous claim that a picture cannot depict *its* form of representation, its own logical form. But Wittgenstein had evidently forgotten the crucial significance of "its (own)", when he drew the following conclusions:

Propositions can represent the whole reality, but they cannot represent what they must have in common with reality in order to be able to represent it—the logical form. *To be able to represent the logical form, we should have to be able to put ourselves with the propositions outside logic, that is outside the world.* Propositions cannot represent the logical form: this mirrors itself in the propositions. That which mirrors itself in language, language cannot represent . . . The propositions *show* the logical form of reality. They exhibit it . . . What *can* be shown *cannot* be said (4.12–4.1212).

Notice that the sentence which I have italicized implies that Russell and Wittgenstein would have to get outside the world in order to achieve the goal of Logical Atomism. For this goal is to provide us with *statements* about the hidden logical form of our everyday or scientific statements; to *state* that the logical form of, e.g., the statement that Pussy is on the mat is so and so, where so and so is what Wittgenstein calls the 'one complete analysis'. Wittgenstein, presumably, did not notice this implication of what he says in 4.12, or he would not have spent so much time discussing the details of the logical notation in which completely analysed propositions should be *stated*. Wittgenstein used his picture simile to draw a conclusion which makes nonsense of Logical Atomism. Though Malcolm does not acknowledge this implication of what Wittgenstein says in 4.12, his interpretation seems to conform with mine. Malcolm's gloss, quoted above, reads: 'it [a picture] cannot get outside itself to depict its own form of representation. Therefore, logical form, the form of reality, which all pictures must possess, cannot be depicted in any picture. This consideration must apply to sentences too'. It should now be clear why I italicized Malcolm's "Therefore" and "any" when quoting this passage earlier.

The fallacy in Wittgenstein's reasoning is obvious. Because a sentence cannot be used to state *its own* logical form, it does not follow that the logical form of the statement it is used to make cannot be stated by means of other sentences, or nonverbal symbols. Wittgenstein could not have made this error, if he had pursued the implications of his picture simile, or had given any clear meaning to "the form of representation". Suppose that we use "picture" to mean picture. What meaning might we then give to "the form of representation"? We might so use it that each of the following would be said to employ different forms of representation:

(a) Pictures which depict a distant man and a nearby man as equally large, etc., and (b) pictures which conform with the so-called laws of perspective.

(a) Single-line outline drawings, (b) monochromatic pictures, and (c) paintings which reproduce all the colours of what is depicted. (And this interpretation is suggested by 2.17 and 2.171.)

(a) Maps which depict the world's surface on a rectangle, (b) those which depict it on two flat circles, and (c) maps drawn on a globe. (And this interpretation is suggested by 4.0141.)

In each of these examples, although, of course, a picture cannot depict its own form of representation, it does not follow that different forms of representation cannot be depicted in a picture. Take my second example. One could produce a large picture, containing in the foreground three easels, each bearing a picture of the multi-coloured objects in the background of this picture, one of the three being an outline drawing, one monochromatic, and one reproducing the colours of the objects in the background. Here, one picture depicts three pictures and the objects depicted by each, and thus depicts three different forms of representation. Similarly one sentence can contain, and be used to make statements about, one or more other sentences. Malcolm presents Wittgenstein's conclusion as being: 'We cannot say what this combination [of words in a sentence] means'. But teachers, linguists and philosophers are forever making statements about the meaning of other statements; and philosophers frequently make statements about the logical forms of statements. And so does Wittgenstein in the *Tractatus*; for example, when he says: 'In a proposition there must be exactly as many distinguishable parts as in the situation that it represents' (4.04). This statement is about the relationship between language and the world, and about *logical form* in the sense in which Wittgenstein usually used this phrase. As Russell said, 'Mr. Wittgenstein manages to say a good deal about what cannot be said' (*Tractatus*, 1922, p. 22).

If anyone thinks it possible to salvage Wittgenstein's picture theory of meaning or to extract from it any important insights, his first task, I suggest, should be to try to find some one clear meaning for "the form of representation" which makes sense of the passages where Wittgenstein uses this expression. Should he succeed, he will still have formidable problems, notably to make sense of the third passage in which Wittgenstein makes use of his picture simile:

> The gramophone record, the musical thought, the score, the waves of sound, all stand to one another in *that pictorial internal relation* which holds between language and the world. To all of them *the logical structure* is common . . . In the fact that there is a general rule by which the musician is able to read the symphony out of the score, and that there is a rule by which one could reconstruct the symphony from the line of a gramophone record . . . herein lies *the internal simi-*

larity between these things which at first sight seem to be entirely different. And the rule is the law of projection which projects the symphony into the language of the musical score. It is the rule of translation of this language into *the language of the gramophone record* (4.014 and 4.0141. My italics).

Mr. J. O. Urmson considers that from this passage 'we can learn a great deal about what was meant by 'picturing'' (*Philosophical Analysis*, p. 88). This was clearly Wittgenstein's intention, for this passage is preceded and followed by the assertion: 'A proposition is a picture of reality' (4.01 and 4.021). It seems to me, however, that all that it shows clearly are the following serious confusions in Wittgenstein's thought. (i) He uses "language" indiscriminately. A musical score, like English, is a system of symbols which, by conventions, signify or represent things or operations; but undulations in the groove of a gramophone record are *not* a language—not symbols for representing sounds, but a mechanism for producing sounds. (ii) He confuses (*a*) rules (conventions) by which symbols signify things and, parasitic on these, rules for translating from one system of symbols to another, with (*b*) causal connections (laws) involving things other than symbols, e.g. those involved in the process of making a gramophone recording or of producing musical sounds by playing a record. (iii) He abuses "logic", by applying "logical structure" to the physical structure of things, e.g. of sound-waves and the groove of a record. (iv) He equates 'the pictorial internal relation . . . between language and the world', and 'logical structure' which is said to be common to language and the world, with 'the internal *similarity* between things', i.e. between symbols and what they signify. Yet he says that the so-called internal similarity *consists* ('herein lies') in there being 'rules for translation' or 'laws for projection'. Now since he uses the latter phrases to include semantic rules, rules for applying symbols to whatever they are, by convention, applicable, this passage does throw light, not on what he *meant* by "picturing", but on what his use amounts to. For this passage reveals that all it comes to is that a sentence is said by Wittgenstein to 'picture' whatever it is conventionally used to signify. Wittgenstein cannot of course have recognized this, or he would not have thought that exciting, or indeed any, conclusions could be drawn from assimilating 'Sätze' and pictures.

It seems gratuitous to argue, as Urmson does, that what Wittgenstein meant by "the internal similarity" between a sentence and what it signifies must be *more* than 'some rule . . . for determining the fact which it states', namely 'something more like intuitively recognizable similarity of structure' (*Philosophical Analysis*, p. 90). In that case, one would have to interpret the picture theory as applying only to elementary propositions; and Urmson rejects this interpretation (p. 93); which is, however, taken for granted in several recent commentaries, including those by Stenius and Black. Black says, as if it were obvious and universally agreed: 'Wittgenstein's final account of the nature of language divides into two parts—the 'picture theory' of elementary propositions, and the 'truth-function theory' of complex propositions' (*Companion*, p. 11). There is an overwhelming case for arguing that this is what Wittgenstein *should* have said. Consider his statement: 'In a proposition there must be exactly as many distinguishable parts as in the situation that it represents' (4.04). If this is what he meant by his less precise statements, 2.13 and 2.131, when he is first introducing his picture theory, the latter should have been applied only to elementary propositions; for only of them could he claim a one-one correlation between the 'elements of a picture' and the corresponding 'simple objects'. It is not surprising, however, that Wittgenstein has commonly been interpreted, e.g. by Ramsey, Urmson, Anscombe and Malcolm, as intending his picture theory to apply to all propositions. For nowhere in the *Tractatus* does he say that the picture theory applies only to elementary propositions, and he frequently says things which clearly imply the opposite. Consider these statements:

A proposition is a picture of reality. A proposition is a model of reality as we imagine it. At first sight a proposition—one set out on the printed page, for example—does not seem to be a picture of the reality with which it is concerned. But no more does musical notation at first sight seem to be a picture of music, nor our phonetic notation (the alphabet) to be a picture of our speech. And yet these sign-languages prove to be pictures, even in the ordinary sense, of what they represent (4.01 and 4.011);

. . . we understand the sense of a propositional sign without its having been explained to us. A proposition is a picture of reality: for if I understand a proposition, I know the situation it represents. And I understand the proposition without having had its sense explained to me (4.02 and 4.021);

Reality is compared with propositions. A proposition can be true or false only in virtue of being a picture of reality (4.05 and 4.06).

Obviously Wittgenstein could not have *intended* such statements to apply only to elementary propositions; it would be so misleading to speak as if we come across the latter 'on the printed page' and understand them without explanation. If one reconstructs the *Tractatus* theory of language as Black does, one must admit, as Black does, that the picture theory is about 'a never-never language', since 'we can produce no elementary propositions and would not recognize them if we had them' (*Companion*, p. 11). But in that case the picture theory no longer has any philosophical interest. If it is not about *our* languages, everyday or scientific, but about a never-never language, it is impossible to use it to set a limit to the expression of our thoughts in language; which Wittgenstein says, in the Preface, is the aim of the book. This point needs emphasis, for it is becoming common for Wittgensteinian scholars to take it for granted that the picture theory was intended to apply only to elementary propositions. Thus Mr. George Pitcher speaks of 'Wittgenstein's insistence that propositions *as ordinarily expressed* are not, in that form, pictures of the situations they describe'; to which clause he appends the footnote: 'Although Wittgenstein sometimes talks as if they were—for example in T. 4.011' (*The Philosophy of Wittgenstein*, 1964, pp. 80–1. His italics). I cannot find any statement in the *Tractatus* where Wittgenstein says what Pitcher says he *insists* on. Nor, apparently, can Pitcher, for the only evidence he offers for the alleged insistence is a single statement from the *Notebooks*: 'First and foremost the elementary propositional form must portray; all portrayal takes place through it.' Admittedly this can be interpreted as it is by Pitcher, but it is less explicit than the statements from the *Tractatus* which I have quoted.

I find it surprising that Russell should have judged 'very powerful' the arguments for mysticism which Wittgenstein derived from his picture simile. It would appear that Russell did not then pause to analyse these arguments. Perhaps he accepted them at their face value because he was much impressed by other things in the *Tractatus*, notably some pertinent criticisms of his own logical notation, e.g. of his sign for "is identical with", and, more important, Wittgenstein's thesis that all necessary propositions are tautologies. The latter must, presumably, have struck Russell as a revelation or a revolution. For Russell had earlier conceived of the subject-matter of logic and mathematics as the contents of a Platonic other world. (See, for example, Chapters IX and X of *The Problems of Philosophy*, 1912). In a book written in prison during the war, Russell had written:

The importance of "tautology" for a definition of mathematics was pointed out to me by my former pupil Ludwig Wittgenstein (*Introduction to Mathematical Philosophy*, 1919, p. 205).

But Russell evidently did not recognize the full implications of Wittgenstein's iconoclastic thesis until he read the *Tractatus*, for he had also written, whilst in prison:

Logic is concerned with the real world just as truly as zoology, though with its more abstract and general features (op. cit., p. 169).

This last statement was omitted from later editions of Russell's *Introduction*. This suggests that Wittgenstein's thesis released Russell both from the spell of Platonism and from a tendency to treat logical truths as *very* general empirical generalizations.[9]

That all necessary truths are analytic propositions, which unfold the (often unforeseen) implications of what men have packed into definitions, is a very important thesis. Its formula-

[9] I invited Earl Russell to comment on my conjectural explanation of the fact that he had formed such a high opinion of the *Tractatus* when he first read it. In his reply, dated 20th December 1968, he describes this explanation as 'very sound'. But what he says next indicates that he did not regard Wittgenstein's thesis as a *welcome* release: 'I felt a violent repulsion to the suggestion that "all mathematics is tautology". I came to believe this but I did not like it. I thought that mathematics was a splendid edifice, but this shows that it was built on sand'. If I may say so, with respect, I suspect that Russell may have been unduly influenced by the pejorative flavour of "tautology"; which suggests triviality, a *mere* repetition in other words or symbols of what has already been said. "Analytic truth (proposition or statement)" is more neutral. Surely mathematics (or *Principia Mathematica*) is no less splendid an edifice because it comprises analytic truths derived from its definitions, which, though not the only possible starting points, are still not arbitrary; and because it is something which men have *constructed*, rather than being a description of what they have *observed* by a non-sensuous kind of cognition. Rather the opposite. Russell also writes in this letter, referring to Wittgenstein's *Tractatus*: 'I did not appreciate that his work implied a linguistic philosophy. When I did, we parted company'.

tion by Wittgenstein was a major contribution to a critique of language (though not a new idea, for it was presented by Hume in psychological dress). This thesis is now an axiom for most empiricists; including myself, *provided that the necessary qualifications are made*. These would include: (i) that we should not assume that if a sentence is analytic at all, it is analytic for all, for 'us'; since it may be analytic as used by me but not as used by you; (ii) that a person's use of a sentence may not be sufficiently precise to enable anyone to give a definite answer to the question: 'Is it analytic for him?' So far as I can see, Wittgenstein's thesis that all necessary propositions are tautologies is the *only* viable contribution to a critique of language to be found in the *Tractatus*.

My selective critique of this remarkable book has not conveyed many of its qualities, e.g. the dramatic impact and mystical aura of many of its more startling assertions; such as:

A proposition can determine only one place in logical space; nevertheless the whole of logical space must already be given by it (3.42);

To give the essence of a proposition means to give the essence of all description, and thus the essence of the world (5.4711);

Logic is prior to every experience (5.552);

Logic fills (erfüllt) the world (5.61);

Logic is transcendental(6.13)

No other philosopher can match Wittgenstein's imaginativeness in using the word "logic". In the Preface he wrote:

the *truth* of the thoughts communicated here seems to me unassailable and definitive. I am, therefore, of the opinion that the problems have in essentials been finally solved.

He also wrote here 'What can be said at all can be said clearly'.

SECTION XIV

Wittgenstein's Later Accounts of Language and of Philosophy

MY MAIN aim in discussing the *Philosophical Investigations*, as it was in discussing the *Tractatus*, is to consider the kind of linguistic study which is equated with philosophy, and to compare this account of philosophy with what Wittgenstein actually does when presumably intending to practise his recommended methods. It will be argued that most of the conclusions which Wittgenstein draws or suggests are not and could not be established by the methods which he commends. One of the difficulties in interpreting the *Investigations* is that it contains many scraps of imaginary dialogue, with both participants speaking in the first person, and sometimes no indication as to which of them is expressing Wittgenstein's current view. Another difficulty is that the reader is so often left to guess the connection, if any, between adjacent remarks, the point of the examples, etc. The philosophers who are most confident that they can read between his lines often disagree widely and vehemently. Wittgenstein's words will be quoted frequently, in order to minimize the perils of paraphrasing; which may be illustrated by Professor Malcolm's rendering of '. . . is none too easy a thing to do' (§ 302), first by 'is a contradiction' and later by 'is unintelligible.'[1]

It would be nearly correct, though misleading, to say that the same conception of philosophy is endorsed in the *Tractatus* and the *Investigations*. This would be correct insofar as both works treat language as the subject-matter of philosophy and claim that the function of philosophy is to eliminate the nonsense, to cure the confusions, produced by earlier philosophers

[1] Malcolm's review of the *Investigations*, reprinted in Mr. G. Pitcher's anthology *Wittgenstein: The Philosophical Investigations*, 1966, pp. 75–6. This review appeared originally in *Phil. Review*, 1954, and was also reprinted in Malcolm's *Knowledge and Certainty*, 1963. When mentioning this review, my page-references will be to Pitcher's anthology.

through their misunderstandings of language: of 'the logic of our language' (*Tractatus*), of the 'grammar' or the 'rules' of language (*Investigations*). But the rôle of philosophers in 'elucidating' what people say officially drops out in the *Investigations*, or at any rate the kind of elucidation envisaged in the *Tractatus*, i.e. so-called logical analysis. It would, however, be misleading to say that the *Tractatus* and the *Investigations* share the same conception of philosophy; for according to the *Investigations* the subject-matter of philosophy really is language and not the logical vacuum of the *Tractatus*; and this makes a vast difference to the kind of study which Wittgenstein commends as philosophy. The *Investigations* equates philosophy with a kind of empirical linguistics, whose subject-matter is things that people actually say and really do with language. One of the new maxims is 'don't think, but look' (§ 66). The revolution in Wittgenstein's thought was mainly due to his acknowledging that a philosopher concerned with language should consider how it *is* used.

One way of classifying the contents of the *Investigation* is:

(1) criticisms of the *Tractatus*,
(2) the new account of language,
(3) the new account of philosophy,
(4) the application of the new philosophical method.

This will be my order for discussion, and to a large extent it is Wittgenstein's too; but he never segregated different topics, and discussion of any one of his themes involves culling and comparing remarks from all over the book. The first three of these topics will be considered in this section.

Criticisms of the Tractatus

(1) Wittgenstein repudiates the error which he had formulated in the *Tractatus* by saying: 'A name means an object. The object is its meaning' (3.203). What he now criticizes is the more general thesis, attributed to Augustine, that the meaning of any word is the object for which it stands (§ 1). This fallacy has misled many philosophers from Plato on. Wittgenstein has no difficulty in showing that it is a fallacy, e.g. for words like "five" (§ 1), "here" and "this" (§ 8) and for 'exclamations'

(§ 27). He asserts that different uses of words are 'absolutely unlike' (§ 10).

(2) The assumption of the *Tractatus* that the ultimate constituents of 'facts', and therefore of the world, are 'simple objects', is repudiated in an important passage (§§ 46–8). Wittgenstein argues here that the notion of absolute simplicity is vacuous; that our application of the correlative terms "simple" and "composite" varies with the context: 'We use the word "composite" (and therefore . . . "simple") in an enormous number of different and differently-related ways' (§ 47). This is an important insight about a pervasive error. Locke's attempt to define "simple idea" was a manifest failure, yet many later philosophers, including Russell and Moore, used the 'simple–complex' dichotomy uncritically to play a key rôle in their theories.

(3) Wittgenstein repudiates the whole conception of logical analysis on which the *Tractatus* was based—the view that 'a proposition has one and only one complete analysis' (3.25), the assumption that all of our statements have a hidden structure, that of a logical calculus. The most important passages in the *Investigations* on this are paragraphs 81 and 88 to 107. He describes his own former vision about language thus: 'it may come to look as if there were something like a final analysis of our forms of language . . . as if there were something hidden in them that had to be brought to light (§ 91); 'The strict and clear rules of the logical structure of propositions appear to us as something in the background—hidden in the medium of the understanding' (§ 102). He asks: 'Where does this idea come from?' and answers: 'It is like a pair of glasses on our nose through which we see whatever we look at. It never occurs to us to take them off' (§ 103). Now, having removed those spectacles, he declares that 'we must stick to the subjects of our everyday thinking' (§ 106) and examine 'actual language' (§ 107).

(4) In the *Tractatus* Wittgenstein had argued as if, apart from his own use of it to 'show' things that cannot be 'said', language is used only for one purpose, making true or false statements, asserting facts. This view is emphatically repudiated, and it is to eradicate this view that his similes between language and tools and games are introduced.

The New Account of Language

The main themes are the variety of our uses of language, the need for a student of language to consider our utterances not in isolation but in their context, and the definition of "meaning" in terms of "use". 'For a large class of cases—though not for all—in which we employ the word "meaning" it can be defined thus: the meaning of a word is its use in the language' (§ 43). We are never told what Wittgenstein thinks are the exceptions; and though this statement is offered as a definition of "the meaning of a *word*", Wittgenstein sometimes speaks of the use or employment of sentences, and apparently he wished to equate their meanings with their uses. 'Look at the sentence as an instrument and at its sense as its employment' (§ 421). The tool-kit simile is introduced early to remind us of the variety of uses of words: 'Think of the tools in a tool-box: there is a hammer, pliers, a saw, a screw-driver, a rule, a glue-pot, glue, nails and screws. The functions of words are as diverse as the functions of these objects' (§ 11). The term "language-game" had already been introduced in paragraph 7, but from the start it is used very ambiguously. In introducing this term, Wittgenstein tells us that he will use it in three apparently different ways—to refer to (a) 'those games by means of which children learn their native language', or (b) 'a primitive language', or (c) 'the whole, consisting of language *and the actions into which it is woven*' (§ 7. My italics). By "a primitive language", Wittgenstein seems to mean not any actual primitive language, but imaginary, extremely simple, language-uses, such as that of the builder described in § 2, which contains only four words and in which uttering "Slab" functions as 'Bring me a slab'. The third use of "language-game" is stretched even further in § 16: which implies that a 'language-game' is to include not only the actions of the people into which the language is woven, but also the things which they use in performing such actions—for Wittgenstein says that it 'causes least confusion' to include among 'the instruments of language' cards used as colour samples (cf. § 1). So stretched, the 'language-game' of cricket will include the bats, ball, pavilion clock, etc. When he is thinking on these lines Wittgenstein speaks of a language as 'a form of life' (§ 19. Cf. § 226).

Wittgenstein's use of "language-game" is, however, reduced

to confusion by what he says in § 23, where he uses this term in a way that does not correspond to any of his earlier statements of intent:

> But how many kinds of sentences are there?—There are *countless* kinds . . . And this multiplicity is not something fixed, given once for all; but new types of language, new language-games . . . come into existence, and others become obsolete . . . Review the multiplicity of language-games in the following examples, and in others:
>
> Giving orders, and obeying them—
> Describing the appearance of an object, or giving its measurements—
> Constructing an object from a description (a drawing)—
> Reporting an event—
> Speculating about an event—
> Forming and testing a hypothesis—
> Presenting the results of an experiment in tables and diagrams—
> Making up a story; and reading it—
> Play-acting—
> Singing catches—
> Guessing riddles—
> Making a joke; telling it—
> Solving a problem in practical arithmetic—
> Translating from one language into another—
> Asking, thanking, cursing, greeting, praying.

This is bewildering. He started this paragraph by talking about different 'kinds of sentences', which he then equates with different 'language-games'. Yet he includes in his list making an object from a drawing, which need not involve using language at all. What his examples illustrate are the different *functions* of a sentence, the different *purposes* for which a sentence may be used. The same sentence can be used for many different purposes of the kinds which Wittgenstein here illustrates. "Would you like to go to Timbuctoo?" may be used as an invitation, a request for information, a polite way of giving an order, a joke, a translation, a way of teasing, etc. What has happened is that Wittgenstein has telescoped the game-simile and the tool-simile. The point of the tool-simile had seemed clear in § 11—to draw our attention to the different purposes for which we use words (or sentences). In § 23, Wittgenstein speaks as if each of the countless different purposes for which one can use a sentence is a different language-game! This telescoping of the two so different similes has generated much confusion in the thought of Wittgenstein, and of others. Apparently they have not noticed that these similes pull in opposite directions. (More about this later.)

Wittgenstein seems to acknowledge that he has been playing fast and loose with the game-simile, when he says, on behalf of his imaginary critic: 'You talk about all sorts of language-games, but have nowhere said what the essence of a language-game, and hence of language, is: what is common to all these activities and what makes them into language or parts of language'. His answer is: 'this is true.—Instead of producing something common to all that we call language, I am saying that these phenomena have no one thing in common which makes us use the same word for all,—but that they are *related* to one another in many different ways' (§ 65). He proceeds to offer his celebrated account of 'family resemblances' (§§ 66–7). He argues that there is nothing common to the activities which we call 'languages', just as there is nothing common to the activities we call 'games' or the things we call 'numbers'; that when we survey and compare different games, we find only 'a complicated network of similarities overlapping and criss-crossing', as in the case of the resemblances between members of a family; and that we extend a concept 'as in spinning a thread we twist fibre on fibre. And the strength of the thread does not reside in the fact that some one fibre runs through its whole length, but in the overlapping of many fibres' (§ 67). He draws the conclusion that the extension of a concept is '*not* closed by a frontier' (§ 68), that we 'do not know the boundaries because none have been drawn' (§ 69).

Notice that in this passage Wittgenstein again uses two similes which pull in opposite directions. Had he confined himself to the analogy between the similarities between the things to which we give the same name and 'the various resemblances between members of a family', this would strongly suggest what is called a resemblance theory of universals, i.e., briefly, that the function of a general (descriptive) word is to indicate some specifiable respect(s) in which the things so called resemble each other. But his spinning a thread simile, if developed, undermines the possibility of any coherent version of a resemblance theory of universals. In the latter simile, each of the overlapping fibres must presumably represent resemblance in some single respect. Then Wittgenstein's account of how we extend our concepts (extend the application of words) can be schematized thus:

Let X represent a word like "game" or "language" or "number".

Let X_1, X_2, etc., represent different types of things to which we apply X.

Let a, b, c, etc., represent resemblances in a single respect. Then the situation, according to Wittgenstein's account is this:

X_1 is like X_2 in respects a b c
X_2 is like X_3 in respects b c d
X_3 is like X_4 in respects c d e
X_4 is like X_5 in respects d e f
and so on.

Here b, c, d and e run through a certain 'length of the thread', but a and f do not; and there is no resemblance between, nothing common to, some types of things called 'X', e.g. X_1 and X_5.[2]

What Wittgenstein says here *seems* to be intended to apply not merely to a minority of words, to slippery customers like "game", but to descriptive words in general. For he uses his account of "game" to illustrate the indeterminacy of linguistic rules in general: 'the application of a word is not everywhere bounded by rules' (§ 84). In that case Wittgenstein seems to be committed to an unacceptable form of Nominalism. In rejecting earlier the view that the meaning of a word is 'the object for which it stands', he rejected by implication what have traditionally been called Realist theories of universals. Wittgenstein's second simile would preclude any coherent version of a resemblance theory, by denying that there is or need be *any* resemblance, *anything* 'in common', between *all* the things to which a general word is applied; and by asserting that there are *no* limits to the 'extension of a concept'. According to the

[2] This implication of the thread simile conforms with Wittgenstein's claim (§65) that there is nothing common to the things which we call 'games' or 'languages', etc.

second simile, we are free to extend the application of "game" as follows:

Shooting pheasants is like playing football in some respects, and so may be called 'a game';
The trapping of insects by a sundew is like shooting pheasants in some respects, and so may be called 'a game';
The eruption of a volcano is like the trapping of insects by a sundew in some respects, and so may be called 'a game'.

If we did permit our 'concepts' to be extended in this manner it would produce linguistic anarchy. Indeed Wittgenstein's account implies that our language is already in this state. But Wittgenstein fails to draw the crucial distinction between cases where a word is being used in the same sense and cases where it is being used in different senses; fails to acknowledge that one is applying a word to two sets of things in the same sense, if and only if there is *some* resemblance between them which one could describe or somehow indicate as the ground for applying the word to both sets.[3] And although he denies that there is anything common to, any resemblance between, games in the sense in which he is using "games", he is conspicuously inconsistent, for the use to which he puts his simile between languages and games involves assuming that games *are* alike, in that they *are played* and that they involve *following rules*. If he had acknowledged this, he would be entitled to say that the reaction of a sundew or a volcano cannot be called 'a game', in the sense in which he is using this word. As it is, he leaves himself unable to give any reason for not extending thus the application of "game". His remarks in the passages which have just been discussed would commit him to a form of Nominalism which permits anything to be called by any word, provided we can find *some* respect in which it resembles *any*thing to which this word is already applied! Wittgenstein does not seem to have thought out the traditional problems concerning so-called universals. At any rate he never makes it clear what solution he wished to adopt. His failure to do this is one of the most serious gaps in his account of language, and, as we shall see later, it is a source of serious confusion in his thought. It also affects the

[3] Otherwise the word is not being used to express *the same* 'concept'.

Tractatus, where he failed to raise the question whether his 'simple signs' are supposed to be proper names or common names.

Without acknowledging that he is doing so, Wittgenstein does treat their being played and their involving the following of rules as *common features* of games. It is in these respects that he assimilates games and the uses of language. He is led to speak of any language-use as *playing* a language-game; which is scarcely appropriate since "play" is contrasted with "work", and we sometimes use words for serious purposes. The feature of his simile which he emphasizes most is that both games and languages involve following rules. But though he frequently invites us to compare the so-called rules of language with games-rules, his own remarks on this do not generate much light. He argues that language-rules and games-rules are alike in not legislating in advance for all contingencies. He draws a parallel between the fact that no boundary has been drawn for the application of the words "game" or "number", and the fact that there are no 'rules for how high one throws the ball in tennis' (§ 68). This is not a happy comparison. It would be pointless, because unenforceable, to make rules about this, or about how much tennis players may perspire. Games-rules are designed with certain purposes in view, the chief of which *is* to try to legislate in advance for all contingencies which could give rise to dissension. If a games-rule is found in practice to be arbitrary or ambiguous in its application, it is revised to try to avoid this. The rules of charades are not imprecise because they prescribe only that each team shall play-act each successive syllable of the word-to-be-guessed, and thus leave endless scope for antics and exhibitionism—leaving scope for this is the purpose of this game.

The game most often referred to by Wittgenstein in trying to throw light on language is chess. But the rules of chess are fixed, and they specify precisely all of the kinds of move which are forbidden, and in these respects they are *un*like rules of language. Another respect in which Wittgenstein's simile between language-rules and games-rules is seriously misleading is that it leads Wittgenstein to speak as if language-rules were prescriptive. Thus, in a passage where he is assimilating language-rules and rules of chess, he says: 'Following a rule is like obeying an order' (§ 206). Games-rules are indeed prescriptive. A player who breaks the rules, even if the game be solitaire, is not playing the game, in both the literal and the metaphorical sense of "playing the game". Wittgenstein's analogy between games-rules and language-rules will, of course, seem apt to anyone who does think that language-rules are prescriptive, and this is what Ryle found most instructive in Wittgenstein's analogy between speaking and playing chess. (See 'The Theory of Meaning', *British Philosophy in the Mid-Century*, ed. C. A. Mace, 1957, p. 255.)

Others may think it more appropriate to speak of linguistic *conventions* or *habits* or *customs*, rather than of *rules*; and in any case they may find Wittgenstein's remarks about linguistic rules tantalizingly vague, and may wonder just how he would have formulated the sort of rules he has in mind. As Heath has said:

> 'syntactical, semantical, social and other so-called "rules" are all amalgamated together under the monistic heading of "use"', and Wittgenstein 'appears content to oscillate, at his own convenience, between uses of "use" suggesting the protean mutability of *speech* according to occasion and context, and . . . the procrustean rigidity of *language* as a public institution' (*Phil. Quarterly*, Jan. 1956, pp. 68–9).

This ambivalence is a natural result of Wittgenstein's fusion of the tool-simile and the game-simile (§ 23). *Playing games does involve obeying prescriptive rules, whereas using the contents of a tool-kit does not.* Wittgenstein assimilates using language to both of these different kinds of activity, without making it clear in which respects it is like, and unlike, each. Hence his oscillation between speaking as if language-rules are prescriptive and precise like the rules of chess, and as if they are as permissive and pliable as the 'rules' for using a knife or a crowbar.

Wittgenstein now repudiates his *Tractatus* view that language-rules are, or are like, the fixed and exact rules of a logical calculus (§§ 81 and 91), but ironically some of the chief examples he uses to illustrate what we mean by "following" or "understanding" a language-rule involve reference to the rules of a calculus. The calculus in question is one whose rules are fixed, precise, unambiguous and understood by all except savages and small children, namely simple arithmetic. From these examples Wittgenstein somehow arrives at two cryptic conclusions which play a crucial rôle in the sequel: 'it is not possible to obey a rule "privately"' (§ 202), and 'The use of the word "rule" and the use of the word "same" are interwoven', that "same" is defined in terms of following a rule, as "proposition" is defined in terms of truth (§ 225). Wittgenstein oscillates between two *very* different kinds of arithmetical examples, but without acknowledging their difference:

(1) In the first type of case, one person, A, sets a problem for another, B, namely 'to write down a series of signs [i.e. numbers] according to a certain formation rule' (§ 143[4], and after digressions §§ 185 ff.). Here, B is given some specific rule for the construction of a series of numbers, e.g. $2x+1$, and to test whether he understands this rule, he is asked to write out the corresponding series.

(2) In the second type of case, B is set a completely different task: 'A writes a series of numbers down; B watches him and tries to find a law for the sequence of numbers' (§§ 151 ff., and after digressions §§ 179 ff.). Here, of course, it is wholly inappropriate to speak of '*the* rule for *the* series', since this would imply that there is only one way of continuing systematically the three or four numbers which A has written down; and this is false, unless "the rule for the series" means the rule which A intended, had in mind, when he wrote down the three or four digits. But Wittgenstein certainly did not intend "the rule for the series" to be so interpreted, for one of the things he uses his arithmetical examples to try to show is that A's unspoken thoughts and intentions are irrelevant to answering the question what 'the rule' is. In discussing his second kind of example, Wittgenstein starts by describing B's problem appropriately as 'trying to find *a* law for the sequence', but proceeds, inconsistently, to refer to 'the series' of which the written numbers are a segment and to speak of 'the principle of the series' (§§ 151–2). (He uses "rule", "principle", "law" and "formula" interchangeably to refer to a construction-rule.)

Wittgenstein evidently confused his two kinds of arithmetical

[4] In §143, Wittgenstein then changes the subject, and proceeds to discuss how a child is taught from scratch to write out the series of natural numbers.

example, overlooked the differences in the problems set for B.[5] When he returns (§ 185) to the type of problem which he first introduced, he starts by saying that 'the pupil [B] has mastered the series of natural numbers'. He then supposes that B is given a specific construction-rule, to start with zero and make a series by adding 2 to each successive member; and that B does so correctly up to 1000—and then writes down 1004, 1008, 1112! But this is inconsistent with his statement that B has 'mastered the series of natural numbers'. The use to which Wittgenstein puts this odd example is to manufacture a paradox—that the steps in such arithmetical series are not determined by the construction-rule. Indeed, he proceeds to speak as if this paradox applies to all rules, including rules of chess and linguistic rules: 'This was our paradox: no course of action could be determined by a rule, because every course of action can be made to conform with the rule' (§ 201).[6] It is to remove this paradox that he produces his dictum that 'it is not possible to obey a rule 'privately''.

In the tangled arguments which led to this conclusion, Wittgenstein fails to distinguish the two *very* different questions:

(a) Whether, in a calculus like simple arithmetic, a rule for constructing a series *determines* the contents of the series? To which the answer is certainly affirmative for the sort of rules Wittgenstein mentions, like 'Keep on adding 2'.

(b) How are children *taught* the rules of arithmetic? To which Wittgenstein gives the unexceptionable answer—by training and practice (§§ 143–5, 189).

Yet Wittgenstein argues as if his answer to question (b) requires us to give a negative answer to question (a); because he confused the two different kinds of arithmetical problem which A set for B, and because, in the second type of problem, the way

[5] In *The Brown Book* (pp. 141–3), Wittgenstein used the first kind of arithmetical example, without confusing it with the second. He then used it simply to make the point that if a teacher told a pupil to form a series by adding one, the sense in which he *meant* the pupil to write 101 after 100, and 1569 after 1568, is given by the hypothetical statement: 'Had you asked me before what I wanted you to do at that stage, I should have said . . .' (p. 142). Cf. *PI* § 187.

[6] The most that his arithmetical examples had shown is that the same 'course of action' can be subsumed under different rules, *not* that different courses of action can comply with a given rule.

in which a sequence of digits should be continued is, from B's viewpoint, indeterminate, even when B *has* mastered the rules of arithmetic.

How odd that Wittgenstein should try to convey what it is like to follow linguistic rules by discussing the rules of a calculus, though one of his main theses is now that linguistic rules are *not* like the rules of a calculus. How astonishing that he should assert that *the* use of "same" (as if there were only one) is logically tied to *the* use of "rule" (as if there were only one) by appealing to the special use of "same" when one says 'go on doing the same thing' as an instruction to someone to continue an arithmetical series! That this is how Wittgenstein was thinking is shown by what he adds to his second cryptic conclusion: 'The use of the word "rule" and the use of the word "same" are interwoven. (As are the use of "proposition" and the use of "true".)', namely:

> Suppose someone gets the series of numbers 1, 3, 5, 7, . . . by working out the series [determined by the rule] $2x+1$. And now he asks himself: "But am I always doing the same thing, or something different every time?" (§§ 225–6).

The passages which I have just criticized are among those which Strawson has praised as being 'of great brilliance and clarity' (*Mind*, 1954, p. 78). (If others have felt qualms about Wittgenstein's reasoning therein, they seem to have suppressed them.) Philosophers who claim to understand Wittgenstein's thought, find in his arithmetical examples justification for premises from which he later derives his paradoxical theses concerning 'a private language'. Thus Professor Malcolm writes that in these examples 'he forges a remarkably illuminating connection between the philosophy of psychology and the philosophy of mathematics'. (Malcolm's review of the *Investigations*, p. 70). What I find illuminating is that Wittgenstein confuses the questions 'How *do* we use it?' and 'How did we *learn* to use it?', *both* when discussing expressions like "Add 2" or "$2x+1$" *and* when discussing expressions like "in pain".[7] I shall say more about this in the next two sections.

[7] Notice how, in § 189, Wittgenstein answers '*How* is it used?' by saying 'people are so trained . . .'.

The New Account of Philosophy

I have already cited some of Wittgenstein's most surprising assertions telling us that philosophy may only describe and not explain the workings of language, must leave everything as it is, and has no concern with anything which is hidden (§§ 109, 124 and 126). Here I shall quote some passages which disclose more fully his views about the origin of philosophical nonsense, and about the methods for curing it which constitute the new philosophy. Berkeley once complained that (other) philosophers raise a dust and then complain that they cannot see. Wittgenstein complained that: 'When we do philosophy [old style] we are like savages, primitive people, who hear the expressions of civilized men, put a false interpretation on them, and then draw the queerest conclusions from it' (§ 194). Philosophers are supposed to do this by getting entangled in rules of their own making: 'we lay down rules, a technique, for a [language-] game, and . . . when we follow the rules, things do not turn out as we had assumed . . . we are therefore, as it were, entangled in our own rules' (§ 125). Thus, philosophy [new-style] is 'a battle against the bewitchment of our intelligence by means of language' (§ 109). Philosophers are alleged to have produced the tangles by forgetting the jobs words do when used in their everyday practical contexts: 'For philosophical problems arise when language *goes on holiday*' (§ 38); 'The confusions which occupy us arise when language is like an engine idling, not when it is doing work' (§ 132). 'What *we* do', he says, 'is to bring words back from their metaphysical to their everyday usage [Verwendung]' (§ 116).

The goal of the new philosophy is described as therapeutic: 'The philosopher's treatment of a question is like the treatment of an illness' (§ 255); 'What is your aim in philosophy?—To show the fly the way out of the fly-bottle' (§ 309); 'The real discovery is the one that makes me capable of stopping doing philosophy when I want to.—The one that gives philosophy peace, so that it is no longer tormented by questions which bring *itself* in question . . . There is not *a* philosophical method, though there are indeed different methods, like different therapies' (§ 133). The goal is to induce a state of mind in which the patient only says things with which no one would disagree: 'In [new-style] philosophy we do not draw conclusions . . . Philosophy only states what everyone admits' (§ 599); 'If one tried to advance *theses* in philosophy, it would never be possible to question them, because everyone would agree to them' (§ 128). The uses of language are sometimes described as part of man's natural history: 'What we are supplying are really remarks on the natural history of human beings' (§ 415). The philosopher's study of this branch of zoology is to be purely empirical: 'One cannot guess how a word functions. One has to *look at* its use and learn from that' (§ 340). And philosophers must not try to explain what they observe: 'Our mistake is to look for an explanation . . . where we ought to have said: *this language-game is played*. The question is not one of explaining a language-game by means of our experiences, but of noting a language-game' (§ 654–5). Since the new philosopher's goal is not that of other natural historians—to order, inter-relate and explain what he observes—his descriptions of language-games need not be systematic. He will consider specific 'bumps' which the old-style philosopher 'has got by running [his] head up against the limits of language' (§ 119). 'The work of the philosopher consists in assembling reminders for a particular purpose' (§ 127). That is, a philosopher's descriptions of language are to be *ad hoc*—the particular purpose being the treatment of a certain 'bump' by reminding the patient how a certain word is 'doing work' when it is used by *non*-philosophers. One would expect that even the new-style philosopher would treat bumps one at a time, but Wittgenstein himself tried to massage many different bumps simultaneously or in rapid succession. Assembling reminders about everyday usage is sometimes presented not merely as a method of curing our confusions, but also as a method of answering our questions about the natures of things: 'Grammar tells what kind of object anything is' (§ 373).

Wittgenstein's conception of philosophy is strikingly original. Yet his admirers sometimes gloss over these remarkable doctrines. Professor Malcolm's article on Wittgenstein in *The Encyclopaedia of Philosophy* does not even mention the bold claims about philosophy made in either the *Tractatus* or the *Investigations*. It is, of course, scarcely in the interests of professional philosophers to represent the task of philosophy as the elimination of nonsense produced by philosophers.

SECTION XV

Wittgenstein's Peculiar Way of Practising his New Kind of Philosophy

THE contents of the *Philosophical Investigations* described so far fill only about a quarter of the book. The remainder is concerned directly or indirectly with the problems which form the subject of Ryle's *The Concept of Mind*: the uses of what I call 'mind-predicates'. Wittgenstein's discussions are extremely tangled and inconsequential. So far as I know both his admirers and his critics have failed to emphasize the gulf between the method of philosophizing commended by Wittgenstein and his own practice. The views about mind-predicates suggested or insinuated by snatches of dialogue, unanswered questions and occasionally by arguments, are certainly not descriptions of what people say when not philosophizing. We find very few reminders about everyday usage, and when Wittgenstein does make assertions apparently intended as such, they are usually false. For example: 'It can't be said of me at all (except perhaps as a joke) that I *know* I am in pain' (§ 246); and 'It is correct to say "I know what you are thinking" and wrong to say "I know what I am thinking". (A whole cloud of philosophy condensed into a drop of grammar)' (p. 222). Yet he says, surprisingly, that we should sometimes be prepared to say 'This man *believes* he is pretending' (p. 229. His italics). Much more frequently, he asks us to consider how a certain expression is or must be learnt or taught. This method of enquiry is not mentioned in his account of philosophy in the *Investigations*. It is, of course, legitimate and important, provided that it is not confused with his professed method of describing the actual use of language. But Wittgenstein does confuse these two kinds of enquiry; and he does not pursue nearly far enough the answers to his own questions about how word-uses are learnt or taught.

Apparently it was Wittgenstein's deliberate policy, when discussing the use of a word, to ask questions about learning situations. A passage which makes this explicit is reported in

Lectures and Conversations on Aesthetics, Psychology and Religious Belief (1966), which contains lecture notes taken by some of his students. Wittgenstein is recorded as saying in 1938:

One thing we always do when discussing a word is to ask how we were taught it. Doing this on the one hand destroys a variety of misconceptions, on the other hand gives you a primitive language in which the word is used. Although this language is not what you talk when you are twenty, you get a rough approximation to what kind of language-game is going to be played. Cf. How did we learn 'I dreamt so and so?' The interesting point is that we didn't learn it by being shown a dream. If you ask yourself how a child learns 'beautiful', 'fine', etc., you find it learns them roughly as interjections. ('Beautiful' is an odd word to talk about because it's hardly ever used) (pp. 1–2).

It remains true that Wittgenstein confuses how-do-we-use and how-do-we-learn questions in the *Investigations*, in that he oscillates between them without acknowledging their difference, and presents answers to questions about learning as if they answered his questions about 'the actual use of language'.

The accounts of mind-predicates which we are offered in the *Investigations* often seem to be distorted by a preconceived theory. Wittgenstein has doffed the spectacles provided by Russell, which had concealed from him what people actually say and had seemed to reveal a logical calculus hidden in our talk; but he now seems to have donned another pair of distorting spectacles, and to see only what can be accommodated by some version of the Verification Principle. I am not, of course, claiming that Wittgenstein's arguments in the *Investigations* were consciously derived from principles which he suppressed. The claim is this: that he offers many remarks or incomplete arguments which seem to be intelligible only if we supply some verification principle as their premise; that he frequently argues *as if* he were applying a VP. The version of the VP which he most frequently *seems* to be using is the one which I have labelled 'the By-Others version'.[1] It can be expressed thus: that the ascription of any predicate to any person, P, is meaningful *for anyone including P*, if and only if *people other than P* can verify its correctness, if and only if the overt behaviour of

[1] This version was distinguished from the By-Me and the By-Someone versions on pp. 37–8 above.

P does or could provide *other* people with 'criteria' for applying it to P. The closest that Wittgenstein gets to formulating this principle (and it is not *very* close) is when he says: 'if I need a justification for using a word, it must also be one for someone else' (§ 378), and 'An "inner process" stands in need of outward criteria' (§ 580). *If* anyone were applying the By-Others version of the VP, he would, when discussing first-person utterances, neglect the standpoint of the speaker, adopt that of the listener/spectator, and determine the meaningfulness, or meaning, of such an utterance by asking whether, or how, others could verify it. Wittgenstein very often does this in the *Investigations*. When he discusses the meanings of expressions like "I understand . . ." (§§ 154–5 and 321–2), "I said to myself . . ." (§§ 344), "I have a red image" (§§ 377–8) or "I dreamt . . ." (p. 222), he habitually neglects (or switches away from) the meaning for the speaker. He asks what justifies us *others* in accepting such a statement, by what 'criteria' we *others* can confirm it. He usually follows in Part One a maxim which he formulates in Part Two: 'Do not ask yourself "How does it work with *me*?"—Ask "what do I know about someone else?"' (p. 206). But he does not always follow this maxim. There are at least two important passages where he seems to be applying a By-Me version of the VP.

The implication of the By-Others version are different from those of the By-Me version, but there is an important resemblance between them which distinguishes them from the By-Someone version: both of them would commit one to accepting some form of Behaviourism. That Wittgenstein would have accepted any kind of Behaviourism is sometimes denied on the grounds (a) that in the *Investigations* he rejects Behaviourism (§§ 307–8), or (b) that his position in *The Brown Book* is not that of Behaviourism. Let us consider these arguments. It is unprofitable to use the word "Behaviourism" without explaining what one means by it. As stated earlier (page 48 above), I use "(Philosophical) Behaviourism" to refer to the theses that the meanings of mind-predicates must be explained in terms of overt behaviour, or, less vaguely, that statements about a person's state of mind can be completely analysed in terms of statements about what other people can or could observe him doing. Many of Wittgenstein's later remarks point towards the former version of Behaviourism, though of course he never formulates this thesis explicitly. It is irrelevant to point out that in the *Investigations* he rejects what *he* calls 'Behaviourism'; for what he says here makes it clear that he is interpreting "Behaviourism" in the metaphysical sense. He equates it with 'denying mental processes' (§ 308), with claiming 'that everything except human behaviour is a fiction' (§ 307); though even here he speaks equivocally when he adds: 'If I do speak of a fiction then it is of a *grammatical* fiction'. Rejecting Behaviourism as a metaphysical thesis need not involve rejecting Philosophical Behaviourism; which does not deny the truth of our everyday statements about minds, mental processes, etc., but offers what most of us would regard as a paradoxical account of their meaning.

Regarding the second argument, what Wittgenstein says in *The Brown Book* is clearly incompatible with any kind of Behaviourism. Indeed a defender of Cartesian dualism could accept everything that Wittgenstein says here. Consider these statements:

There is a kind of general disease of thinking which *always* looks for (and finds) what would be called a mental state from which *all* our acts spring as from a reservoir. Thus one says, "The fashion changes because the taste of people changes". The taste is the mental reservoir. (p. 143. My italics);

We don't use the word "taste" as the name of a feeling. To think that we do is . . . undue simplification . . . It is advantageous . . . to consider, *parallel with the feeling or feelings* characteristic for having a certain taste, changing one's taste . . . the facial expression (gestures or tones of voice) characteristic for the same states and events. (p. 144. My italics);

There may be cases where *the presence of a sensation* other than those bound up with gestures, tone of voice, etc., distinguishes meaning what you say from not meaning it. But *sometimes* what distinguishes these two is nothing that happens while we speak, but a variety of actions *and experiences* before and after (pp. 144–5. My italics);

The problem which we are concerned with we also encounter in thinking about volition, deliberate and involuntary action . . . I deliberate whether to lift a certain heavyish weight, decide to do it, I then apply my force to it and lift it . . . One takes one's ideas, and one's language, about volition from this kind of example and *thinks that they must apply . . . to all cases which one can properly call cases of willing* (p. 150. My italics).

In these passages and others, Wittgenstein's remarks about the use of mind-predicates involve references to 'experiences', 'sensations' and 'feelings', as well as to overt behaviour and the context of use. He nowhere says or suggests that none of our acts are caused by mental processes, or that private experiences should or can be ignored in giving an account of our uses of mind-predicates. What he attacks here as 'a kind of general disease of thinking' is the view that *all* our actions spring from the mental reservoir, that *each* mind-word is used simply to name a private experience. The thesis which he neatly sketches here seems now to be almost universally accepted among English-speaking philosophers. The general acceptance of this thesis was mainly due, I think, to Ryle's *C of M*; but this very important insight evidently originated from Wittgenstein. Only in the last few paragraphs of *The Brown Book* is there a hint of the passages in the *Investigations* which led Heath to ascribe to Wittgenstein 'some form of crypto-behaviourism' (*Phil. Quarterly*, Jan. 1956, p. 70), and which led Strawson to speak of Wittgenstein's 'hostility to the doctrine of privacy' and to ascribe to him the thesis 'that no words name sensations (or 'private experiences')' (*Mind*, Jan. 1954, p. 98 and p. 94). The fact that what Wittgenstein said in 1934 is incompatible with any kind of Behaviourism is, however, no ground for denying that many of his later remarks imply Philosophical Behaviourism. *The Brown Book* represents the first stage in his rethinking the philosophy of mind, in his curing himself from what he calls a 'disease of thinking'. That he, like other contemporary philosophers, had suffered from this disease, is indicated in a letter he wrote to Russell in 1919: '"Does a Gedanke consist of words?" No! But of psychical constituents that have the same relation to reality at words' (*Notebooks*, p. 130).

I shall not claim in what follows that a clear or consistent formulation of Behaviourism (or of any other theory) can be found in the *Investigations*; or that all of its contents could be reconciled with this theory. It has been an embarrassment to some of Wittgenstein's admirers that he claims to be simply reminding us of our everyday ways of talking and yet *seems* to be advocating some form of Behaviourism. Much ingenuity has been devoted to constructing alternative interpretations. There are many possible permutations, depending on which of the remarks one treats as crucial and which one ignores, dismisses as slips or explains away. Section XVII will give samples of the variety of the interpretations which have been offered, and will illustrate the ways in which they are supported. Here I shall examine the passage in the *Investigations* which has provoked most controversy, a passage in which he discusses more or less continuously our use of 'names of sensations', and especially of "pain". Wittgenstein returns to this topic several times in the sequel, but the main discussion is in paragraphs 243 to 315. He introduces this passage as a discussion of the possibility of a 'private language', that is, of a language in which 'a person could write down or give vocal expression to his inner experiences—his feelings, moods and the rest—for his private use', and in which the individual words 'are to refer to what can only be known to the person speaking; to his immediate private sensations' (§ 243).

The first task is to expound what are usually treated as the most significant remarks in this passage. This will be done in a way which conveys what strikes me as the pattern of the implicit reasoning; but attention will be drawn to statements which seem to provide scope for alternative interpretations. It will be argued that, whichever interpretation one adopts, Wittgenstein's remarks violate his own programme for doing philosophy. Since these remarks appear in a rather random order, I shall take the liberty of expounding them in a different order, starting with what Wittgenstein (unusually) offers as his 'conclusion'. If one assumes that he meant what he here says, this much reduces the number of possible interpretations. This is the conclusion:

> [Imaginary Critic:] "But you will surely admit that there is a difference between pain-behaviour accompanied by pain and pain-behaviour without any pain?"—[Reply:] Admit it? What greater difference could there be?—[Imaginary Critic:] And yet you again and again reach the conclusion that the sensation itself is a *nothing*—[Reply:] Not at all. It is not a *something*, but not a *nothing* either! The conclusion was only that a nothing would serve just as well as a something about which nothing could be said (§ 304).

Notice that the conclusion is not to deny the occurrence of

sensations like pain, considered as private experiences—nor to deny their importance to us—but to deny that anything could be *said about* them. The remainder of § 304 must now be quoted, since it provides an escape-clause or qualification which at first sight might appear to make an important difference:

> We have only rejected the grammar which tries to force itself on us here. The paradox disappears only if we make a radical break with the idea that language always functions in one way, always serves the same purpose: to convey thoughts—which may be about houses, pains, good and evil, or anything else you please.

In the light of this, Wittgenstein's conclusion could be interpreted thus: that nothing could be 'said about' the sensation itself IF we assume that "pain" is used to 'convey thoughts about', to refer to, the sensation itself, in the way in which "house" may be used to convey thoughts about a public object; and that what we are meant to conclude is that the latter view about the function of "pain" is mistaken.

What Wittgenstein presents as his alternative conclusions in § 304 seem to coincide with those reached in § 293. Here he starts by considering the view 'that it is only from my own case that I know what the word "pain" means', and he asks 'how can I generalize the *one* case so irresponsibly?' He then writes:

> Suppose everyone had a box with something in it: we call it a "beetle". No one can look into anyone else's box, and everyone says he knows what a beetle is only by looking at *his* beetle.—Here it would be quite possible for everyone to have something different in his box. One might even imagine such a thing constantly changing.—But suppose the word "beetle" had a use in these people's language?—If so it would not be used as the name of a thing. The thing in the box has no place in the language-game at all; not even as a *something*: for the box might even be empty.—No, one can 'divide through' by the thing in the box; it cancels out, whatever it is (§ 293).

The conclusion here seems to be identical with that of the earlier part of § 304—that nothing could be said about the sensation itself, the thing in the box. But here again a qualification is added:

> if we construe the grammar of the expression of sensation on the model of 'object and name' the object drops out of consideration as irrelevant.

This clause seems to correspond to the qualification added in § 304, in that it hints that there is a way of construing 'the grammar of the expression of sensation' other than treating "pain" as a name. However, the rôle of class-names is to refer to and/or to describe things. So a denial that "pain" is the *name* of something private[2] implies that "pain" is not used to refer to or describe, to 'convey thoughts about', the sensation itself.

Wittgenstein's conclusions in paragraphs 293 and 304 are worded as if they were intended to fulfil his professed purpose—description of our actual use of language, of 'grammar'—and so, naturally, they have often been interpreted thus. The apparently different and alternative conclusions presented here are:

(a) that nothing can be said about the sensation itself, which 'has no place in the language game'.

(b) that "thinking about" and "naming" (and therefore "talking about", "referring to", "describing", etc.) do not perform the same rôle, when followed by "a pain", as they do when followed by "a house".

These conclusions about how we do not or cannot use words like "pain", prompt the question: how *do* we use them? If we interpret Wittgenstein as adopting conclusion (b), we must ask: what is the special rôle of the verbs in such locutions as "*talking about* or *referring to* a pain"? We must now consider Wittgenstein's only answer to this question. This had been given earlier, in § 244, and it is extremely brief.

Wittgenstein starts with the question 'How do words *refer* to sensations?' He then immediately substitutes for this the very different question 'how does a human being learn the meaning of the names of sensations?', and offers this answer:

Here is one possibility: words are connected with the primitive, the natural, expressions of the sensation and used in their place. A child has hurt himself and he cries; and then adults talk to him and teach him exclamations and, later, sentences. They teach the child new

[2] I say 'something private' deliberately, in place of "(private) object", for all of Wittgenstein's arguments hinge on the epistemological privacy of the sensation itself, and *not* upon whether we classify sensations as 'objects' or 'processes' or 'occurrences', etc.

pain-behaviour. "So you are saying that the word 'pain' really means crying?"—On the contrary: the verbal expressions of pain replaces crying and does not describe it.

So the suggestion is that an utterance like "I am in pain" is simply a substitute for unlearned behaviour like crying or groaning; which implies that it is no more a *statement* than is a groan. Though Wittgenstein offers this account only as 'one possibility', he does not offer any other possibilities in Part One. And he offers the same sort of account of other kinds of first person utterances. For example: 'Now I know how to go on' (i.e. how to continue the series), is described as 'an exclamation', as corresponding to 'an instinctive sound, a glad start' (§ 323). And later he explicitly accepts an implication of assimilating sensation-reports to groans and thereby treating such utterances as not being literally *reports*: the implication being that the "I" in "I am in pain" is not used to refer to oneself. He says: 'Now in saying this ['I am in pain'] I don't name any person. Just as I don't name any person when I groan with pain' (§ 404).[3]

What Wittgenstein says in § 244 can apply only to first person utterances. We are left to assume, apparently, that ascriptions of pain to *other* people are to be treated as statements about their actual or potential behaviour. At one point Wittgenstein seems to suggest that such third-person utterances may (also?) have the function of expressing the *speaker's* emotional attitudes:

I tell someone I am in pain . . . Let us assume he says: "It's not so bad".—Doesn't that prove that he believes in something behind the outward expression of pain?—His attitude is a proof of his attitude. Imagine "It's not so bad" replaced by instinctive noises and gestures (§ 310).

Malcolm interprets this to mean:

The thought that behind someone's pain-behaviour is the pain itself does not enter into our use of "He's in pain", but what does enter

[3] He supports this assertion by saying: '"I" is not the name of a person' (§ 410). This is a very bad argument, for though "I" is not anyone's name, it is of course used to refer to someone, to the speaker. Compare what Wittgenstein says in §§ 404 and 410 with his earlier statement: 'To say, "I have a pain" is no more a statement *about* a particular person than moaning is' (*BBB*, p. 67. His italics).

into it is our sympathetic, or unsympathetic, reaction to him (Malcolm's review of the *Investigations*, op. cit., p. 91).

If Malcolm's interpretation is correct, Wittgenstein is clearly adopting the theory which I call 'Philosophical Behaviourism'.

Wittgenstein's arguments, as expounded so far, do not warrant the conclusions presented in paragraphs 293 and 304. The beetle in the box metaphor is a forcible way of presenting a familiar challenge to the argument from analogy, but the most that it could establish is that we cannot *communicate* about 'inner experiences'; on the ground that no one is acquainted with what, if anything, others are talking about when they use expressions like "my (or "this") pain". To establish that nothing can be *said about* the sensation itself, it would be necessary to show that it is impossible for a person to talk *even to himself* about *his own* sensations. This radical thesis does, however, seem to have been endorsed by Wittgenstein. At any rate, he uses arguments which would, if valid, demonstrate this thesis in his celebrated Diary argument, which we must now consider. This passage is introduced by way of the question whether it makes sense to suppose that a child who is a genius had invented a name for a sensation, 'that he had 'named his pain'' (§ 257). The first stage of the argument runs:

Let us imagine the following case. I want to keep a diary about the recurrence of a certain sensation. To this end I associate it with the sign "E" and write this sign in a calendar for every day on which I have the sensation.—I will remark first of all that a definition of the sign cannot be formulated.—But still I can give myself a kind of ostensive definition.—How? Can I point to the sensation? Not in the ordinary sense. But I speak, or write the sign down, and at the same time I concentrate my attention on the sensation—and so, as it were, point to it inwardly . . . in this way I impress on myself the connexion between the sign and the sensation.—But "I impress it on myself" can only mean: this process brings it about that I remember the connexion right in the future. *But in the present case I have no criterion of correctness. One would like to say: whatever is going to seem right to me is right. And that only means that here we can't talk about 'right'* (§ 258. My italics).

The italicized sentences form the crux of this argument. Wittgenstein is evidently claiming that even the diarist cannot claim to be *right* in applying "E" to a present sensation, since he cannot know that he is *correctly* remembering that the sensation on which he had originally conferred "E" was like his present sensation. That this is how he was thinking is confirmed by the fact that he goes on to argue that memories of an inner experience may not count as a 'justification' of a belief; for, he says, 'justification consists in appealing to something independent', and if a person appeals 'from one memory to another', this is not an independent test, but is 'as if someone were to buy several copies of [the same] morning paper to assure himself that what it said was true' (§ 265). Before making this last move, Wittgenstein had extended his argument from "E" to "pain". He makes the diarist protest 'But I can (inwardly) undertake to call THIS 'pain' in the future' (§ 263); and in the sequel he alternates between discussing "E" and "pain", and argues as if the same conclusions must be drawn about both; as indeed they should on his premises. For if memory is discounted as not providing 'a criterion of correctness', a person who seeks to use any symbol as a name for a species of his own sensations can never verify whether he is fulfilling his intention or is applying the symbol at different times to sensations (or other inner experiences) which have nothing in common. From which it would follow (*if* we accept "the" VP) that a person cannot 'name', and cannot significantly talk even to himself about, his own inner experiences. One would hesitate to attribute to Wittgenstein such a paradoxical thesis, were it not that it fits in with so much that he says. Apart from his conclusions in paragraphs 293 and 304, consider his imperative: 'Always get rid of the idea of the private object in this way: assume that it constantly changes, but that you do not notice the change because your memory constantly deceives you' (p. 207). According to this injunction, what each of us must 'get rid of' is the idea of, his beliefs about, *his own* 'private objects'. Wittgenstein is not here, as in the beetles metaphor, merely stressing the inaccessibility of *other* people's 'private objects'.

I have now expounded what strike me as the main arguments, or thoughts, which lead to what Wittgenstein presented as his conclusion (§ 304). I must now stress certain statements which have so far been mentioned only in passing. As stated earlier, Wittgenstein introduced his beetles metaphor as if he were exploring the implications of the view that 'it is only from my own case that I know what the word "pain" means' (§ 293); and he prefaces the Diary argument with the supposition that a child-genius invents for himself a name for a sensation. In view of this, it may be, and it has been argued, that *the* purpose of the whole private language passage is to demonstrate the impossibility of maintaining the thesis that *we* learn to use sensation-words by doing what Wittgenstein described his diarist as trying to do. There seems to be no doubt that this was *one* of Wittgenstein's purposes. This prompts the question whether anyone has ever affirmed the thesis which Wittgenstein is challenging. Many philosophers have answered this question by suggesting, or flatly asserting, that what Wittgenstein was attacking, and rightly attacking, is Cartesian Dualism. This view seems to me to be a by-product of regarding Wittgenstein's remarks through spectacles provided by Ryle, whilst forgetful of what Descartes wrote and of what "dualism" here means. I shall enlarge on this later. The point that I want to stress here is that, according to the interpretation that we are considering, Wittgenstein has *changed the subject*, i.e. his own chosen subject—describing the actual use of words like "pain", and is discussing instead how we learnt to use such words. He presents his conclusions as theses about grammar, about our actual use of "pain". Yet in the key passages which lead to his conclusions he argues as if the latter can be established by considering how we did learn, or more often how we could not have learned, to use "pain".

Let us suppose that Wittgenstein's conclusions were intended as reminders about our actual use of words like "pain". In that case, it is easy to show that they are indefensible. No one could or would defend as such a reminder the statement that nothing could be said about the sensation itself. The alternative conclusion is that "thinking about", "talking about" or "referring to" play an importantly different rôle when followed by "this pain" than they do when followed by an expression referring to a public object like "that house", or to a public process like "that noise". If any one sought to defend this claim as a reminder about everyday language, we may remind him of one of Wittgenstein's examples: '"You said, 'It'll stop soon'—Were you thinking of the noise or of your pain?"' (§ 682). In such a question, "thinking of" could be replaced by "talking about" or "referring to". If anyone claims that these verbs are used in importantly different senses when completed by "the noise" and by "your pain", he will have to seek support from some source other than everyday usage; for he is certainly not describing such usage. According to Wittgenstein, 'Grammar tells what kind of object anything is'. But what kind of grammar could be used to support either of the alternative conclusions of § 304? Now consider Wittgenstein's account of reports of sensations in § 244. Obviously, saying 'I am in pain' usually is an expression of pain, and may function like a groan in inviting or soliciting sympathy and help. But *reporting* one's pain is a unique way of expressing it. Saying 'I am in pain' is unlike a groan in being true or false. It is a grammatical fact that 'I am in pain' said by me, and 'You are not in pain' said at the same time to me, are contradictory statements. But Wittgenstein's account implies that these utterances cannot contradict each other because to say 'I am in pain' is not to make a statement at all.[4]

If Wittgenstein *had* considered grammar, he could scarcely have failed to notice the distinctions which we draw in ordinary language between the following types of sentence:

(1) "John feels pain or is in pain",
(2) "John is behaving as if in pain or showing symptoms of pain",
(3) "John is simulating pain or pretending to be in pain",
(4) "John is hiding or concealing his pain",
and (5) "John is expressing his pain".

As we use such sentences, the logical relations between the statements which we use them to make are:

that (1) and (2) are logically independent;
that (3) implies that (2) is true and that (1) is false;
that (4) implies that (1) is true and that (2) is false;
that (5) implies that (1) and (2) are both true.

This is to state the obvious. It seems necessary to do so because Wittgenstein and others have offered paradoxical accounts of our uses of mind-predicates, have claimed to be doing grammar,

[4] Malcolm says that in § 244, Wittgenstein 'is bringing to light the arresting fact that my sentences about my present sensations have the same logical status as my outcries and facial expressions'. (Malcolm's review of the *Investigations*, op. cit., p. 82.) What can "logical" mean here? Cf. Ryle's 'logical tone of voice'.

yet have ignored these elementary grammatical facts. If grammar, our established uses of language, is to be the test, all forms of Behaviourism fail simply by virtue of the fact that (1) and (2) are logically independent. Wittgenstein, however, exploits the expressions "to express one's pain" and "expression of pain"; he exploits the fact that 'John is expressing his pain' is true if and only if it is true both that John feels pain and is showing symptoms of pain. He uses sentences of type (5), and fails to discuss their relationships to sentences of the other four types.

Grammar provides many other reasons for rejecting Wittgenstein's conclusions. A pertinent question, which I owe to Mrs. Andrea McKeown, is to ask: what do the adjectives that we attach to "pain" (e.g. "throbbing", "dull" or "stabbing") describe, if they do not describe the sensation itself? Or suppose we advance from shallow to 'deep' grammar, i.e. ask what we *mean* by our utterances. It would be absurd to treat as a long-delayed groan a person's descriptions of his past pains for the information of his doctor or his biographer. Or again (an example which I owe to Mrs. McKeown): What do we *mean* when we describe a person as feeling nervous? It would be illegitimate for us to speak of *the* natural expression(s), *the* behaviour-pattern(s) characteristic, of nervousness. For nervousness may be manifested in different people, or in the same person at different times, in contrary ways: in talking more loudly, or less loudly, than usual, in being more aggressive, or less aggressive, than usual, more sociable, or less sociable, than usual, and so on. The items of behaviour which we class together as symptoms of nervousness are so classed, not because of their similarities *as behaviour*, but because they are believed to express similar introspectible states of mind—of the kind(s) which one reports by saying 'I feel nervous'.

According to Wittgenstein's account of philosophy, his discussion of "pain" should have been confined to assembling reminders about how we *do* use this word, to 'noting', and refraining from any attempts to *explain*, the relevant language-games. In fact he embraced conclusions which it is absurd to represent as such reminders, or as pieces of grammar deep or shallow. This was the result of his telescoping and confusing the questions 'How *do* we use "pain"?' and 'How did we *learn* to use it?' What he says in § 244 is a first step towards answering the latter question.[5] Yet he proceeds as if this answered the former question, and, by implication, as if it revealed the answers to questions about our uses of all the mind-predicates of which anyone might want to say that a person has privileged access to what they refer to or describe.

Let us now look more closely at the Diary argument. If we measure a philosopher's stature by his success in provoking thought by posing really difficult puzzles, Wittgenstein was a great philosopher (and we should also add some cubits to Zeno's stature). It needs a kind of genius to produce, in three and a half pages, arguments which have persuaded so many philosophers to accept a conclusion so radical and so paradoxical. And many who have not been so persuaded, have found it very difficult to diagnose the errors. Disentangling the Diary argument is a challenge. I suggest that it owes its influence to the facts that it is, in effect, a two-pronged application of "the" VP, and that, for many philosophers, the latter has become an unconscious axiom. The first stage of the Diary argument involves arguing *as if* from the By-Me version which Wittgenstein adopted in 1929: 'if I can never completely verify what the sentence means then also I cannot have meant anything by the sentence.' (See p. 161 above.) In § 258, Wittgenstein puts himself in the diarist's shoes and uses the first person singular. Admittedly he switches from "I" to "we" in the last sentence, 'here we can't talk about 'right''; but nobody doubts that he meant us to conclude that the diarist himself cannot, by adopting a private rule, use a sign as the name of a sensation. The reason given is: 'I [the diarist speaking] have no criterion of correctness . . . whatever is going to seem right to me is right'; implying that the diarist has no means of verifying conclusively such a statement as 'the sensation on which I formerly conferred "E" was the same as this present sensation'. In the conclusion ('here we can't talk about 'right''), "can't" must presumably mean 'cannot *meaningfully*'. He could scarcely have intended this conclusion to be a reminder about our everyday talk, a claim that it is a breach of grammar to speak of a memory of a sensation being 'correct' or 'right'. One may

[5] The first two sentences of § 257 contain his only other step. The hint given here is, however, important and will be discussed later.

argue that it is redundant to add "correctly" or "rightly" after "remember", on the ground that "to remember" is an achievement-verb. But it is certainly not improper to say, e.g. for emphasis or in answer to others' doubts, what is usually superfluous. Thus the first Diary argument does not conform to Wittgenstein's programme of simply describing 'the actual use of language'. It is a would-be demonstration that it is *meaningless* to purport to use a sign simply as a name of a species of sensations of one's own, on the ground that one cannot *conclusively verify* that one's use of the sign is consistent.

The Diary argument contains a stage which I have so far neglected (§ 261). This involves arguing *as if* from the By-Others version of the VP. Wittgenstein switches to the viewpoint of the listener/spectator. He asks: 'What reason have we [i.e. we others] for calling [the diarist's] "E" the sign for a *sensation*?' He answers that 'the use of this word stands in need of a justification which everybody understands'; meaning, presumably, that nobody (including the diarist) is entitled to apply "sensation" to what the diarist purports to call "E", unless this could be 'justified' by everybody, i.e. unless people other than the diarist could *verify* that "sensation" is then being applied correctly.

The Diary argument is often treated, in effect, as showing that certain would-be statements are *meaningless* because they are *unverifiable*. Consider Mr. Rush Rhees' gloss on stage one of this argument. Having raised the question 'if it means anything to say I am in pain again', he writes:

> If it were something I knew only in myself, then I might say "This is something different now" or "This is the same again" . . . and in any case it would not make any difference. This is not a question of whether I can trust my memory. It is a question of when it makes sense to speak of remembering. If I thought I could not trust my memory, then of course I might look for confirmation. But there cannot be any question of confirmation here, nor any question of doubting either. There is just no rule for what is the same and what is not the same; there is no distinction between correct and incorrect; and it is for this reason that it does not make any difference what I say. Which means, of course, that I say nothing (*PAS*, Supp. Vol. XXVIII, 1954, p. 83).

Rhees interprets Wittgenstein as claiming that, because my

claim to remember a sensation cannot be confirmed, such a claim does not make sense. This flies on the face of everyday language, for it involves denying meaning to familiar statements, like saying to the doctor 'It is the same pain as I had yesterday—I remember it clearly'. Rhees denies here that what is in question is 'whether I can trust my memory', but this cannot be allowed. "I trust my memory" *means* 'I am sure that my memory is *correct*, that I am remembering *aright*'. Wittgenstein's conclusion is that "right" or "correct" cannot be used in the context in question.

The beetles metaphor too owes its persuasiveness to the fact that it makes an implicit appeal to "the" VP—to the By-Me version. This metaphor is a way of posing the question: When another person uses "my pain", is he having an inner experience of the sort which *I* call 'my pains'? It is because no answer to this question can be conclusively verified that one may be tempted to dismiss the question as meaningless.

I shall now give two more examples to illustrate the peculiar ways in which Wittgenstein implements his programme of assembling reminders about everyday language. Both involve arguing *as if* from the By-Others version of "the" VP. The first example consists of some cryptic remarks concerning a person's reports about his mental imagery:

> [Imaginary Critic:] "Before I judge that two images which I have are the same, I must recognize them as the same". [To which L.W. replies:] And when that has happened, how am I to know that the word "same" describes what I recognize? Only if I can express my recognition in some other way, and if it is possible *for someone else* to teach me that "same" is the correct word here.
>
> For if I need a justification for using a word, it must also be one for someone else (§ 378. My italics).

Let us consider the implications of this passage by taking an example. Suppose I visualize two round white objects. Wittgenstein's words imply that I am entitled to claim to recognize them as 'the same', only if 'I can express my recognition in some other way' (that is, presumably, other than simply telling you that they are the same in shape, colour and size); and only if someone else can then 'teach me that "same" is the correct word here'. Well, apart from describing my images in words, no other way of 'expressing my recognition' to you seems to be available, except my painting a reproduction of my images. But if you then judge the two things in my painting to be 'the same', this confirms *my* recognition that my two images were the same, only on the assumption that the things in my painting are the same as, are faithful reproductions of, my images. But only *I* can recognize this! In any case why should I attach more weight to *your* judgement of the resemblance between the things that I have painted than I do to my own? As so often, when one tries to unfold Wittgenstein's opaque remarks, they do not make sense[6].

The second example comes from paragraphs 153–5, where Wittgenstein is discussing the question: what is meant by "Now I understand" or "Now I can go on" (i.e. can continue the series)? His puzzling conclusion is presented from the standpoint of the listener/spectator:

> FOR US it is *the circumstances* in which he [the speaker] had such an experience [i.e. a supposed experience accompanying his saying of a formula] that justify HIM in saying that he understands, that he knows how to go on (§ 155. His italics. My capitals.)

If Wittgenstein had written "us" instead of "him", his statement would have been intelligible and defensible. His use of "him" is hard to explain—except by pointing out that it conforms with the By-Others version of the VP. This example illustrates the close attention that needs to be paid to the pronouns which Wittgenstein uses, when one is trying to identify the meanings of his remarks.

I am not the first to interpret Wittgenstein's arguments as being dependent on an unfamiliar version of "the" VP. Dr. Judith Jarvis Thomson has done so too in her interesting paper 'Private Languages' (*Amer. Phil. Quarterly*, 1964). The climax of Dr. Thomson's paper is her thesis that what 'the denial of the possibility of private languages amounts to' is 'a revised formulation of something very familiar indeed, namely the Principle of Verification', to wit:

[6] Notice that, in § 378, Wittgenstein seems to be telescoping the three different questions: how I recognize that two of my images are the same, how others can verify (get evidence of the truth of) my claim to have done this, and how a child could be taught to use "the same" in such contexts.

A sign "K" is not a kind-name in a man's language unless it is possible to find out whether or not a thing is of the kind associated with "K" (over and above its seeming or not seeming to him to be so) (p. 29).

This was certainly an unfamiliar version of "the" VP. Dr. Thomson does not, however, tell us which principle she would regard as *the* VP. The lacuna in her new version is in its failure to specify *by whom* it must be 'possible to find out whether or not a thing is of the kind associated [by whom?] with "K"'. One only needs to ask this to see that her new VP splits into (at least) two, depending on whether one answers 'by whom?' by saying 'by himself' or by saying 'by others'. Whereas the By-Someone version of the VP (Ryle 1936, Ayer 1956) left a lacuna in not asking the question 'meaningful for whom?', Dr. Thomson's version fails to ask the question 'verifiable by whom?'

It is of interest that, having shown that Wittgenstein's arguments depend on a version of the VP, that this is what his thesis about a private language 'amounts to', Dr. Thomson ends by saying:

. . . about the new form of the Principle of Verification, it seems to me very clear that Wittgenstein himself would never for one moment have subscribed to it. It is astonishing that a man who repeatedly insisted that he put forward no theses in philosophy should constantly be credited with having proved this or that thesis . . . (p. 31).

What surprises me about this conclusion is that so perceptive a critic of Wittgenstein's remarks should apparently feel committed to denying that Wittgenstein could ever have been inconsistent. The relevant inconsistency is not, of course, that of *proving* any version of the VP. Indeed it would scarcely seem justifiable to say that Wittgenstein *used* any VP, for that would suggest that he did so deliberately. We may say, like Dr. Thomson, that his thesis concerning a private language 'amounts to' acceptance of some VP, or, better, that his key arguments would be valid only if some verification principle is supplied as a premise.

Where Wittgenstein is most inconsistent is in professing simply to describe how we do talk and then drawing obviously false conclusions as to what we cannot say. Insofar as these conclusions *depend* upon any version of the VP, they may be classified as covert *a priori* linguistics. Notice another conspicuous inconsistency. Just as, in the *Tractatus*, Wittgenstein managed to say things which he said there *could* not be said, e.g. about 'logical form', so in the *Investigations* he manages to do what he says here *cannot* be done, namely to make references to, 'convey thoughts about', sensations themselves. If he had failed to do this, we should not know what he was talking about in the private language passage, what his diarist was setting out to do in recording 'the recurrence of a certain sensation'.

SECTION XVI

Some Answers to Important Questions Raised by Wittgenstein

IT WOULD be unjust to dwell upon Wittgenstein's inconsistencies without acknowledging the importance of many of the questions which he raised. The aim of this section is to offer solutions to some of the problems posed by his discussion of 'names of sensations'. But first we may ask why Wittgenstein presents this discussion as one concerning the possibility of a 'private language', defined, in effect, as a language which could only be understood by one person, its inventor. This seems an odd way of introducing his discussion of 'words of our common language' like "pain", whether his purpose was to describe the actual use of such words or to explain how we learnt to use them.

I submit that what Wittgenstein says about a private language is vitiated by failure to distinguish between different senses in which a language or a word may be supposed to be private, notably (a) that what it is used to refer to or describe are private experiences; and I shall call this 'privacy of reference'; (b) that its meaning(s) can be known only by its inventor; the 'privacy of incommunicability' as I shall call it. My definition of "private" in sense (a) may sound circular in that it uses the word "private". But here "private" is attached to "experience" and what I mean by calling a person's experience 'private' is that the person has non-inferential knowledge of it, in a way that no one else does. To know that I am in pain, you need evidence, but I do not. Wittgenstein seems to be trying to outlaw this notion of private experience by a piece of *a priori* linguistics, when he says: 'if as a matter of logic you exclude anyone else from having something [e.g. your pain], it loses sense to say that you have it' (§ 398). This produces a head-on collision with ordinary language, in which we do use possessive pronouns, e.g. '*my* pain', '*his* imagery', and we speak of '*having* pains, intentions, etc.'. This leads Wittgenstein to express *disapproval* of 'the expressions of ordinary language'—about whose use he is supposedly assembling reminders (§ 402).

Consider the passages where he introduces his notion of a private language:

But could we also imagine a language in which a person could write down or give vocal expression to his inner experiences—his feelings, moods, and the rest—for his private use?—Well, can't we do so in our ordinary language?[1]—But that is not what I mean. *The individual words of this language are to refer to what can only be known to the person speaking; to his immediate private sensations. So another person cannot understand the language.* (§ 243. My italics).

Notice the force of "So". Wittgenstein apparently takes it for granted that if a person uses words which are private in their reference, they must be private in the sense that their meaning is incommunicable.[2] A few pages later he writes:

Now what about the language which describes my inner experiences and which only I myself can understand? How do I use words to stand for my sensations?—As we ordinarily do? Then *are my words for sensations tied up with*[3] *my natural expressions of sensation? In that case my language is not a 'private' one. Someone else might understand it as well as I* (§ 256. My italics).

In these passages Wittgenstein, in effect, *defines* "a private language" as one in which communication is impossible. This would guarantee a negative answer to one of the questions which could be intended by asking: 'Can there be a private language?'—namely: Is it possible to communicate about private experiences? Yet this is one of the main questions which he proceeds to discuss.

In § 256 Wittgenstein legislates that if a person's 'words for sensations' are 'tied up with natural expressions', in the way that he has suggested that "pain" is, these words are not to be called 'private'. What could be his point in restricting "private

[1] This question is sometimes quoted as if it constituted a clear affirmation that we can talk about, i.e. refer to, our private experiences. But Wittgenstein has not yet explained how *he* interprets "give vocal expression to", i.e. in § 244.

[2] Wittgenstein's reasoning here suggests that he had not, after all, freed himself from the fallacy of equating the meaning of a word with the thing(s) which it is used to refer to.

[3] Here "tied up with" means, presumably, 'as learnt substitutes for'; as has now been suggested in § 244.

language" in this way? A possible answer is suggested in the next paragraph:

What would it be like if human beings showed no outward signs of pain (did not groan, grimace, etc.)? Then it would be impossible to teach a child the use of the word "tooth-ache" (§ 257).

This suggests that his intention, in denying the possibility of a private language, might only be to deny the possibility of talking about types of private experience which, unlike pains, have no natural expressions. But if this was his intention, he forgot it immediately. For the kind of sensation he proceeds to discuss is pain, and it is with reference to pain that he draws his conclusions in §§ 304 and 293. And when he does discuss talk about private experiences which in fact have no natural expressions, he does not mention this fact about them. The distinction hinted at in § 256, between private experiences which do and those which don't have natural expressions, is ignored in the rest of the book.

Why then does Wittgenstein introduce his discussion of words like "pain" as being concerned with the possibility of a private language? I suspect that he was reasoning thus: privacy of reference implies privacy of incommunicability (§ 243), and, since we do use words like "pain" to communicate information, such words cannot have privacy of reference. In any case, it is very surprising that he does not distinguish (i) a language the only function of all whose words is to refer to 'what can only be known to the person speaking', and (ii) a language some of whose words may be used for this purpose. Since his aim is, presumably, to throw light on *our* uses of *our* languages, it is (ii) which he should be discussing. Yet it is with (i) that he equates a 'private language' in paragraphs 243 and 256.

I return now to unfinished business—trying to break the spell cast by the Diary argument. Many have accepted the thesis that a person cannot confer names on sensations of his own, on the ground that he would have no way of verifying that he is using such a would-be name consistently, since he has no way of checking this except his own memory, but has no independent way of testing such memories, and so 'has no criterion of correctness'. This argument commits one to scepticism concerning memory-beliefs about private experiences. Wittgenstein seems to have been willing to accept this corollary, for he says:

Always get rid of the idea of the private object in this way: assume that it constantly changes, but that you do not notice the change because your memory constantly deceives you (p. 207).

Could we, consistently, accept such a conclusion?

Wittgenstein's argument ignores the fact that even in the case of a word which applies to publicly observable objects, a person cannot get independent confirmation of the correctness of his use of it, except by relying upon his own ability to recognize, *without criteria*, the contents of his own experiences. Suppose that I have recently learnt to use the word "magenta", wish to verify that I am applying it correctly, and say to someone: 'That's magenta, isn't it?' My confirmation will consist in *my* hearing sounds *which I have to recognize* as a token of a sentence, e.g. "Yes it's magenta". I should regard this as confirmation because, in recognizing the sounds I hear as a sentence, I take it for granted that the speaker is having a private experience of seeing what we are both looking at, and that he has performed a private act of ostensible recognition, an act of the kind that I had just tentatively performed.

Wittgenstein argues as if a sign cannot be a word for me, cannot have a meaning for me, unless I can get independent confirmation of the correctness of my use of it. But, as we have seen, the possibility of my getting such confirmation presupposes that I can recognize what I see, hear, etc., and that there are other people who can recognize what they hear and see. Unless I put some trust in my own acts of recognition, why should I put any trust in yours? Wittgenstein keeps appealing to the established uses and rules of language. But no one could ever know that other people's, or his own, use of any word is *regular*—that they, or he, follow a *rule*—except by trusting his own memory, by relying on his own capacity to recognize the contents of his own experience. And the *sounds* which we recognize as sentences are more transitory than most pains. The capacity to recognize things straight off without criteria—what Professor H. H. Price calls 'primary recognition' (*Thinking and Experience*, Ch. 2)—is pre-verbal. Possessing this capacity is a condition of being able to learn to use any word. One could not learn to use "apple", unless one could recognize both specimens of this fruit and the sounds or marks which are tokens of the word "apple". And in practice we have no more difficulty in recognizing certain private experiences like pains, than we have in recognizing colours or apples or tokens of the word "apple". If one needed 'a criterion' for recognizing a pain, one would need a criterion for recognizing the word "pain"; and what could "criterion" then mean? What can Wittgenstein have meant by "criterion" when he made his diarist say 'in the present case I have no criterion of correctness'?

Recognizing something need not, of course, involve remembering in the sense of recollecting past experiences. I can recognize something as a so-and-so, without recollecting, and perhaps without being able to recollect, experiences of other so-and-sos. Perhaps one reason why the Diary argument has seemed compelling to many philosophers, is that they have ignored primary recognition, and dwelt upon cases where one tries to recollect the specific qualities of a particular past sensation and to compare these with the specific qualities of a present sensation. One would rarely be prepared to give a firm affirmative answer to the question: Was it *exactly* like this present sensation? But Wittgenstein's argument implies that we can *never* know the answer to such a question, and this is surely false. There are some situations in which I know the answer to such a question as surely as I know anything, e.g. if a severe and distinctive pain keeps recurring at short intervals. The implication of Wittgenstein's thesis—that even in such a case I cannot rely on my memory of, and therefore cannot talk significantly about, my sensations—destroys his thesis.

We very often lack complete confidence about the precise, the determinate, qualities of what we are recollecting; but this does not apply only or specially to cases where what is recollected is a private experience. It applies also, and in my own case equally, where one is recollecting the qualities of public objects, e.g. the colour of someone's eyes or the shape of a flower. In any case, such uncertainty is usually irrelevant for Wittgenstein's purpose, for what he is discussing are *class*-names, e.g. "E" or "pain". Pains are not all exactly alike any more than dogs are. Those who find the Diary arguments convincing often follow Wittgenstein's habit of using "the same" without discrimination, without attempting to analyze the sense in which the things to which a class-name is applicable can be said to be 'the same'. Consider Rhees' claim, quoted earlier, that if I use "pain" to refer to something to which only I have access, 'there is just no rule for what is the same and what is not the same . . . [so] it does not make any difference what I say'. Or consider Malcolm' similar statements:

when one has given oneself the private rule 'I will call this same thing [sic] "pain" whenever it occurs', one is then free to do anything or nothing. That 'rule' does not point in any direction . . . What I choose to call the 'same' will *be* the same . . . But a sound that I can use *as I please* is not a word (Review of the *Investigations*, op. cit., p. 73).

There is an element of truth in what Malcolm says here, *if* one is considering the imaginary situation in which Wittgenstein places his diarist, and *if* we identify the diarist with the child-genius of the previous paragraph who invents a name for a sensation. In that case, it is indeed indeterminate, from his viewpoint as well as ours, what the diarist would count as 'the same as this' and therefore to be called 'an E' or 'a pain'. But what Malcolm, Rhees and others have failed to recognise is that this indeterminacy has nothing to do with the diarist's language being private either in its reference or in its 'rules' being secret. The indeterminacy as to what will count in future as 'the same as this' stems from *the absurdity of supposing that in giving an ostensive definition of a general word, it could suffice to point, or attend, to a single exemplar*. Any attempt to define thus a general word would leave its meaning indeterminate, whether the 'pointing' be done 'inwardly' or outwardly, whether it be done by oneself or by one's teacher. Suppose that Wittgenstein's diarist cum child-genius had set out to name some, to him, unfamiliar public object, e.g. one which we call a 'peregrine falcon'. If we suppose him to give himself 'a private rule', we must not formulate this rule as Malcolm does: 'I shall call *this same thing* "E"', for these words would only be appropriate if "E" was to be a proper name.[4] Since it is class-names which are under discussion, the private rule would need to be 'I shall call this kind of thing "E" in future'. But this resolution leaves it indeterminate, undecided, in what respects and to what degree other things need to resemble the object in question in order to qualify as E's; whether the diarist would apply "E"

[4] The same goes for Wittgenstein's way of wording the diarist's rule: 'I . . . (inwardly) undertake to call THIS "pain" in the future' (§ 263).

only to other peregrine falcons, to any hawk, to any bird with a hooked beak, to any bird, to anything that flies, etc.

Wittgenstein should not have overlooked this, for at one point he emphasizes the ambiguity of any ostensive definition which involves only a single exemplar. A language learner, he says, 'might equally take the name of a person, of which I give an ostensive definition, as that of a colour, or a race, or even of a point of the compass' (§ 28). But then, instead of considering how ostensive definitions can be and are used in teaching the meaning of a general word, Wittgenstein contents himself with saying: 'an ostensive definition can be variously interpreted in *every* case'; which at least suggests that there is a mystery about how we learn and teach the use of general words, on the ground that this cannot be achieved by ostensive definitions. The conclusion which ought to be drawn is that in order to convey the meaning of a general term by ostensive definition, it is necessary to refer to a collection or series of exemplars which resemble each other in the relevant respects and to the required degree, but are unlike each other in other respects. Thus the meaning of "spherical" may be conveyed by pointing in succession to spherical objects which differ in colour, size, material, etc. Teaching the use of a general word ostensively is incomplete without also pointing to things which resemble the exemplars in only some of the relevant respects or to an insufficient degree, and saying: 'Not spherical, but egg-shaped', 'Not a peregrine, but an eagle', 'Not a pain, but a tickle', etc. One has not learned the use of a general word unless one has learned the boundaries of its application. These may, of course, be indeterminate. For example, each colour-word covers a range of distinct shades, and some shades are about equally similar to standard exemplars of different colour-names. But this too can be conveyed by ostensive definition: 'That is blue-green' or 'reddish purple'.

That teaching the meaning of a general word ostensively must involve a plurality, and a variety, of exemplars is self-evident if one accepts what is called a Resemblance theory of universals. For according to this theory, general words whose function is to describe fulfil this function by saying what a thing *is like*, i.e. what other things this thing resembles; and to talk of "a kind" or "a class" of things is a short way of referring to things which have certain specifiable resemblances, which we, for some purpose or other, have chosen to distinguish and to name. But even if you hold a Realist theory of universals and regard each descriptive word as the proper name of a single transcendental entity (à la Plato) or of a single essential property (à la Aristotle), it would still be absurd to claim that, in order to convey the meaning of a class-name, it could suffice to point to a *single* exemplar. For however you conceive universals, you must admit that anything that can be pointed at, be it public or private, is an instance of many universals. Socrates was a human, a biped, a philosopher, etc. This is a pain, a sensation, something that has been going on for over a minute, etc.

If Wittgenstein's diarist is the child genius and is inventing a name for some unfamiliar sensation, then of course he could not *fix* the meaning of "E" or "pain", simply by concentrating his attention on a particular sensation and saying: 'I undertake to call THIS 'pain''. But if the diarist is like us, in that he has for years been experiencing a variety of sensations, some pleasant and some unpleasant, he is at least in a position to compare his present sensation with others, and to make decisions as to the respects, and the degree, in which future sensations must resemble this one before he will call them 'Es'. And if he does this, he will be in the same position as a Robinson Crusoe who invents names for *public* objects, e.g. unfamiliar flora and fauna, and is unable to appeal to the memory of anyone except himself to confirm that he is using these names consistently. No one would doubt that Defoe's Crusoe would be able to do this, for he had learned the language-game of class-names before his shipwreck. In discussing the Diary argument, Ayer envisaged a Crusoe who had survived after being isolated on a desert island before he had learnt any language. (*PAS*, Supp. Vol., 1954). Ayer thus introduced a new interpretation of Wittgenstein's ambiguous question 'Could there be a private language?', namely: could a person invent a language without any stimulus or help from others? Since this was intended as a logical and not a psychological question, Ayer's affirmative answer must surely be accepted; though we need not debate this thesis, if we assume that what the Diary argument was intended to illuminate is how *we* use, *or* learn to use, words like "pain" or "das Schmerz".

Were the Diary argument valid, the Beetles metaphor would be superfluous. It would be pointless to ask whether your utterance could enable another to understand your reference to one of your sensations, if *you* cannot use it to *make* such a reference. Were the Diary argument valid it would have been superfluous for Wittgenstein to argue separately that a person is not saying anything about his private experiences when he makes statements like 'I understood . . .', 'I meant . . .', 'I imagined . . .', 'I dreamt . . .', etc. The beetles metaphor is a useful one because it depicts the situation in which we find ourselves—we cannot observe other people's 'beetles', their private data. And this applies to the data provided by our sense-organs as well as to sensations like pains. Each of us[5] has learned to apply "red" to the shades which he himself sees when he looks at human blood, ripe tomatoes, etc., and no one can verify that the colour he sees when he looks at a tomato is the same as the shade seen by another who is looking at this tomato. But surely Wittgenstein went too far when he said 'the box might even be empty', implying that for all I know other people's boxes may be empty, that others may not have any private experiences. Admittedly I cannot *demonstrate* that other people are not automata, but I have a strong evidence that, like me, they are conscious. I have evidence that others see things as variously coloured, for they will, on request, describe or draw things which we are both looking at, and their drawings and descriptions tally closely with what I see; and presumably they could not *discriminate* the objects which I and they are looking at, unless they saw them, as I do, as differently coloured.[6] Similarly with pains, I cannot demonstrate that what you feel when you have a dental abscess is the same as what I feel when I have one. But your behaviour and your description of your pain may leave me no room for doubting that you feel a localized sensation for which you feel strong aversion; and that is all I need to be sure about to have a reason for, e.g., giving you my last aspirin; and I should have no reason for acting thus unless I believed that there are in you,

[5] Including those of us who are colour-blind, even dichromats for whom things that are red, yellow, green and brown are indistinguishable in hue.

[6] This may be challenged by means of reminders about operations by machines, operations which some want to call 'perceiving', 'discriminating', 'recognizing', etc. Such arguments do reduce the weight of the argument from analogy—but not to zero. Wittgenstein had a short reply to such arguments: 'Only of what behaves like a human being can one say that it has pains' (§ 283); which provokes the reply: Like in what respects and to what degree? As like as a jelly-fish?

'behind' your behaviour, sensations in *some* degree similar to *some* species of what I call 'pains'. The traditional argument from analogy is not a demonstrative proof, but it does not follow that it has no weight at all. Consider these statements: that human beings are alike in that similar physiological conditions usually make them experience similar sensations and that they tend to express similar sensations by similar behaviour. Nearly everyone believes that these statements are true and would interpret "sensations" therein, not behaviouristically, but as referring to occurrences or 'objects' to which their owners have privileged access. The versions of "the" V P implicit in Wittgenstein's later remarks imply that, so interpreted, these statements are meaningless. So much the worse for such versions of "the" V P.

The argument from analogy should not of course be taken as an account of how, as children, we inferred what we believe about the inner lives of others; but as a way of defending the reasonableness of such beliefs against the arguments of the sceptic. Until we read some philosophy or psychology, we take it for granted that the private experiences of others are like our own. Indeed some theorists have taken this for granted. Thomas Hobbes, for example, in his Introduction to *Leviathan* wrote:

> for the similitude of the thoughts and passions of one man, to the thoughts and passions of another, whosoever looketh into himself, and considereth what he doth, when he does *think*, *opine*, *reason*, *hope*, *fear*, etc., and upon what grounds; he shall hereby read and know, what are the thoughts and passions of all [all!] other men upon like occasions . . .

Hobbes went on to infer that all humans are like himself in desiring for their own sake only self-preservation, power and pleasure. To take another example, J. B. Watson, having searched, by introspection, for 'imagery in the Galtonian sense' without success,[7] inferred, despite the testimony of others, that everyone else is like himself in this respect.[8] Hobbes and Watson provide examples of the most naïve use of the argument from analogy. Though all of us may tend to take it for granted that the inner lives of others are like our own, we sometimes get convincing evidence that this assumption is false. The results of

[7] *Psychological Review*, vol. XX, 1913, pp. 173–4. [8] *Behaviourism*, 1925, p. 213.

Francis Galton's questionnaire concerning mental imagery illustrate this:

> 'To my astonishment', he wrote, 'I found that the great majority of the men of science to whom I first applied protested that mental imagery was unknown to them, and they looked upon me as fanciful and fantastic in supposing that the words "mental imagery" really expressed what I believed everybody supposed them to mean . . . They had a mental deficiency of which they were unaware, and naturally enough supposed that those who affirmed that they possessed it, were romancing' (*Inquiries into Human Faculty*, (1883), fifth paragraph in the section on 'Mental Imagery').

People who have clear and vivid visual imagery are equally astonished when they first discover what Galton's men of science reported. Now the very fact that we can sometimes do what Galton did, i.e. discover that our assumptions about other people's private experiences were mistaken, establishes an affirmative answer to the question: 'Can we communicate about our private experiences?' This is one way of interpreting Wittgenstein's ambiguous question: 'Can there be a private language?' The conclusion which Wittgenstein seems to draw from the beetles metaphor is that this question must be answered in the negative. Presumably no one would claim that we can communicate everything about our inner experiences, e.g. about the specific qualia of various algic or erotic sensations. But obviously we can tell each other something about our pains, or about what (if anything) we 'see in the mind's eye' when visualizing the breakfast table. When a person answers Galton's questions concerning the brightness, definition, colouring and apparent distance of his visual images, we interpret his utterances as *statements referring to* his private data. How else *could* we interpret them? We cannot apply to such utterances the account Wittgenstein gave of "I am in pain", for there is no 'natural', unlearnt, non-verbal behaviour which expresses what is reported by saying 'I am picturing a blue table-cloth', and for which this utterance could be a substitute.

Let us turn now to Wittgenstein's question: how do we (or must we) learn or teach the use of "pain"? (And of other mind-predicates.) Wittgenstein made a very important opening move when he said:

if human beings showed no outward signs of pain . . . it would be impossible to teach a child the use of the word "tooth-ache" (§ 257).

This is one of his most pregnant remarks; though, under his midwifery what it gave birth to was the Diary arguments. The insight to which it points is that unless *some* of our private experiences had 'natural expressions', which provide publicly observable referents for ostensive definitions or ostensive teaching of mind-predicates, the language-game of reporting one's inner experiences could not get started. Consider a passage in which Mr. C. H. Whiteley takes seriously Wittgenstein's invitation to consider how we learn to use words like "pain", "drowsy" or "depressed":

I think that if we look closely at the way language is learned, and are not too much impressed by an over-simple notion of "ostensive definition", we can see how such words come to be understood, and how the connection is established between the inner and outer factors in our mental concepts [i.e. how an association is established between a word like "pain" and *both* felt pain *and* the kinds of observed behaviour which is a spontaneous expression of pain].

Let us suppose that A and B are experienced users of a language and C is a learner who is in their company and hears them speak; and let us suppose that A and B from time to time use, say, the word "drowsy" both with reference to one another and with reference to C. Their criteria for using it of one another and of C will, of course, be purely behavioural. Now C, in the course of learning the language, will observe that A says of B "B is drowsy" whenever B behaves in certain characteristic ways. C will also observe that A says of [to] him "You are drowsy" whenever he, C, has certain characteristic feelings. The connection between drowsy feelings and drowsy behaviour is established in C's mind by the fact that A uses the same word in connection with them both. I do not see how else it could be established. (*Mind*, 1961, p. 167).

Whiteley's last-quoted statement presupposes, what he has argued (p. 166), that children could scarcely *reach* beliefs about the experiences of others by analogical inferences. At the age of learning to use words like "pain", a child suffering pain is preoccupied with what he feels, and is rarely in a position to recognize the resemblance between his present behaviour as it appears to others and the behaviour which he has observed in others when they were said to be in pain. The conclusion which

Whiteley draws is that, as the result of teaching, we come to connect certain inner experiences and certain behaviour patterns 'as parts of a whole' (p. 167), that 'mental concepts comprise factors of two kinds, an inner or private and an outer or public', and that 'both factors in the concept are integral to it in the way in which both being covered with fur and having a propensity to mew are integral to the concept of "cat"' (p. 164).

Whiteley's account of the learning process is correct as far as it goes, but surely it does not go far enough. He describes only the first stage. There is no difficulty in seeing how the child is led to associate a word like "anger" both with what he feels when others apply the word to himself and with the types of behaviour he observes in others when he hears the word applied to them. But learning our language does not stop at this stage. The next stage involves learning that the feelings and behaviour-patterns which one has associated do not always accompany each other. The child learns this through being taught to inhibit expression of anger or pain, by hearing a person saying 'I'm in pain' without displaying any pain-behaviour, or saying 'he looks angry, but he isn't, he's just pretending', and so on. Children do not take very long to learn our five-way distinctions between 'feeling anger', 'behaving angrily', 'pretending to be angry', 'concealing one's anger', and 'expressing one's anger'. It is misleading to speak, as Whiteley does, as if it were true of all mind-words that 'inner and outer factors' are both essential, and equally important, parts of their meaning; as if we adults so use all such words that they are not correctly applied unless two independent conditions are fulfilled. Whiteley's account leads him to draw the untenable conclusion, that it is 'anomalous' to say that someone 'feels drowsy but behaves alertly' or 'behaves sympathetically without feeling sympathy' (p. 164).

No single pattern of analysis fits our *uses* of all mind-predicates. These form a spectrum with respect to the relative importance of 'inner and outer factors'. 'Is John tired?' is not primarily, if at all, a question about John's feelings. It is solely or primarily a question about John's capacity to go on working or playing, etc. We can obtain conclusive evidence for answering this question by observing John's non-verbal behaviour or by physiological tests. 'Is John drowsy?' is different. Here, surely, the experiential and the behavioural or physiological factors are both (and about equally) relevant; for surely we should not say that a person *is* drowsy unless we believe that he feels drowsy and he is also showing some signs of drowsiness. 'Is John in pain?' is again different, for surely everyone except a doctrinaire Behaviourist would understand this as asking if John *feels* pain, regardless of whether he is displaying or concealing it.

The characteristic error of rival 'philosophies of mind' is to try to squeeze all mind-predicates into the same mould. Thus a traditional view, attacked by Wittgenstein, assimilates all mind-predicates to "pain". Behaviourists make the opposite mistake of assimilating all mind-predicates to dispositional terms like "intelligent" or "obstinate"; and, noticing that their ascription to a person does not *imply* anything about his current experiences, they deny or gloss over the fact that the dispositions in question are often manifested in private experiences, e.g. unexpressed thoughts and feelings. Strawson allows us two patterns of analysis, one for dispositional terms and one for predicates such that one's own experience provides 'an entirely adequate basis' for self-ascription (*Individuals*, p. 107). But two moulds are not enough. The predicates which Strawson squeezes into the latter mould are as heterogeneous as "tired" and "depressed" and "in pain". If we think of mind-predicates as forming a spectrum with respect to the relative importance in their meaning of 'inner and outer factors', those for which inner and outer factors are about equally important form only a small part of the spectrum.

Ryle, in *C of M*, gave pride of place to dispositional terms, as if they provided paradigms for the analysis of all mind-predicates, and he said as little as possible about the many mind-words which are used mainly or solely to describe private experiences. Wittgenstein, in the *Investigations*, devoted much time to discussing sensation-words like "pain", which are a major stumbling-block for Philosophical Behaviourism. His most important contribution was in indicating that overt behaviour must in practice play an indispensable part in teaching and learning the uses of such words. Unfortunately Wittgenstein says things which imply or suggest a mistaken conclusion—that there is a *logical* connection between ascriptions of pain, etc., and overt behaviour; and this is the important lesson which he is supposed by many to have taught us.[9] A place where a logical connection might, with some plausibility, be located is in the learning process. It might be argued that it is logically necessary that, in the process of learning our use of "pain", each of us had to associate "pain" with behaviour-patterns which he sees and hears.

I do not wish to endorse the view that the necessity in question is properly called 'logical'. It is not clear that Wittgenstein intended "impossible" to mean 'logically impossible' when he said: '. . . if human beings showed no outward signs of pain . . . it would be impossible to teach a child the use of the word "toothache"' (§ 257). One who claims that it is *logically* necessary that teaching the use of "pain" must involve ostensive reference to overt behaviour, may be challenged on the ground that it would be possible to teach a child the meaning of "pain", even if the child never displayed or observed natural expressions of pain; that the teacher could do this by burning, beating and pricking the child and saying each time 'That's pain'. To this argument he could reply: (a) that if the child never reacted to such maltreatment with the expected behaviour, the teacher would be left in doubt whether the child were abnormal in not *feeling* pain: (b) that this method of teaching might well lead the child to equate "pain" with cruelty or cruelty-to-me, and therefore not apply "pain" to headaches, tummy-aches, etc. But if the challenge is expressed thus: What right have you to treat as *a priori* what is surely not an analytic statement, namely that teaching the use of "pain" *must* involve ostensive reference to overt behaviour?, it is not easy to see how this challenge could be met.

The thesis that there is a logical connection between 'inner processes' and overt behaviour seems to be implied by Wittgenstein's claims that behaviour provides 'the' or 'our criteria' for ascribing mind-predicates. His statement 'An "inner process" stands in need of an outward criterion', could, of course, be interpreted in a way that makes it innocuous. If this meant only that the only *evidence* that *others* can have for ascribing pain to John, is John's behaviour, including what John says, this thesis (if we ignore the possibility of telepathy) is not controversial.

[9] 'that pain behaviour is an essential part of the concept of pain' is Pitcher's familiar way of formulating this conclusion, which Pitcher endorses (*The Philosophy of Wittgenstein*, pp. 306–7).

But according to the only definition he gave of it, Wittgenstein used "criterion" to mean evidence which is conclusive, conclusive by virtue of the meanings we give to the words we use. In *The Blue Book*, he contrasts "criterion" and "symptom", and says that the criterion for applying a word is 'the defining criterion', i.e. the property specified by the definition of this word; and he says: 'I call "symptom" a phenomenon of which experience has taught us that it coincided, in some way or other, with the phenomenon which is our defining criterion' (p. 25). This distinction between "criterion" and "symptom" is reaffirmed in the only passage in the *Investigations* in which he says anything *about* his use of "criterion", i.e. in paragraphs 354-5. Admittedly, Wittgenstein speaks here of the 'fluctuation in grammar between criteria and symptoms'; but that phrase presupposes that "criterion" and "symptom" are still being contrasted in accordance with the Blue Book definitions. As Wittgenstein recognized in *The Blue Book*, it is a tautology to make a statement of the form 'if x is P, then x is A', if P is, in his sense, the criterion for applying the predicate "A".

In the *Investigations* Wittgenstein uses "criterion" in several different ways. In some passages, the context requires that "criterion" be interpreted in the *OED* sense, as meaning simply empirical evidence (e.g. §§ 269, 344 and 633). In some passages the context requires that "criterion" be interpreted in accordance with his own definition, notably when he speaks of our *fixing* or *introducing* criteria (§ 322, pp. 212 and 222[10]). What we *fix* is not the evidence (unless we are cheating) but defining rules, which in turn determine what shall count as empirical evidence for applying the predicate in question. In some cases it is *very* difficult to see what Wittgenstein could have meant by "criterion", e.g. when he speaks of 'a criterion of identity of a sensation' (§ 288), or asks: 'What is the criterion of my learning the shape or colour of an object from a sense-impression?' (p. 185). But there is one significant passage which reveals a further, and very peculiar, use of "criterion". This is where Wittgenstein is discussing what is meant by "doing sums in one's head" or "talking to oneself":

When I say ABC to myself, what is the criterion of my doing the

[10] But note that in the baffling passage on pages 222–3, he is oscillating between different senses of "criterion".

same as someone else who silently repeats it to himself? It might be found that the same thing took place in my larynx and in his . . . But then *did we learn the use of the words*: "to say such and such to one-self" *by someone's pointing to* a process in the larynx or the brain? (§ 376. My italics.)

Wittgenstein's rhetorical question implies that he is here using "the criterion for applying "A"" to refer to whatever sort of thing is (has to be?) pointed to in the process of ostensively teaching the use of "A".

How are we to explain the fact that many philosophers have treated it as an important truth, learnt from Wittgenstein, that there is a *logical* connection between any ascription of any mind-predicate and overt behaviour? Presumably they, like Wittgenstein, are telescoping the questions 'How *do* we use . . .?' and 'How did we *learn* to use . . .?'; a natural by-product of which is the strange meaning given to "criterion" in § 376. Apparently, like Wittgenstein, they use "criterion" to mean sometimes 'empirical evidence' and sometimes 'defining property' and sometimes even to mean 'what has to be pointed at in teaching . . .'. It is easy to see how telescoping these different meanings of "criterion" yields the conclusion in question: that criteria (*qua* empirical evidence) for ascribing a mind-predicate constitute logical grounds for its ascription ('logically adequate criteria' as Strawson puts it). If this diagnosis is rejected by those who accept the view in question, they are invited to explain how they reached it, and how they would justify it.

The view that there is a logical connection between ascriptions of mind-predicates and overt behaviour seems to be based on confusing different theses. It is one thing to say (*a*) that it is logically necessary that our learning to use "pain", *as we have learnt it via ostensive definitions*, involves going through a stage of someone pointing to, and our associating "pain" with, behaviour-patterns. It is a very different thing to claim (*b*) that ascribing pain to a person logically implies statements about his behaviour. (*a*) is surely true, but (*b*) is obviously false. As we do use "pain", to say 'John is in pain' does not entail any statements about John's behaviour, now or in future. Although, as language-learners, we go through the stage of associating "pain" as much with behaviour-patterns as with sensations, the former connection is not permanent and indissoluble, not 'logical'. We later learn to use "pain" in such a way that the experiential factor becomes dominant in its meaning and the behavioural factor becomes peripheral, becomes a symptom as Wittgenstein uses this term. And there are many other mind-words of which this is true. For example "to recognize". When a poacher turns and runs, we regard this not as constituting his recognition of the game-keeper, but as evidence that (it is probable that) he has *consciously* recognized the keeper. All of us, all the time, are recognizing things without behaving in ways from which our acts of recognition could be detected. Any attempt to give an account of "recognize" consistent with Philosophical Behaviourism would be even less plausible than doing this for "pain", Suppose that "recognizing something" is redefined as acquiring a state of readiness to behave in certain ways, this move will not serve its purpose. For John's state of readiness to say that he has seen an osprey is no more observable by others than is his perceptual experience; and so cannot provide others with a *criterion* for ascribing to John an act of recognition, whether "criterion" means empirical evidence, *or* logically conclusive evidence, *or* what has to be pointed at in teaching the use of the word.

The paradoxical conclusions which Wittgenstein drew about 'names of sensations' were apparently connected in his mind with his obscure conclusions concerning 'rules' which he derived from his arithmetical-series examples:

> The use of the word "rule" and the use of the word "same" are interwoven. (As are the use of "proposition" and the use of "true") (§ 225); [and] it is not possible to obey a rule 'privately': otherwise thinking one was obeying a rule would be the same thing as obeying it (§ 202).

Malcolm expounds the Diary argument as a deduction from these axioms. That is why Malcolm said that Wittgenstein had forged 'a remarkably illuminating connection between the philosophy of psychology and the philosophy of mathematics'. It seems to me that in applying these cryptic conclusions to the philosophy of mind, Wittgenstein produced only confusion. He had illustrated the connection between "rule" and "same" by reference to arithmetical series. He treated an operation like adding two as a paradigm case of '(doing) the same (thing)'.

This illustrates *exact* similarity: for the operation of adding two to zero is exactly similar to that of adding two to 1000. But "the same" does not mean 'exactly similar' when we speak of pains or colours being 'the same'. To say that things are 'the same', meaning 'of the same kind', is to say that they resemble each other in specifiable respects and degrees. And this applies whether we are talking about non-linguistic things or about the sounds and marks that we class as instances of the same word. Sometimes Wittgenstein even seems to confuse the radically different uses of "the same", to mean *of the same kind* and to mean *the same individual or particular entity* (see §§ 253 and 443); though in the former case "the same" is used to refer to a relation between *different* things and in the latter to say that two different descriptions apply to *one* thing.

Wittgenstein's conclusion that 'it is not possible to obey a rule 'privately'' was reached via the thoughts that rules of our arithmetical notation are fixed by our conventions, our public and agreed procedures that these have to be taught, and that no one is free to adopt his own interpretations:

> there is a way of grasping a rule which is *not* an *interpretation*, but which is exhibited in what we call "obeying the rule" and "going against it" in actual cases . . . And hence also, 'obeying a rule' is a practice (§§ 201–2).

But this shows that Wittgenstein is here using "private" as the opposite of "publicly known and agreed". So no conclusions can be drawn, from what he says here, about the impossibility of language being private *in its reference*, i.e. used to refer to private experiences; nor, of course, about the impossibility of rules being 'obeyed privately' in the more obvious interpretation of this phrase; that is, when one follows rules (e.g. does calculations) in one's head. Wittgenstein and his followers oscillate at their own convenience between using "private language" in different senses. (See §§ 243, 256, 269.) It is unfortunate that Wittgenstein did not make use of his simile between using language and playing games when considering his ambiguous question whether language can be private. Games may be private *qua* secret, for one can invent new forms of solitaire, and obey one's own rules without divulging them. Games may also be private in the sense that they involve making references to private experiences. As

Wittgenstein acknowledges at one point: 'There is a game of 'guessing thoughts'' (p. 223). But though he acknowledges this fact, he does not recognize its 'depth grammar', its implications. He dismisses these with a characteristic piece of *a priori* linguistics: 'To say "He alone can know what he intends" is nonsense' (p. 223).

Lest I should be misinterpreted as saying 'Wittgenstein was a behaviourist', I shall repeat something said earlier. I have not been claiming that the *Investigations* contains a clear or consistent statement of Philosophical Behaviourism. What I have tried to show is that some of Wittgenstein's most celebrated remarks would commit him, if he were consistent, to Behaviourism as I have defined this term. There are, however, a few passages in the *Investigations* where he says things which are incompatible with this theory, and which suggest the moderate position of *The Brown Book*. The following would be an example, *if* we make the unverifiable assumption that it is not the imaginary critic who is supposed to be talking:

> The essential thing about private experience is really not that each person possesses his own exemplar, but that nobody knows whether other people also have *this* or something else. The assumption would thus be possible—though unverifiable—that one section of mankind had one sensation of red and another section another (§ 272).

This passage illustrates, incidentally, the connection between Philosophical Behaviourism and "the" Verification Principle, for these remarks which are incompatible with the former involve rejecting the latter.

There are indications that when Wittgenstein wrote Part II of the *Investigations* his views were changing. We find a few passages suggesting that he was then prepared to admit that an utterance might be a *report* of the speaker's state of mind, the clearest of these being at the end of Section IX:

> A cry is not a description. But there are transitions. And the words "I am afraid" may approximate more, or less, to being a cry. They may come quite close to this and also be far removed from it.
>
> We surely do not always say someone is complaining, because he says he is in pain. So the words "I am in pain" may be a cry of complaint, *and may be something else* (p. 189. My italics).

In view of the remarkable extent to which Wittgenstein's

thought developed and changed throughout his life, and was apparently still changing until the end, I suggest that Wittgenstein would have been dismayed at the way in which his admirers have tended to treat his later remarks as containing final solutions to the problems of philosophy. This tendency will be one of my main topics in the next section.

SECTION XVII
Wittgenstein's Legacy

PROFESSOR Malcolm tells us in his Memoir that Wittgenstein

> believed that his influence as a teacher was largely harmful . . . He once concluded a year's lectures with this sentence: "The only seed I am likely to sow is a certain jargon" (*Ludwig Wittgenstein*, pp. 62–3).

That remark was *much* too modest. We are indebted to him for some very important insights. But he has bequeathed some jargon, and one of the most popular items is "criterion". Despite their abundant use of this word during the last twenty years or so, philosophers have scarcely ever defined or explained their uses, and it is often unclear just how they would wish to do so. Even Strawson seems to have been perpetuating Wittgenstein's amalgamation of different senses of "criterion", when he wrote that 'behaviour-criteria' are 'not just signs . . . but are criteria of a logically adequate kind . . .' (*Individuals*, p. 106). The article on 'Criterion' in *The Encyclopaedia of Philosophy* (1967) by Mr. Anthony Kenny is wholly devoted to Wittgenstein's use of this word. But although Kenny quotes passages which illustrate Wittgenstein's incompatible uses of the word, he does not show signs of recognizing the dangers of confusing them.

Consider these statements made by Mr. A. M. Quinton in expounding Wittgenstein's Diary argument:

> Wittgenstein maintains that our mental vocabulary does not refer to inner acts and states. It is not so much that he denies the existence of private experiences as that he denies that they could serve as criteria for the employment of mental words;

and on the next page:

> But what could be meant, he [Wittgenstein] asks, by the question whether a given sensation was the same as *the one chosen as the criterion*? ('Excerpt from "Contemporary British Philosophy"', reprinted in G. Pitcher's anthology *Wittgenstein*, 1966, pp.17–19. My italics.)

Quinton seems to be introducing yet another use of "criterion", according to which a person's criterion for employing a word is *the* original exemplar by reference to which the word had for him been ostensively defined. Perhaps Quinton intended to render more precise the use of "criterion" indicated in § 376 of the *Investigations*, which I have rendered as: whatever *sort* of thing is (has to be?) pointed to in the process of ostensively teaching the use of a word. But Quinton's use of "criterion" seems to be endorsing, by implication, the error of arguing as if a general word could be ostensively defined by reference to a *single* exemplar. (see pp. 225–6 above.)

Wittgenstein's amalgamation of his § 376 use of "criterion" and his use of it to mean 'defining property', is closely connected with his amalgamation of the questions: 'How do we use "—"?' and 'How did we learn to use "—"?'. Wittgenstein's habit of offering answers to the latter question as if they were answers to the former, has reintroduced what has sometimes been called 'the genetic fallacy': the assumption that, by considering how an idea is acquired (or a word-meaning is learnt), we can discover the correct analysis of the idea (the correct use of the word). Presumably all philosophy teachers who still teach some history of philosophy still point out that Locke, Berkeley and Hume made this mistake. Have any of them pointed out that Wittgenstein makes it? And that other philosophers have followed suit, when discussing 'the logic of concepts' and the 'criteria' for their application? Malcolm's *Dreaming*, to which I refer below, provides a conspicuous example. Wittgenstein and his followers have given us useful, if unintended, reminders that the 'genetic fallacy' really is a fallacy.

Another unfortunate feature of Wittgenstein's legacy is that many philosophers feel obliged to quote his remarks as 'texts' before giving us their own arguments, or to present their own theories as explications of his insights. I shall give two examples, the first from Professor Peter Winch's *The Idea of a Social Science* (1958), the second from a paper by Mr. R. Bambrough. Winch introduces the reader to some of Wittgenstein's insights in a section headed '*Rules: Wittgenstein's Analysis*' (pp. 24–33); the insights being those cryptic theorems which Wittgenstein derived from his arithmetical examples and misapplied in discussing 'a private language' (*PI*, §§ 202 and 225). Winch's paraphrase of the second of these theorems is: 'It is only in terms of a given rule that we can attach a specific sense to the words 'the same'' (p. 27). To explain this, he says that the word "same" is systematically ambiguous, and then quotes from the *Investigations*:

But isn't *the same* at least the same?

We seem to have an infallible paradigm of identity in the identity of a thing with itself. I feel like saying: 'Here at any rate there can't be a variety of interpretations. If you are seeing a thing you are seeing identity too.'

Then are two things the same when they are what *one* thing is? And how am I to apply what the *one* thing shows me to the case of two things? (§ 215)

These dark sayings do indeed illustrate the ambiguity of "the same", by seeming to confuse numerical and qualitative identity. Winch does not mention this ambiguity. He quotes this obscure passage as if, by itself, it would clarify for students the connection between "the same" and "rule".

I shall now quote the passage in which Winch passes from Wittgenstein's second theorem to the first, that 'it is not possible to obey a rule 'privately'' (§ 202):

What is the difference between someone who is really applying a rule in what he does and someone who is not? A difficulty here is that any series of actions which a man may perform can be brought within the scope of some formula or other if we are prepared to make it sufficiently complicated. Yet, that a man's action *might* be interpreted as an application of a given formula, is in itself no guarantee that he is in fact applying that formula. What is the difference between these cases?

Imagine a man—let us call him A—writing down the following figures on a blackboard: 1 3 5 7. A now asks his friend, B, how *the* series is to be continued. [My italics.] Almost everybody in this situation, short of having special reasons to be suspicious, would answer: 9 11 13 15. Let us suppose that A refuses to accept this as a continuation of his series, saying it runs as follows: 1 3 5 7 1 3 5 7 9 11 13 15 9 11 13 15. He then asks B to continue from there. At this point B has a variety of alternatives to choose from. Let us suppose that he makes a choice and that A again refuses to accept it, but substitutes another continuation of his own. And let us suppose that this continues for some time. There would undoubtedly come a point at which B, with perfect justification, would say that A was not really following a mathematical rule at all, even though all the continuations he had made to date *could* be brought within the scope of some formula. Certainly A was following a rule; but his rule was: Always to substitute a continuation different from the one suggested by B at every stage. And though this is a perfectly good rule of its kind, it does not belong to arithmetic.

Winch's variation of Wittgenstein's arithmetical examples is open to obvious objections. The important one is not that A's rule 'does not belong to arithmetic', but that A is cheating or playing a joke on his friend B; that A wantonly misleads B by asking him how *the* series is to be continued, instead of saying 'guess the rule which I have in mind'. And since A *need* never divulge what this rule is, Winch's argument scarcely supports Wittgenstein's first theorem that 'it is not possible to obey a rule 'privately'' (§ 202). Perhaps Winch recognized this. For, whereas he quotes Wittgenstein's second theorem he does not quote the first, but reformulates it in a way that Wittgenstein never did: 'it is only in a situation in which it *makes sense* to suppose that somebody else could *in principle* discover the rule which I am following that I can intelligibly be said to follow a rule at all' (p. 30. My italics). But whatever one may think of Winch's exposition of what Wittgenstein said about linguistic rules, why should he think it necessary or appropriate to expound this in introducing students to the idea of a social science?

Let us now consider Mr. R. Bambrough's paper 'Universals and Family Resemblances' (*PAS*, 1960–1, reprinted in Pitcher's *Wittgenstein*, to which page-references will be made). Bambrough has, I think, done something remarkable. He has made an entirely new move in a debate that has gone on for 2500 years. Yet he insists in fathering it on Wittgenstein, without even explaining why. He opens by saying:

'I believe that Wittgenstein solved what is known as "the problem of universals", and I would say of his solution . . . that it is "one of the greatest and most valuable discoveries that has been made of late years . . ."' (p. 186).

The contents of much of Bambrough's paper are not new: he starts by expounding Wittgenstein's remarks about family resemblance, and ends by outlining a familiar type of resemblance theory. Presumably he does not think that Wittgenstein invented the latter, which was held, if not developed, by Hobbes[1] and by Hume.[2] Bambrough's novel move comes in the middle of his paper (pp. 193–9), and seems to be unrelated to, and indeed incompatible with, the remainder. It consists in treating as 'an important philosophical truth' such platitudes as 'what all chairs have in common is that they are chairs' (p. 197). Bambrough writes:

> Now the platitude that all games have in common that they *are* games is denied by the nominalist, who says that all games have nothing in common except that they are *called* games.[3] And it is not only the nominalist, but also his opponent, who misunderstands the central importance of the platitude . . . When he is provoked by the nominalist's claim . . . he feels that he must look for something that games have in common apart from *being* games. This feeling is entirely misplaced. The very terms of the nominalist's challenge require only that the realist should point out something that games have in common apart from *being called* games, and this onus is fully discharged by saying that they *are* games (pp. 195–6. His italics).

Do others get an Alice-in-Wonderland feeling at being told that realists can dispose of nominalism simply by saying emphatically '(all) games *are* games'? Bambrough does not claim to have discovered this insight. He writes: 'Wittgenstein says that games have nothing in common except that they are games' (p. 199). If Wittgenstein ever said this, one would like to know where and when; and whether he tried to reconcile this with what he does say in *The Blue Book* and the *Investigations*, where he spoke very differently. For he recognized there that the so-called problem of universals concerns our use of general *words*. Wittgenstein did not, in this context, confuse using and mentioning the word "game". He speaks of 'the general term "game"' (*BBB*, p. 17), of 'the proceedings that we call "games"' (*PI*, § 66). At one point Bambrough seems to

1 'One universal name is imposed on many things, for their similitude in some quality or accident' (Hobbes, *Leviathan*, Ch. IV).

2 'When we have found a resemblance among several objects, that often occur to us, we apply the same name to all of them. . . .' (Hume, *Treatise*, I, I, VII).

3 If this is what 'the nominalist' says, has any philosopher been a nominalist?

recognize this, when he says that Wittgenstein 'asserts . . . the realist's claim that there is an objective justification for the application of the word "game" to games . . .' (p. 199). Since this is what the debate has been about, i.e. justifying or explaining the use of general words, what on earth can one make of the assertion 'games *are* games', where the word "games", is, presumably, in both instances, being *used*? Bambrough's new move is Wittgensteinian in some ways—it is bold and baffling—but no reason has been given, nor I think could be, for attributing it to Wittgenstein.

Another part of Wittgenstein's legacy which may be mentioned in passing is the latitude which his admirers often allow themselves in affirming what he, or others, have said or meant, without giving adequate, or sometimes any, documentation. Thus Bambrough gives no reasons or references to justify ascribing his own new move to Wittgenstein. More commonly, philosophers assert that Wittgenstein said or held so and so and cite page or paragraph numbers; but when one consults the passages in question, they often seem to say things *very* different from the gloss. Wittgenstein's critics are also sometimes guilty of this. Thus Mr. H. N. Castaneda claims to find in the *Investigations* the most extreme kind of Nominalism, the thesis that 'the similarities and samenesses that we find in things do not exist *in rerum natura*' but 'consist of the fact that we "call" the things in question the same' ('Private Language Argument', *The Encyclopaedia of Philosophy*, 1967, Vol. 6, p. 463). In support of this he refers us to the following paragraphs of the *Investigations*: 146, 149, 185–90, 208–23, 348–52. A few of the remarks therein would permit, but none requires or clearly points to, Castaneda's interpretation. The present section will contain further illustrations of the lax standards which are common in Wittgensteinian exegesis.

Another manifestation of Wittgenstein's influence is that some philosophers have taken texts from him, interpreted these literally and worked out their implications, regardless of the resulting paradoxes and of the fact that their conclusions conflict with ordinary uses of language. I shall give two examples, the first Professor Malcolm's book *Dreaming* (1959). The texts which inspired this book are a few remarks in the *Investigations*, notably:

Now must I make some assumption about whether people are deceived by their memories or not: whether they really had these images while they slept, or whether it merely seems so to them on waking? And what meaning has this question? (p. 184).

Malcolm seems to have taken the last sentence as a rhetorical question, as a way of saying that the preceding question is meaningless; presumably on the strength of Wittgenstein's later remark:

The question whether the dreamer's memory deceives him when he reports the dream after waking cannot arise, unless indeed we introduce a completely new criterion for the report's 'agreeing' with the dream . . . (pp. 222–3).

Many readers of Malcolm's book may have got the impression that he is claiming that 'we do not dream but only wake with delusive memories of experiences we never had' (as Ayer put it). Malcolm rejects this interpretation in 'Professor Ayer on *Dreaming*' (*J. of Phil.*, 1961, a reply to Ayer's 'Professor Malcolm on Dreams', *J. of Phil.*, 1961). But if Malcolm does not wish to embrace that paradox, he has embraced many others, for example: 'that in the familiar concept of dreaming there is no provision for the duration of dreams in physical time' (p. 79). This is plainly false.[4] The premises of Malcolm's *a priori* linguistics are less concealed than they were in Wittgenstein's *Investigations*. They are: (i) some unidentified version of the Verification Principle, as revealed in Malcolm's statement: 'I have stressed *the senselessness, in the sense of the impossibility of verification*, of the notion of a dream as an occurrence 'in its own right'' (p. 83. My italics); (ii) oscillation between the different senses in which Wittgenstein had used "criterion", and particularly the failure to recognize that in the present context one must choose between using "criterion" to mean merely *empirical evidence* and to mean *evidence that is conclusive*, 'that settles the question with certainty' (p. 60); (iii) the genetic fallacy, as practised by Wittgenstein: deducing the answer to 'How *do* we use "dream"?' from his own answer to 'How did we *learn* to use "dream"?' Malcolm's inadequate answer to the latter question is: 'the concept of dreaming is derived, not from

[4] It is neither ungrammatical nor meaningless to ask, e.g., for how many minutes a person had been dreaming.

dreaming, but from the familiar phenomena that we call 'telling a dream' (p. 55); or as he sometimes puts it: '*The* criterion of someone's having a dream . . . is that upon wakening he tells the dream' (p. 49. My italics). It is remarkable that anyone should not just ignore, but deny, the fact that one's own *experience* of dreaming plays a part in one's forming 'the concept of dreaming'; and that any philosophical expositor of ordinary language should define "dreaming" in a way which implies that deaf-mutes, dogs and as yet speechless infants cannot significantly be said to dream. Recall Malcolm's statement: 'A philosophical statement cannot be paradoxical and not be false' (*The Philosophy of G. E. Moore*, pp. 361–2).

The philosophy of religion is another field in which we find bizarre examples of the working out of the literal implications of Wittgenstein's texts. The philosophy of religion has, for many, been liberated from awkward problems concerning the truth or coherence of, or the evidence for, religious beliefs. In this case, the liberating text is:

> Our mistake is to look for an explanation where . . . we ought to have said: *this language game is played.* The question is not one of explaining a language-game by means of our experiences, but of noting a language-game (*PI*, §§ 654–5).

Mr. D. Z. Phillips' *The Concept of Prayer* (1965) is representative of the new and popular way of doing philosophy of religion. He starts by quoting our now familiar text: 'Philosophy may in no way interfere with the actual use of language . . . It leaves everything as it is'. He acknowledges that many philosophers would say that he is 'taking the most important issue for granted, namely the existence of God' (p. 12), and he then proceeds to explain how this issue may be by-passed. Philosophers who make that criticism, we are told, 'assume that they know the conceptual category[5] to which the reality of God belongs' (p. 13). To this Phillips replies: 'to answer this question one must determine the depth grammar of the concept to be investigated' (p. 13). Examining the depth grammar reveals a new version of the Ontological Argument, which shows 'that it *makes no sense* to say that God might not exist' (p. 14. His italics). This new argument was discovered by Malcolm, from

[5] With what kind of category is a *conceptual* category being contrasted?

whom Phillips quotes the following passage and describes it as 'penetrating':

In the Ninetieth Psalm it is said: 'Before the mountains were brought forth, or ever those hadst formed the earth and the world, even from everlasting to everlasting, thou art God'. Here is expressed the idea of the necessary existence and eternity of God, an idea that is essential to the Jewish and Christian religions. In those complex systems of thought, those 'language-games', God has the status of a necessary being. Who can doubt that? Here we must say with Wittgenstein, 'This language-game is played' (p. 18).

Phillips explains that this shows that 'To have the idea of God is to know God' (p. 18). It transpires that "to have the idea of God" means to know how to use the word "God", yet *also* (surprisingly) means *to know God*! We are told:

the religious believer must be a participant in a shared language. He must learn the use of religious concepts. What he learns is religious language; a language which he participates in along with other believers. *What I am suggesting is that to know how to use this language is to know God* . . . [that] *He* [God] *is to be found in the language people learn when they come to learn about religion* (pp. 50–1. My italics).

Other philosophers who adopt Phillips' method of disposing of questions about God's existence, do not always express it so clearly and simply. When stated so clearly, this way of defending one's faith seems simplistic. Those who use this short-cut must then recognize the limitations of their method, notably that *all* living religions or cults are equally justified thereby. Not all new-style philosophers of religion are liberal enough to accept the implications of their premises—that witchcraft, Spiritualism and Voodoo are language-games which have as much authority as the game(s) which they themselves have been taught to play.

The last feature of Wittgenstein's legacy which will be illustrated is one which was anticipated by Professor Heath, when he wrote in 1956 that the *Investigations* provides 'a goldmine for commentators'. Since then many able philosophers have devoted much effort and ingenuity to trying to interpret the remarks in this album. Mr. Pitcher's recent anthology, subtitled 'A Collection of Critical Essays', contains a sample of nineteen papers, selected from the 174 works listed in the incomplete Bibliography. Readers of this anthology who are new to this game may be struck by the confident and sometimes dogmatic tone in which some commentators tell us what Wittgenstein meant; but, noticing that those most confident that they can read between Wittgenstein's lines disagree very widely with each other, perhaps they will suspect that there is something arbitrary and unprofitable about this game. In Section XVI, several alternative interpretations of the 'private language' passage were described. The prevailing range of disagreement in interpreting this passage will now be indicated by reference to four recent papers which have not so far been mentioned. In the course of doing this, attention will be drawn to some short-comings in the quality of their arguments and scholarship. I have chosen interpretations which differ substantially from my own, rather than ones with which I am more or less inclined to agree, e.g. those of Ayer, Strawson, Quinton and Pitcher. The papers discussed below, apart from Mr. Holborow's, are included in Pitcher's anthology, to which page-references will be made.

Mr. L. C. Holborrow has recently presented as 'obvious' an interpretation of Wittgenstein that no one else seems to have thought of before ('Wittgenstein's Kind of Behaviourism', *Phil. Quarterly*, 1967). He tells us that what Wittgenstein was denying, in denying the possibility of a private language, was that 'there could be a language which referred to experiences which were *radically private*, i.e. completely without "natural expressions"' (p. 347). He tells us that Wittgenstein distinguished two 'utterly different types' of private experience, those which do and those which don't have natural expressions. The only evidence that he offers for this thesis is given in this assertion:

> The "immediate private sensations" considered in 243, and contrasted with the inner experiences that can be referred to in language, are obviously intended to be "private" in the sense that they lack a "natural expression" (p. 346).

Yet he does not quote § 243! I have quoted the relevant part of it on page 221 above. Does any one else find it obvious that Holborow has read correctly between the lines, obvious that

Wittgenstein is contrasting, and not using as synonyms, "inner experiences" and "immediate private experiences"? In fact, there are two remarks by Wittgenstein which could have been cited as seeming to suggest Holborow's interpretation, i.e. in paragraph 256 and the opening of 257. But if the thought then in Wittgenstein's mind was what Holborow finds *obvious*, Wittgenstein forgot it immediately; for the kind of sensation he proceeds to discuss is pain: in the Diary argument, the Beetles metaphor, the passage where he presents his conclusion (§ 304) and in many intervening remarks. Had Holborow been correct, Wittgenstein would not have gone on and on about pain, but would have focussed on expressions like "having an image", "dreaming", "hearing a singing in one's ears", etc., which describe experiences which do not have natural expressions in the way that pain has. Holborow's paper was written as a reply to mine (*Phil. Quarterly*, 1966) in which I argued that some of Wittgenstein's remarks would commit him to what I then called 'Linguistic Behaviourism'. Yet Holborow does not discuss the remarks which I had emphasized in this context, notably paragraphs 293 and 304. If commentators are to be bold enough to ignore what is given as 'the conclusion', this leaves room for novel interpretations less implausible than Holborow's.

Mr. John W. Cook's 'Wittgenstein on Privacy'[6] is long, complex, subtle and closely reasoned. He puts under a microscope a few paragraphs preceding the Diary Argument and finds more in them than any one had done before. I shall not discuss what he found here beyond expressing my surprise at the fact that an exponent of everyday language should still feel obliged to try to justify some of Wittgenstein's least justifiable would-be reminders; and at the manner in which Cook does this. (i) He claims that when one adds "I know that" to "I am [or, presumably, "am not"] in pain", one produces a *meaningless* utterance and not a more emphatic statement. Cook argues (pp. 291 ff.) as if the only point of saying 'I know I am in pain' could be to contrast my present state of mind with cases where I would say 'I doubt whether I am in pain', which is dismissed as meaningless. He fails to recognize that the point

[6] Published originally in *The Philosophical Review*, 1965.

would normally be to rebut doubts or challenges expressed by others: '*I* know I am in pain' as a reply to 'I know you are shamming' or 'I know that can't hurt'. Consider the contexts in which a person does thus emphasize his own *authority* to make reports about his sensations, feelings, desires, intentions, thoughts, etc.[7] (ii) Cook defends, as one of Wittgenstein's insights, the thesis that a sentence like "All the pains [or, presumably, "the desires or intentions"] I have are mine" should be 'recognized as spurious, as not belonging to the language game' (p. 304); implying that such sentences are *meaningless*, and not, as they surely are, analytic.

Cook's preoccupation with the theses just described leads him to treat very casually the passages which most commentators have put in the centre of the picture; and he writes rather dogmatically of other philosophers' 'misunderstandings' and 'errors'. Consider what he says about Pitcher's alleged errors[8] in *The Philosophy of Wittgenstein*. Cook says that it has been argued, erroneously, by Pitcher

> that since sensations are private, and since Wittgenstein denies the possibility of naming private objects, he must be denying that ordinary language contains any genuine names of sensations: on Wittgenstein's view "private sensations do not enter into pain language games" (p. 289).

Compare this with the passage near the end of Cook's paper where he finally explains the nature of Pitcher's alleged error:

> since the view that sensations are private allows sensations to have "no place in the language-game" and thereby makes it impossible to give any account of the actual (that is, the "public") use of sensation words, we must, if we are to give an account of that language game, reject the view that sensations are private (p. 322).

The main difference, then, between Pitcher and Cook is that Pitcher assumes that Wittgenstein was not the most extreme kind of behaviourist; that he was saying, in effect: 'I deny, not that we have private sensations, but that we can talk about them'; whereas Cook baldly rejects 'the view that sensations are private' (as he puts it). Cook seems committed, then, to

[7] See Ayer's discussion in *The Concept of a Person*, pp. 58–64.

[8] Pitcher ignores the escape-clause in § 304, and therefore attributes to Wittgenstein, without qualification, what, in Section XVI, I labelled 'conclusion (a)'.

interpret Wittgenstein as an extreme Behaviourist. He ends by citing Wittgenstein's suggestion that words are used in place of natural expressions of pain (§ 244). He shows no sign of recognizing any of the glaring difficulties in accepting this as an account of how we *do* (as distinct from how we *began to learn* to) use words like "pain".

Consider now the *grounds* that Cook offers for saying that Pitcher has misunderstood a passage which really involves rejecting the view that sensations are private. The passage is the one concerning the beetles (§ 293). Pitcher had said of Wittgenstein's sentence, "The thing in the box has no place in the language-game at all", that 'The analogy with pain is perfectly clear'. (It has seemed so to most readers.) Cook's comment is: 'But so far from this being Wittgenstein's view, it is what he calls a "paradox" (*PI*, 304)' (p. 321). *Yet Cook does not quote § 304.* Had he done so the arbitrariness of his assertion would have been obvious. The relevant passage is:

> It [the sensation itself] is not a *something*, but not a *nothing* either. The conclusion was only that a nothing would serve just as well as a something about which nothing could be said. We have only rejected the grammar which tries to force itself on us here. The paradox disappears only if we make a radical break with the idea that language always functions in one way . . .

How on earth could Cook *know* that what Wittgenstein referred to here as 'the paradox' is not his own self-contradictory statement, 'it is not a *something*, but not a *nothing* either', but is a very different statement made eleven paragraphs earlier?

Mr. Alan Donagan's paper 'Wittgenstein on Sensation' makes an original contribution to Wittgensteinian exegesis, by discovering a possible new interpretation of paragraph 301. According to Donagan, Wittgenstein was denying that one can form a 'picture' (*Bild*) of another person's pain, but is allowing that one can have an 'imaginative representation' (*Vorstellung*) thereof. This interpretation is based on paragraphs 297–301, and does indeed seem to be the most plausible interpretation of this passage, particularly of the statement: 'The (*Vorstellung*) of pain certainly enters into the language-game in a sense; only not as a (*Bild*)'. On the strength of this, Donagan offers an interpretation of Wittgenstein's general position which would make it a moderate and reasonable one, acceptable, I think, to Descartes: that sensations are private occurrences, distinct from their behavioural expressions, if any; that we may use a word like "pain" to *refer to* such an occurrence, but that "pain" is, in effect, a description which involves reference to behaviour, for "pains" means: sensations which people tend to express by such and such behaviour. On this interpretation, the main lesson which Wittgenstein was trying to teach us is that a person can never know whether other people's private experiences are like his own, but that such ignorance makes no difference, since, as Donagan puts it:

> provided that what a man truthfully reports as pain is always what he would naturally express by pain-behaviour, it matters not at all what it is that he truthfully reports as pain (p. 346).

My reaction to this interpretation is: if that is what Wittgenstein meant, why did he not say so, instead of saying so many things which point in different directions?[9] However, what I want to consider here is one of the main arguments which Donagan uses to support his conclusion that his interpretation is *the* correct one. Donagan says that Wittgenstein 'unequivocally affirmed that sensations are a nondispositional accompaniment of behaviour' (p. 349). He offers, as such an unequivocal affirmation, words which Wittgenstein put within quotation marks and were evidently intended as an interjection by his imaginary critic:

> "Yes, but there is *something* there all the same accompanying my cry of pain. And it is on account of that that I utter it. And this something is what is important and frightful" (§ 296).

Wittgenstein's final answer to this imaginary critic, who kept on butting in, consists in saying:

> It is not a *something* but not a *nothing* either. The conclusion was only that a nothing would serve just as well as a something about which nothing could be said (§ 304).

Donagan quotes the first of the two sentences I have just quoted, and says it is the 'chief problem in expounding Wittgenstein's theory', *but then just ignores the second sentence*. And he

[9] Paragraph 272 could be cited in support of Donagan's interpretation, though Donagan does not do so.

disposes of the similar conclusion of paragraph 293 ('The thing in the box has no place in the language-game at all; not even as a *something*') by describing it as a *slip* on Wittgenstein's part (p. 346). Paragraphs 293 and 304 are surely, by Wittgenstein's standards, unequivocal statements that we cannot talk about the sensation itself *or* that "talking about x" in this context does not involve *referring to* x. Donagan is prepared to dismiss their implications, yet he treats as an unequivocal affirmation what Wittgenstein put into the mouth of his imaginary critic.

Finally, let us consider a passage from Mr Anthony Kenny's paper 'Cartesian Privacy' in order to illustrate a distortion of history which has become common among Wittgenstein's apologists. Kenny sets out to examine the claim which, as he says, is frequently made: 'that one of the achievements of Wittgenstein was to provide a refutation of Cartesian dualism' (p. 352). Wittgenstein had defined "a private language" as one in which there can be no communication. In order that his thesis that such a language is impossible should seem to have some philosophical purpose, many of his expositors have supposed or asserted that Wittgenstein's target was Descartes or Cartesian dualism. If we suppose that Wittgenstein's target was things written by other philosophers, his target could have been all of those British empiricists from Locke to Ayer who have assumed that the immediate data of perception are private—ideas, impressions or sense-data; and some of these philosophers are and some are not dualists. Alternatively, Wittgenstein's target might have been what Rudolf Carnap called 'the protocol language' (*The Unity of Science*, 1934). Why pick on Descartes or his theory as Wittgenstein's target? The result of doing so has been that, in the interest of making Wittgenstein's arguments sound pertinent for their postulated purpose, his expositors have claimed that acceptance of Cartesian dualism requires acceptance of the preposterous view that we learn language in the way that Wittgenstein's child-genius-cum-diarist attempted to do so. Kenny endorses this thesis. After a scholarly discussion of various features of Descartes' thought, he makes the following bald statements:

it seems clear that if a Cartesian *res cogitans* uses a language it must be a private language in the sense defined by Wittgenstein . . .

If the language contains words for sensations, then the connection between the words and the sensations must be set up without the intermediary of the natural expression of sensation in bodily behaviour; for the words of the language are supposed to have meaning at a stage at which it is doubtful whether there are any bodies at all (p. 362).

What seems clear to me is that Kenny is arguing as if Descartes' philosophy started with the first Meditation and ended with the second; as if Descartes never resolved his doubts about the existence of physical things; as if Descartes, to whom it never occurred to doubt the existence of other people, was a solipsist.

It ought not to be necessary to remind professional philosophers that Cartesian dualists believe in bodies as well as minds. The feature of Descartes' thought which *might* have led him to conclude that the language used by a *res cogitans* must be a private language à la Wittgenstein is *not* his dualism but his method of doubt. Admittedly Descartes used his method of doubt to try to justify the kind of mind-body dualism which he accepted as part of his religious faith; and during the earlier stages of Descartes' thought-experiment, he doubted the existence of all bodies including his own. Had Descartes been rigorous and consistent in applying his method of doubt, he would have been obliged to doubt the existence of other minds. He would then have faced the question: How did I learn to talk and write French and Latin? Had he found it impossible to escape from solipsism, he would presumably have been obliged to conclude that he himself had *given* meanings to the Latin and French words which he used—to *all* of them, and not just to 'words for sensations'. But *if* Descartes had got stuck at this stage and with this conclusion, *he would not have been a dualist.* When Kenny and others argue that it is a corollary of Descartes' kind of mind-body *dualism* that each of us has created his own sensation language, their critical powers seem to have been blunted by a desire to make sense of Wittgenstein's remarks about a private language.

Consider Mr. Donagan's procedure in this matter in 'Wittgenstein on Sensation'. He *starts* by saying:

The position I shall call "Cartesian" is that each man has,

in the Rylean phrase, "privileged access" to his own sensations (p. 324).[10]

His next move is:

Cartesians *are tempted to infer* that, in order to name a sensation of a given kind . . . each man must wait until he has a sensation of that kind, and then privately confer the name . . . on it (p. 325. My italics).

The next stage is:

"I speak or write [a word] down, and at the same time I concentrate my attention on [a] sensation—and so, as it were, point to it inwardly" (*PI*, 258). *It is in some such way, Cartesians would hold*, that words like "pain" are connected with the inner processes of which they are the names (p. 337. My italics).

The *final* stage is to speak, without qualification, of

the Cartesian doctrine that sensation words are names privately conferred on processes inwardly observed (p. 349. My italics. Cf. p. 338).

Notice that Donagan starts by so defining "Cartesian" that the vast majority of philosophers, at all times including the present, are Cartesians; namely all who are not Behaviourists. This makes it all the more preposterous to end up by describing as 'the Cartesian doctrine' the thesis that 'sensation words are names privately conferred on processes inwardly observed'. For it implies that hard-headed physicalists who are not behaviourists, like J. J. C. Smart or H. Feigl, are committed to this doctrine. Mr. Cook, on the other hand, in 'Wittgenstein on Privacy', is more cautious. He describes Wittgenstein's target as 'the [*the*!] philosophical idea of a private language', but prudently refrains from committing himself to saying that any philosopher has actually held this view; which he formulates as the thesis that 'each of us must give these [sensation-] words their meanings independently of other people' (pp. 287–8).

What I have said about these four papers illustrates one of the most lamentable features of Wittgenstein's legacy—the standards of scholarship and argumentation that he has inspired.

[10] Notice that Donagan here equates 'Cartesian dualism' with 'the doctrine of privileged access'—Ryle's fallacy, discussed in Section IV above.

With such standards, it would be possible to 'prove' almost any interpretation of Wittgenstein's enigmas. The confident assertion of so many irreconcilable interpretations of Wittgenstein's remarks (and there are many more) should make students ask themselves whether it really *matters* what Wittgenstein meant by this or that remark. Mediaeval philosophers were not free to present their own thoughts as their own. Whatever their thoughts, they had to be presented as interpretations of sacred texts, Biblical or Aristotelian. Surely it is time for philosophy to free itself from, to quote Ayer, 'the scholasticism which has been threatening to overtake it' (*The Concept of a Person*, p. 35).

Perhaps Strawson would not now endorse the statement which he made fifteen years ago: 'It is difficult to disagree with the first philosopher of the age'. Let us hope that efforts will be made to overcome this difficulty in view of the results of such misplaced reverence. So many philosophers have devoted themselves to digging for the gold hidden beneath those elusive remarks, have propounded so many incompatible theses as Wittgenstein's insights, and have commonly done so in the dogmatic manner of his own *earlier* assertions. This sort of thing would surely have confirmed Wittgenstein's belief, reported by Malcolm, that 'his influence as a teacher was largely harmful'. So long as Wittgenstein continues to be regarded as the first philosopher of the age, other philosophers and their students will be tempted to emulate his obscurantism and to share his lack of interest in the achievements of earlier philosophers.

Conclusion

SECTION XVIII

A Plea for Speculative Metaphysics

THE aim of this section is to suggest something constructive in place of linguistic philosophy, but it will start with a summary of some of my main criticisms of the latter. As we have seen, a good deal of linguistic philosophy has been done by the high *a priori* method. Like Rationalist metaphysicians, its practitioners have not let mere empirical facts cast doubt upon what they grasped as self-evident. Wittgenstein's *Tractatus* and Ayer's *Language, Truth and Logic* are examples of this approach. It seems impossible to reconcile this way of doing philosophy with acceptance of Empiricism. If those who practise *a priori* linguistics are still empiricists, they should make their thinking conform with their theory of knowledge. If those who still do *a priori* linguistics have abandoned Empiricism, it is a new and strange species of Rationalism which they are practising. For they argue as if they believed that their study of everyday English reveals the logical structure of all human thought.

Some linguistic philosophy conforms more or less closely with the kind of empirical linguistics which Wittgenstein recommended, but did not practise, in the *Investigations*: description of 'the actual use of language' uncontaminated by explanation. Much of Austin's work conforms closely with Wittgenstein's programme for philosophy. Austin warned philosophers against introducing technical terms like "sense-datum" and against 'tampering' with ordinary English words (*Sense and Sensibilia*, pp. 62–3). He explained why we should not tamper with our mother-tongue—that there cannot be *much* wrong with it since it has 'stood up to the long test of the survival of the fittest' (*PP*, p. 130). Though Austin disapproved of other philosophers' technical terms, he introduced his own. For example "illocutionary act" (what you do *in* saying something), "perlocutionary act" (what you do *by* saying something) and "illocutionary forces".[1] This last phrase might suggest that Austin was constructing an

[1] *How to do things with Words*, 1962.

explanatory theory about language, involving hidden forces, but it is really just a new name for the different *uses* that we make of language, such as to give a description, to ask a question, to make a promise or to give a verdict. It is just another way of making Wittgenstein's point that the functions of words are as diverse as those of the contents of a tool-box.

Wittgenstein's assimilation of words and tools is, I think, the most fertile of his similes. Austin brought it to life, showed how it can be developed and applied. He thereby added a new dimension to grammar, for books on grammar by linguists were still too inhibited by traditions going back to Aristotle. That was an important achievement. Many (most?) branches of knowledge which are now pursued in autonomous University departments have originated from philosophers' observations, speculations and questions. But when the answers to philosophers' questions can, and can only adequately, be verified by systematic observation or experiment, it is time for philosophers to do what they have done in the past, namely to leave it to specialists to pursue their questions; *without, however, losing interest in what the specialists discover*. Austin envisaged 'a revised and enlarged *Grammar*', a 'comprehensive *science of language*' which would be independent of philosophy (*PP*, p. 180). Need this development be postponed, as Austin suggested, until the next century? Should not philosophers who wish to devote themselves to describing and classifying word-uses apply now for posts in expanding departments of linguistics, where this work can be pursued with all modern conveniences?

It is a recent and, I think, an eccentric conception of philosophy which assumes that its subject-matter must be something not studied in other University departments: concepts and categories and the logic thereof. Philosophers who use "the concept of A" would, presumably, if they are empiricists, cash this phrase as meaning 'the (or this) use of the term "A" and of its synonyms, if any'. If its subject-matter were word-uses, philosophy would be a sub-department of linguistics. This would indeed be a revolutionary departure from the traditional conception of philosophy. But why should anyone think that philosophy excludes all other studies to which Universities have given names? Those other studies are allowed to overlap (Bio-Physics, Psycho-Linguistics, Economic Geography, etc.), so why should philosophy not be allowed to overlap with them? Surely it does overlap with nearly all of them, since it includes by definition the theory of knowledge; so all knowledge, knowledge of all subjects and the methods of getting it, should be grist to our mills. If *homo sapiens* does not destroy himself before the end of this century, the Linguistic Revolution in Philosophy will, I think, be recognised by then as one of the most curious curios in the history of ideas.

In urging philosophers to extend their interests again beyond grammar, I am not urging them to abandon an interest in grammar. The Philosophy of Language should, of course, continue to be cultivated as *one* important branch of philosophy, though not more important than the Philosophy of Science, or the Theory of Knowledge or Metaphysics. Nobody would dispute Austin's statement that 'words are our tools, and, as a minimum, we should use clean tools'. Philosophers need to be sensitive to the language in which they develop and try to communicate their thoughts, and (*pace* Wittgenstein) they should go on sharpening their tools. But surely this should be merely a preliminary to using verbal tools in thinking about topics other than the verbal tool-kit. There are many interesting problems about language, but there are lots of other problems, some of them more pressing. Yet many British and American philosophers are still writing and lecturing as if the only problems that concern them as philosophers are those of describing English usage and distinguishing and labelling the different purposes for which we use words, with the help (?) of their own versatile, multi-purpose tools—"concept", "category", "logic" and "criterion". As John Stuart Mill has said, what is valuable only as a means may come to be valued as 'part of the end'. Many philosophers have been treating as *the* end for philosophy what is only a means thereto, and only one of the means. Another indispensable means is acquiring knowledge of empirical facts about non-linguistic matters; facts which philosophical theories should also be designed to explain.

It is not, of course, being argued that philosophers *need* expel "concept" and "category" from their professional vocabulary. Only that if they depart, as they have been doing, from everyday usage, they should acknowledge what the everyday uses are, and their own technical uses of such terms should be defined and explained in Chapter One and the first lecture. Anyone who wishes to go on using "the concept of A" or "the logic of the concept" has a duty to his audience to explain his own usage. For "concept" has many everyday uses, and "the logic of the concept" has none. Perhaps students deserve some blame for putting up with the fashionable jargon for so long, and not pressing for explanations of the contents of their teachers' tool-kits. Philosophers like Strawson who use the current jargon in the name of making 'a close examination of the actual use of words' are presumably willing to paraphrase what they are saying *about* everyday language *in* everyday language.

"Category" can be given a useful role, provided that it is not used vaguely as a synonym for "concept" or "class", and that it is made clear what categories are categories *of*. Ryle seems to have regarded his own use of "category" as a development, a generalisation, of Aristotle's use. But whereas Aristotle acknowledged only ten categories, Ryle denies that there can be any complete or finite list ('Categories', *PAS*, 1938–9, p. 200); though presumably he did not recognise that his 1938 criterion could put *all* non-synonymous pairs of expressions into different categories. If, like myself, you read Ryle on Aristotle on Categories before reading Aristotle, you may be surprised at how little Aristotle actually said. It is not at all clear what were the intended theoretical implications of the bald statement in which Aristotle gave his decalogue of categories:

> Of things said without any combination, each signifies either substance or quantity or qualification or a relative or where or when or being-in-a-position or having or doing or being-affected (*Categories*, 1b 25; J. L. Ackrill's 1963 translation).

This provokes a host of questions which are not answered in the sequel. What are we to make of the category of 'having' which Aristotle illustrates only by 'has-shoes-on' and 'has-armour-on'? What are we to make of Aristotle's inclusion in the category of 'qualification' (or quality) of shapes, while he excludes roughness and smoothness? Many difficulties of interpretation are discussed in Ackrill's Notes. Disregarding details, however, the reason for the frugality in Aristotle's list of categories seems to be that he conceived categories as *summa genera* in his species-genus hierarchies. At any rate he is commonly interpreted thus.

And if we do use "category" to mean *summa genera*, this provides a relatively clear way of distinguishing between categories and other classes (or other 'concepts'); a distinction which is otherwise difficult to justify, as has been argued by Professor John Passmore in Chapter 7 of *Philosophical Reasoning* (1961).

I think then that we are generalising what Aristotle started if we use "category" to refer to any *summum genus* in our classificatory or explanatory schemes. Presumably it is in this sense that Strawson uses "category" in *Individuals*. We might then offer as exemplars: Thing (or Substance), Event, Process, Time, Space, Cause, Body, Mind, Person. Any such list invites criticism. Some philosophers would say that both Body and Mind should be subsumed under Thing (Substance); some would identify Mind and Person; some have subsumed Time under (treated it as a dimension of) Space, and so on. Aristotle's list was also open to criticism. In view of the properties of a person which he assigned to the category of 'qualification', e.g. 'states' and 'conditions', why should he have assigned to two other categories 'is-in-a-sitting-position' and 'has-shoes-on'? Categories, in our present imprecise sense, form inter-related networks; and there is not just one way in which we can make them mesh together. The exploration of ways of relating categories to each other, of alternative categorial-systems, has in the past been one of the main pursuits of metaphysics; and why should this enterprise not continue?

If, however, we use "category" in the manner just suggested, having introduced it by reference to *summa genera* in our classificatory or explanatory schemes, we must answer the question which has been addressed to those who use the concept-idiom without explanation: what is the subject-matter of category-classification—words and their uses, or the non-linguistic things which we use words to talk about? I should, of course, give the latter answer,[2] and in this respect too I believe that I am following Aristotle's trail. Ryle, however, in expounding Aristotle's account of categories, gave the impression that he was interpreting Aristotle's intention as being to classify predicates *qua linguistic expressions*; for Ryle used inverted commas or italics when

[2] Strawson does so too. Although it is 'terms' which he assigns to categories, he introduces "terms" as 'non-linguistic items' (*Individuals*, p. 140), and he equates 'categories of terms' with 'kinds of objects' (p. 154).

referring to the items which are to be assigned to categories. Ryle wrote:

"Who has it?" or "What . . . has it?" The answers to these questions will name or indicate particulars, like "Socrates", "Fido" . . . So *Socrates* is in the category of Substance, whereas *snub-nosed* is in the category of Quality . . . ('Categories', p. 191).

I wish to distinguish a 'categorial scheme' and a 'categorial system'. I shall use the latter to refer to the goal of the more ambitious metaphysicians of the past: a complete and comprehensive world-view, a system which explains how *all* our, and/or their own, categories are inter-related; and I shall use "a categorial scheme" to refer to something less ambitious, more piecemeal—a description or revision of the inter-relations of some but not all of our categories. My main theses are:

(1) That for a metaphysician the whole point and purpose of a categorial scheme or system is not that it should classify words and their uses, but that it should apply to, fit, and make sense of non-linguistic facts, what is currently known or believed about the world and ourselves; that a categorial scheme or system should be designed in the light of the empirical facts which we want to make intelligible.

(2) That we are not free to fool around with our categories *ad lib.* (It was the standard uses of everyday English words which Austin warned us not to fool around with *ad lib.*) Thus a categorial scheme must be rejected if it yields absurdity or internal contradiction, or if it conflicts with other parts of one's own categorial system.

(3) That a categorial scheme or system may not be accepted so long as it cannot be reconciled with all the relevant empirical facts.

In illustrating these theses, I shall indicate briefly the kind of metaphysics which I am advocating.

Thesis (1). No metaphysical questions can be settled by appealing to the current uses of English or any other language. According to the linguistic criterion which Ryle seemed to be using in *C of M*, cherry-blossom and the singing of a song belong to the same category, because each may be said, apparently unambiguously, to be 'transitory' or 'not to last very long'; and the same goes for a millimetre and a second, because each may be said to be 'a unit of measurement' or 'a short interval'. Our reluctance to accept such conclusions is not, surely, attributable to grammatical considerations, to the uses of "blossom" and "singing", or, more generally, of thing-words and process-words; but rather because of the obvious differences between what we use thing-words and process-words to talk about. The reluctance of most of us to put millimetres and seconds into the same category is because of the obvious differences between what we use space-words and time-words to talk about, between the spatial and temporal features of our experience. If we allowed ourselves to be influenced by the grammar of English, or of other languages or symbolisms, we should be inclined thereby to assimilate Time and Space. We are forever using non-verbal symbols, graphs and diagrams, which represent Time as a horizontal line; and in nearly all languages nearly all time-words incorporate spatial metaphors. We speak of the "passing" of time, and this suggests movement along a pictured line (down the River of Time); we speak of temporal intervals being 'filled' with, or 'empty' of, incidents, and we speak of such intervals (and of what fills them) as 'overlapping' or being 'adjacent' or 'far apart', etc.—the same words that we use to describe spatial relations between sticks or bits of paper. If we concentrated on time-*language*, this would dispose us to do what many physicists and some philosophers (mainly logicians) now do explicitly, i.e. put Time and Space into the same category, and think (or profess to think) of Time as a fourth dimension of Space; saying even that Time is 'at right angles to each of the other three dimensions'. (What could this mean except a recipe for drawing diagrams or doing sums?) This new categorial scheme, call it 'the 4-D world scheme', is a bold and revolutionary attempt to revise our common-sense scheme. This brings me to my second thesis.

Thesis (*2*). The 4-D World scheme seems to be too revolutionary. Those who profess to adopt it rarely explore its ramifications for the rest of their categorial system. It is not legitimate simply to say: I hereby conceive of the whole physical universe as a four-dimensional solid, and of the present state of the universe as a three-dimensional time-slice of this 4-D solid, and to stop there, or carry on doing pure mathematics or logic. For this proposed categorial scheme has drastic repercussions on everything else in one's categorial system. The 4-D World scheme implies that it makes no sense to ascribe motion or any other kind of change to anything within the physical world; for what we describe as past and future things and incidents, must, in the new scheme, be thought of as timelessly co-existent pieces of a 4-D solid. This implies that the most fundamental categories in our common-sense system are totally inapplicable to the world or its contents; notably the categories of Physical Thing, Motion, Event, Process, Causation. For as we normally conceive of them, *physical things* are liable to move, change in position, and to change in various other respects; and an *event* is a change in one or more such things; and *processes* start, continue and then stop; and *causal relationships* hold between such things, events or processes. How many people are really prepared to jettison all such categories, and are really able to think of the physical world as a 4-D solid, among whose various parts there are only timeless *geometrical* relationships? Professor Smart[3] claims that he can do this, that the 4-D World scheme is consistent with his whole categorial system. But surely he has left himself out of his picture; for even if he can think of everything else as parts or segments of a changeless 4-D solid, surely he cannot so think of himself. Smart's views on this philosophical problem—the nature of Time—have changed. Presumably he can remember having different thoughts about this when he wrote an article condemning the spatialisation of time and said: 'things change, events happen' ('The River of Time', *Mind*, 1949). It would be self-contradictory for him to ascribe *his own changing thoughts and experiences* to a 4-D solid *to which it is meaningless to ascribe change*. And there is nothing else to which Smart can ascribe the changes he experiences, for he is a Physicalist. He maintains that his conscious experiences are identical with adjacent 3-D slices of his 4-D brain. A Dualist might without self-contradiction adopt the 4-D World scheme, if, like Descartes, he identified himself with an immaterial substance, and explained his changing experiences by saying that he (an immaterial self) becomes *successively* aware of a series of adjacent 3-D slices of the 4-D World. I italicise "successively" in the last sentence, to stress that a Dualist who said this would still have to acknowledge a time-order distinct from the one which he has

[3] *Philosophy and Scientific Realism*, 1963, Ch. vii.

spatialised, namely the order of his own successive experiences. This seems enough to show that attempts to assimilate Time and Space are altogether too revolutionary. Even if one tries to revise the rest of one's categorial system as required, one cannot avoid absurdity and contradiction. Surely it is absurd to think that Science could authorise a theory which implies that nothing can move or change. Physicists construct their theories in order to try to explain their observations; but what they observe are things *moving* and otherwise *changing*.

Thesis (*3*). Behaviourism is an example of a categorial scheme which cannot be accepted because it fails to accommodate empirical facts. (Unless Behaviourism is *merely* a methodology for the practice of Psychology. Psychologists are free to limit their professional interests as they please.) Behaviourism involves an attempt to revise the categories of Mind and Person. It attempts to describe all the relevant facts about people (and of course animals), while denying, or more commonly ignoring, private experiences—thoughts, feelings, wishes, etc., which people often conceal; i.e. leaving out what is for most people most interesting about people and what often makes other people hard to understand. Perhaps the behaviourists' categorial scheme should be transferred to my previous paragraph and dismissed as absurd. An example of a categorial scheme which more obviously belongs to this paragraph is Strawson's account of 'the concept of a person'. (It is not clear to me whether, in describing this concept as 'logically primitive', he meant to convey that it is a category.) As we have seen in section XI, Strawson's account is incoherent. The main objection may be summarised thus. Let "DF" mean 'depression as felt', and let "DB" mean 'depressive behaviour'. Strawson asserts

(i) that DB may be logically conclusive evidence of DF,
(ii) (even more ambitiously) that DF and DB are identical; and yet he acknowledges
(iii) that depression can be 'faked'.

But (iii) means that DB can occur in the absence of DF. There seems to be no way of reconciling (iii) with (i) or (ii).

Here are two alternative categorial schemes which accommodate the empirical facts which Strawson failed to discuss:

(a) We may say that you can observe only the signs or symptoms (if any) of my pain, and must then acknowledge that your evidence that I am in pain falls short of my certainty that I am; and this surely is our scheme, if the "our" refers to the majority of English-speakers.

(b) We may say that you and I both observe different effects of my pain, *my pain* being identified with a (hypothetical) state of my brain or central nervous system, which produces both the ache that I feel and my overt behaviour which you can observe.

Each of these categorial schemes seems to be capable of being made to fit all the empirical facts. The latter is not our common-sense, English-language, scheme, if I am correct in thinking that all of us do use "my pain" to refer to the felt ache, and not to the postulated brain-state. We each learned to use "my pain" long before we knew anything about the grey stuff inside our heads. But we seem to be free to accept scheme (b) as a *revised* scheme. At least I am, so long as I am permitted to introduce another word to refer to my felt aches, etc., i.e. to do what I have hitherto done with "my pain". Whether scheme (b) yields any contradictions within *your* categorial system will depend on what that is; and whether you will want to adopt it will depend on whether you sometimes feel aches, etc., and have occasion to talk about them, and feel conservative in wanting to go on calling them 'pains'.

Strawson's proposed identification of what a person feels with his overt behaviour seems to point to some form of Physicalism; but this is not the position he adopts. He allows that we can intelligibly talk and think about disembodied spirits or 'former persons'; though his short discussion of this topic suggests that he regards this as idle metaphysics, or at any rate boring metaphysics. He makes it clear that he thinks that the only kind of existence which could be enjoyed (endured) by former persons would be dreary and solitary. This topic evidently did not excite Strawson's imaginative powers as much as that of describing the existence of purely auditory beings (an existence which beings who were not music lovers might find tedious). I am not attached to belief in Spirits, and not anxious to become one; but whether Strawson or I will have some such existence in due course is a question of fact which does not depend upon what we wish—unless, of course, the Universe is so designed that a person will become a former person if and only if he wants to; which is how we might arrange things if we bore the responsibilities of a benevolent and omnipotent God. But the category in question, Former Person, would not merit much philosophical discussion if it were merely a *logical* possibility that it might apply to something. This category, however, still has some work to do, since this logical possibility is not yet known to be causally impossible. There are some empirical facts, or alleged facts, which count in favour of it—messages from the dead, etc.; there are many empirical facts which weigh heavily, but not yet decisively, against it, notably the effects of brain-damage. (If brain-surgeons were permitted to fool around *ad lib.* with people's brains, we might soon get well-nigh decisive evidence against it.) I am not digressing. The point that I want to stress is that such empirical facts are relevant in any *philosophical* discussion of the Mind-Body Problem, the Nature of Man, the Concept of a Person. Contemporary philosophers, including Strawson, who, when they write or lecture on such topics, normally ignore all empirical facts except facts about English word-uses, are gratuitously decimating their subject-matter. Philosophers like Strawson who still do some metaphysics need not feel obliged to confine themselves to 'our [common-sense, nonscientific, agnostic, English-language] conceptual scheme'; plus the occasional adumbration of a *logically* possible alternative like a purely auditory world. Surely the most important kind of metaphysics is to explore possible categorial systems or schemes *in the light of the empirical facts which we want them to fit, the facts which limit our freedom of choice, what is known about the world and ourselves*. This is the kind of metaphysics which empiricists should be doing. Should we leave it to scientists to do it, each for his own restricted field, sometimes repeating errors made by earlier philosophers?

It is not the philosopher's job to solve scientists' problems, but it is surely one of our jobs to go on asking important, awkward questions which scientists have swept under their carpets. For example: can the now orthodox theory of Evolution, according to which chance mutations provide the *only* inheritable differences between individuals upon which natural selection operates, really account for the building into the DNA molecules of a Manx Shearwater all that is needed to explain its instinctive behaviour; notably its migrations over thousands of miles of ocean, guided, we are told,[4] by the sun and the stars as its compasses? For this explanation requires that the bird has, in effect, built-in maps of the changing starry heavens for both hemispheres for the times of year when it migrates. Has there been any other period when so many philosophers ignored the problems thrown up by contemporary science? Admittedly few linguistic philosophers have ignored Freud's (semi-scientific) theories; but perhaps only because some of his key-words have, with unusual speed, become part of Everyman's vocabulary. Perhaps too many professional philosophers have come to philosophy via study of the Classics. The study of those dead languages and ancient civilisations seems to foster a frame of mind which is backward-looking, and sometimes a propensity to think, or to act as if, all change is for the worse. As Professor J. Passmore has said: 'classically-trained men are always likely to place great stress on 'correctness', which has a reasonably clear meaning within a dead language' (*A Hundred Years of Philosophy*, p. 439). It seems desirable to train as philosophers more people who have studied the sciences at school or University, a background which, one hopes, would make them forward-looking, empirical and experimental in their thinking. However, we shall not recruit many scientists to our courses so long as philosophy is, or is represented as being, a study of everyday uses of language.

It must be admitted that what linguistic philosophers do is sometimes more interesting than what one would expect from their own accounts of what they are doing. Perhaps some of them will claim that they have all along been doing what I have described as speculative metaphysics, that this is what they mean by "conceptual analysis" or "the logic of concepts". Well if this has been their goal, they have certainly not made this at all clear; and I am not alone in being misled. Warnock, when defending linguistic philosophy, represents many of its practitioners as holding

> that philosophy is the study of the concepts that we employ, and not of the facts, phenomena, cases, or events, to which those concepts might be or are applied (*English Philosophy Since 1900*, p. 167).

[4] For an outline of the experimental evidence, see Chapter 12 of R.M. Lockley's *Animal Navigation* (Pan, 1967).

Suppose that a linguistic philosopher claims to have been doing speculative metaphysics by virtue of having given some non-obvious analyses of concepts. My reply would be that this is not enough. For I have explained "speculative metaphysics" in terms of "categories", and "categories" in terms of "*summa genera*". We may stretch "*summa*" to include what is near, though not at, the top of our classificatory and explanatory schemes. My complaint is that too many linguistic philosophers get bogged down among words that are much too near the bottom; and do not see the wood for the trees. If we stretch "metaphysics" so far that it includes any not-obvious-to-everyone analyses of the meanings of words, we make metaphysics trivial; or at least we confuse what is important with what is relatively trivial and not our professional concern; with a kind of investigation which, apart from Austin at his best, we do not do very well. If anyone stretches "metaphysics" that far, I should re-word my criticism and ask why linguistic philosophers are so unadventurous in their excursions into what they now call 'metaphysics'. Most of them retain some interest in the theory of knowledge, but why should they confine this interest, officially at least, to knowledge so ancient that it has become incorporated in everyday English usage?

Traditionally metaphysics has usually been treated as being independent of moral philosophy, though the converse is not true. Metaphysics was normally conceived as the primary enterprise because it involves ontological questions. But the kind of metaphysics which I am advocating need not exclude ethics. Kant was devising a new categorial scheme when he divided obligations into two irreducibly different classes—Categorical and Hypothetical Imperatives; and so was Bentham when he adumbrated his notion of a hedonic calculus. Our students might welcome the return to a study of morals which is (in our present sense) more metaphysical, after twenty years or so of searching for the precise meanings or uses which we (average English speakers) give to the moral items in our vocabulary; a pursuit which, as J. S. Mill said of Intuitionism, makes ethics 'not so much a guide as a consecration of men's actual sentiments' (*Utilitarianism*, para. 4). Having rejected the Intuitionism of Prichard and Ross, Oxford moral philosophers found a new method of inculcating conservatism; a way of studying ethics adapted to fulfil Wittgenstein's wish that philosophy should leave everything as it is; one which relegates a moral reformer like Bentham to the status of a mere moralist—except, of course, that he did some inaccurate philosophy when he gave the wrong definitions of "right" and "wrong".

I have indicated one of the most important jobs which philosophers ought surely to be doing—speculative metaphysics, which is only one step ahead of, or back from, Strawson's descriptive metaphysics. None of us, presumably, would wish to go back to dogmatic *a priori* metaphysics, which is nearly as objectionable as dogmatic *a priori* Anglo-linguistics. The great metaphysicians—Plato, Descartes, Spinoza, Berkeley, Ayer (1936) and company—have a trait in common: each has had an apparently irresistible tendency to take it for granted that the categorial-system which he had constructed is IT, is how the universe *must* be. This fault is venial. Everyone is biased in favour of his own creations. The recent disillusionment with metaphysics seems to be due to equating metaphysics, as Warnock does,[5] with the dogmatic assertion of an *a priori* theory which is designed to explain everything. But metaphysics need not be dogmatic, it may be exploratory; it need not present an all-embracing system, for a theory may explain something without explaining everything; and of course it cannot usefully be practised as an *a priori* science, for the whole point of any theory is to explain the relevant empirical facts.

This sketch of an alternative to linguistic philosophy is, of course, much too sketchy. This book is incomplete without Part Three, in place of this section which merely adumbrates a programme. What needs to be done is to show in some detail that there are important philosophical problems which are not about words, not generated by misuse of ordinary language and not soluble by the method recommended by Wittgenstein. A prior commitment to write a book about perception has precluded the writing of Part Three. I have, however, tried in this other book[6] to practise the kind of Empiricism which I have advocated here, and to show that problems about *perception* are more interesting and difficult than problems about "look", "see" & co.

[5] See p. 136 above.

[6] *Perception: Facts and Theories* to be published by Oxford University Press, in the Oxford Paperback University Series.

Index

"*A priori* linguistics" defined, 15
A priori linguistics, preliminary illustrations, 4–6, 16–19
  Austin's non-practice of, 78–9, 89
  Ayer's criticism of, 5
  Ayer's practice of, 27–34, 40, 160, 261
  Malcolm's practice of, 247–8
  Ryle's practice of, 5, 40, 42–3, 45, 54–65
  Sommers' practice of, 74–6
  White's practice of, 5, 17–19
  Wittgenstein's practice of, 5, 159–60, 166–84, 200–20, 239, 261
A priori physics, 146–7
A priori psychology, 60–1, 92–3, 172, 248
Achievement-verbs, 18–19, 62, 79, 120, 215
Ackrill, J. L., 264
Agitations, Ryle's category of, 55–9
Albritton, R., 119
Analogy, the argument from, 31, 34, 46, 140, 141–2, 209, 228, 229–30
Analysis, logical, 115–16, 160, 166–84, 186, 187
  philosophical, 5, 25, 65–6, 154–8
  the paradox of, 155–7
Anglo-linguistics, 19, 95, 120–33, 261, 263, 273
Anscombe, G. E. M., 166, 181
Aristotle, 15, 17, 68, 70, 77, 227, 262, 264–5
Arithmetical series, Wittgenstein on, 194–7, 237–8, 242
  Winch on, 243–4
Augustine, 187
Austin, J. L., 1, 8, 11, 15, 21, 78–90, 94, 106, 117, 120, 122, 132, 135, 137–138, 141, 149, 261–2, 266, 273
Austin's Razor, 11
Ayer, A. J., 5–6, 12, 14, 23, 24–40, 54, 79, 86, 93, 105, 131, 136, 137, 153, 160, 227, 247, 250, 252, 255, 258, 261, 274

Bambrough, R., 242, 244–6
Beetles, Wittgenstein's, 206–7, 209, 210, 216, 227–9, 230, 251
Behaviourism, 31, 38, 45–9, 51–2, 60, 64, 67, 134, 202–4, 209, 213, 233, 237, 239, 250–1, 252–3, 257, 269
  in psychology, 46–8, 60, 67
  Ryle's apparent, 46, 49–52, 64, 67
  Wittgenstein's apparent, 46, 64–5, 201–4, 208–9, 213, 233, 239, 250–251, 252–3
"Behaviourism", the author's definition of, 48, 202
Bentham, J., 273–4
Berkeley, 30, 91, 198, 242, 274
Berlin, I., 134–5
Black, M., 74, 165, 166, 181–2
Bosanquet, B., 135
Bradley, F. H., 106, 135, 153

"Can", Austin on, 85–6
Carnap, R., 32, 47, 255
Cartesian dualism, 41, 45, 46, 52, 53, 66, 67, 76, 93, 138, 139, 147, 203, 211, 255–7
Cary, H., 128, 131
Castaneda, H.-N., 246
"Category", Aristotle's use of, 77, 264–5
  Ryle's use of, 41–5, 54–60, 68–74, 77, 264–6.
  Strawson's use of, 125, 145, 265, 269
  the author's uses of, 68, 265–71, 273
Category-mistake, 40, 41–5, 54–5, 68–77, 95, 126
  Ryle's 1938 criterion, 44, 57, 69–71, 74
  Ryle's 1949 criterion, 44, 60, 68, 71–74
  Sommers' criterion, 74
Chess, 64, 114, 193–4, 196
Chinese language, 125
Chomsky, N., 115, 116
Cohen, L. J., 6–7, 96–8, 100
"Concept", recent philosophers' uses of, 1, 42, 55, 61, 91–109, 103, 105, 134–5, 138, 145, 156–7

"Concept"—*cont.*
Ayer's use of, 93, 105
Berlin's use of, 134–5
Körner's use of, 98–9
Moore's use of, 156–7
Ryle's use of, 42, 55, 61, 92–4, 103
Strawson's use of, 93, 103, 138, 145
Warnock's use of, 135
the author's questionnaire concerning, 1, 100–2, 107–9
Conceptual Analysis, White on, 96
Conceptual plane, Cohen on the, 96–8
"Conscious", Ryle on, 50–1, 67
Cook, J. W., 251–3, 257
Copi, I. M., 176
"Could have", Austin on, 85
"Criterion", recent philosophers' uses of, 118–19, 142, 143–4, 223–4, 234–7, 241–2, 247
Wittgenstein's account of, 235–6
the author's use of, 44
Culture-words, Cohen on, 97

Daniel, J. L., vii
Democritus, 87
Depression, Strawson on the concept of, 143–5, 269–70
Descartes, 5, 41, 53, 61, 66, 73, 93, 211, 254, 255–7, 268, 274
Determinism, 84–6
Diarist, Wittgenstein's, 209–10, 211, 214–16, 219, 222–8, 231, 237, 251, 255–7
Donagan, A., 253–5, 256–7
Dreaming, Malcolm on the concept of, 246–8

Family-resemblances, Wittgenstein on, 190–3, 244–5
Favrholdt, D., 166
Feelings, Ryle's category of, 55–9
Feigl, H., 257
Findlay, N., 5
Flattery, P. A., 77
Flew, A. G. N., 20–1, 96, 112–13, 114, 115
Fowler, H. W., 19, 106
Frege, G., 102
Freud, S., 272

Galileo, 87
Galton, F., 60, 230
Games, Wittgenstein's simile between languages and, 162–3, 187, 188–194, 238–9
Gellner, E., 7, 12, 24
Genetic Fallacy, 2, 197, 200–1, 207, 242, 247–8
Goodman, G., 106
God, Phillips on the conceptual category to which His reality belongs, 248–9
Grammar, depth, 113, 115, 213, 248
logical, 112–13
"Grammar", recent philosophers' misuses of, 6, 112–17, 200, 212–13
Greek, Ancient, 127–9
Griffin, J., 166

Haak, S., 76–7
Hampshire, S., 5, 63–4
Hare, R. M., 14
Heath, P. L., 6, 90, 91, 164, 194, 204, 249
Hegel, 112
Hobbes, 20, 229, 245
Holborow, L. C., 250–1
Holroyd, M., 106
Hume, v, 39, 40, 75, 94, 135–6, 164, 168, 184, 242, 245

Identification of particulars, Strawson on, 145–8
"If", Austin on, 83, 84–6
Imagination, Ryle on the concept of, 59–61
Inclinations, Ryle's category of, 55–9
"Inferring", Ryle on, 62
Intelligence, Ryle on the concept of, 50, 66
Intention, White on the concept of, 17–19
"Introspection", Ryle on, 50, 67

Jackson, R., vii
Jesperson, O., 113, 114, 115
Jowett, B., 128, 130, 131, 132

Kant, 77, 149, 273
Kennick, W. E., 6, 105
Kenny, A., 119, 241, 255–6
Kneale, W. and M., 5, 117, 123, 160
Knowing how, Ryle on the concept of, 49–50
Körner, S., 98–9, 100

Langford, C. H., 154–8
Language police, 15, 114
Lazerowitz, M., 6, 105
"Legislative linguistics" defined, 16, 21, 23
Legislative linguistics, illustrated, 19–23, 25–6, 28–9, 42, 45, 50–1, 53, 54–66 (esp. 62–3), 72, 103–4, 105–6, 125–6, 142–5
Leibniz, 106, 149
Linguistic phenomenology, Austin's, 80–2, 89, 132, 149
"Linguistic philosophy" defined, 11–12
Linguistics, real (genuine), 16, 113–17
Locke, John, 29, 36, 87, 91, 187, 242, 255
Lockley, R. M., 272
"Logic", recent philosophers' misuses of, 5, 26–7, 58, 72, 110–19, 180, 184, 212, 233–7
Logical atomism, 116, 166–84 (esp. 168–71, 174, 177–8)

Mace, C. A., 47–8, 194
MacGuinness, B. F., 167, 169, 176
McKeown, A., 213
Malcolm, N., 13, 154–5, 159, 160, 174–176, 178, 181, 185, 197, 199, 208–9, 212, 225, 237, 241, 242, 246–8, 248–9, 258
Marsh, R. C., 168
Maslow, A., 166
Matthews, P. H., 116
Mayo, B., 111–12, 113
Metaphysics, 17, 27–9, 112, 134, 135–6, 138, 148–9, 153–4, 266–74
Microglot, Austin's, 80
Mill, J. S., 135–6, 263, 273
"Mind-predicate", the author's use of, 48
Mitford, J., 106
Moods, Ryle's category of, 55–9, 65
Moore, G. E., 15, 84–5, 114, 115, 134, 153–8, 187
Moral Science without history, 15
Motives, Ryle's category of, 53, 55–9

Neutrality, ideological, 14, 39, 136–7, 145
  ontological, 145–8
Newton, 106
Nominalism, 191–2, 245, 246
Nowell-Smith, P. H., 84–5

"Obligation", Anon on, 94–5
Ogden, C. K., 169, 176
"On purpose", Austin on, 83
Ontological argument, Malcolm's version, 248–9
"Ontological", Strawson's redefinition of, 145–8
Ordinary language, Austin on, 80–2, 89–90
  Ayer on, 6, 27
  Cohen on, 7
  Heath on, 6
  Malcolm on, 13, 154–5, 248
  Moore and, 153–5
  Ryle on, 20–2, 92
Ostensive teaching of general words, 225–7, 231–2, 236, 242

Para-mechanical hypothesis, Ryle on the, 42, 53, 56
Paraphrasing, 113, 115–17, 158
Passmore, J., 158, 265, 272
Paul, G., 24
Pears, D. F., 167, 169, 176
Performative-verbs, 78–9, 120
Person, Strawson's concept of a, 17, 75–6, 124, 138–45, 269–71
Phenomenalism, Ayer's *a priori* proof of, 29–30
Phillips, D. Z., 248–9
Picture theory of meaning, Wittgenstein's, 159–61, 166–7, 174–82
Pitcher, G., 4, 166, 182, 185, 234, 241, 249, 250, 252–3
Plato, v, 8, 15, 91, 107, 127–32, 157, 186, 227, 274
Platonism, 54, 91, 129–31, 153, 183
Polar Principle, 17
Pollard, J., 127
"Predicate", Strawson's use of, 125–6
  the author's use of, 68–9
Price, H. H., 79, 223
Prichard, H., 273
Privacy, convenient, Ryle on, 52
Private language, Wittgenstein on, 197, 205–19, 220–2, 237–9, 255–7
Privileged access, the doctrine of, 41–2, 45–7, 50–2, 56, 58–9, 63, 67, 134, 141, 214, 229, 257

Quinton, A. M., 241–2, 250

Ramsey, F. P., 181

"Real", Austin on, 86–7
Recognition without 'criteria', 223–4
Resemblance theory of universals, 101, 190–3, 226–7, 245
Rhees, R., 215–16, 224–5
Ross, W. D., 273
Rouse, W. H. D., 131
Rules, linguistic, 113–14, 121–4, 193–7, 198, 223
Russell, 11, 34–6, 39, 54, 77, 113, 115, 116, 134, 135–6, 160, 167, 168, 170, 172, 173, 174, 176, 177, 179, 182–3, 187, 201, 204
Ryle, 5, 16, 17–19, 20, 21–3, 33, 36, 38, 40, 41–77, 89, 92–5, 103, 114, 120, 126, 127, 128, 134, 137, 141, 194, 200, 204, 211, 212, 233, 257, 264, 265–6

"Same", Wittgenstein's use of, 195–7, 216–17, 224–5, 237–8, 243
Sartre, J.-P., 14
Scheur, K., vii
Schilpp, P. A., 154
Schlick, M., 30, 161
"'Seeing'", Ryle's use of, 59–61
"Self", Ayer on, 32
  Mayo on, 111–12, 113
Semantics, 115
Shorter, J. M., 140
Showing things, Wittgenstein on, 175, 187
Skinner, B. F., 47, 48
Smart, J. J. C., 70, 257, 268.
Socrates, 46, 88, 127, 129, 131, 133
Sommers, F., 72, 74–7
Spinoza, 274
Stenius, E., 166, 181
Strawson, P. F., v, 3, 17, 75–6, 93, 103, 120–6, 138–49, 158, 197, 204, 233, 236, 241, 250, 258, 265, 269–71, 274
"Symptom", Wittgenstein's use of, 235

Talk, Austin on how to, 80
"Team-spirit", Ryle on, 73
Therapeutic philosophy, 137–8, 163–4, 185, 198–9
Thomas, A. R., 126
Thomas, L. E., 161
Thomson, Judith, 217–18
Time, on spatializing, 267–9
Tools, Wittgenstein's simile between words and, 13–14, 78, 162–3, 187, 188–90, 194, 262
Tsu-Lin Mei, 125–6
"Tweaks" and "twinges", Ryle on, 51, 56, 58

Universals, *see* Resemblance theory and Nominalism and Platonism
Urmson, J. O., 23, 78, 116, 158, 180–1
"Use" and "Usage", Flew on, 20–1
  Ryle on, 21–3
Use, Wittgenstein's equation between meaning and, 5, 16, 20, 22, 188–190, 194

Verification principle, 2, 26–40, 44–5, 63–5, 146–7, 159, 160–1, 201–2, 210, 214–19, 229, 239, 247
  Ayer's 1936 version, 30–1
  Ayer's 1956 version, 36
  By-Me version, 37–8, 30–3, 35–9, 64, 161, 202, 214, 216
  By-Others version, 38, 64–5, 201–2, 215, 216, 217
  By-Someone version, 37–8, 33, 36–7, 64, 202, 218
  Hampshire's version, 64
  Ryle's 1936 version, 33
  Ryle's unidentified 1949 version, 44–5, 63–5
  Schlick's version, 30
  Thomson's version, 217–18
  Wittgenstein's 1929 version, 160
  Wittgenstein's unidentified later versions, 201–2, 210, 214–19, 239
Vienna Circle, 30, 160–1, 167
"Volition", Ryle on, 62, 66
"Voluntarily", Austin on, 82–3
"Voluntary", Ryle on, 61, 66

Waismann, F., 15, 161
Warnock, G. J., 78, 86, 134–8, 158, 272, 274
Watmough, J., 113
Watson, J. B., 46–8, 60, 67, 229
Welsh language, 126–7
White, A. R., 17–19, 62, 89, 96
Whitehead, A. N., 116, 160
Whiteley, C. H., 231–2
Winch, P., 242–4
Wisdom, John, 3, 112, 154

Wittgenstein, v, 2–3, 4, 5, 12, 13, 14, 15, 16, 22, 39, 43, 49, 65, 78, 88, 89, 113, 114, 116, 118, 119, 132, 134, 137, 149, 153, 154, 158–258, 261, 262, 274
his earlier account of philosophy, 166–7
his later account of philosophy, 163–164, 185–6, 198–9
Wooster, B., 71, 111
Woozley, A. D., vii, 83, 122
Wright, G. H. von, 159

Yawn, Austin's, 82–3

Zeno, 214
Zoology, philosophy as, 199